THE

SIEGE OF RICHMOND:

A NARRATIVE

OF THE

MILITARY OPERATIONS OF MAJOR-GENERAL GEORGE B. McCLELLAN

DURING THE MONTHS OF MAY AND JUNE, 1862.

BY

JOEL COOK,

SPECIAL CORRESPONDENT OF THE PHILADELPHIA PRESS WITH THE ARMY OF THE POTOMAC.

PHILADELPHIA:
GEORGE W. CHILDS,
628 & 630 CHESTNUT ST.
1862.

Entered according to Act of Congress, in the year 1862, by

GEORGE W. CHILDS,

in the Clerk's Office of the District Court of the United States in and for the Eastern District of Pennsylvania.

STEREOTYPED BY L. JOHNSON & CO.
PHILADELPHIA.

CONTENTS.

CHAPTER VIII.

CHAPTER IX.

CHAPTER X.

CHAPTER XI.

CHAPTER XII.

INTRODUCTION.

An eminent English author once said, "All histories are but splendid fictions." The student, perplexed by conflicting statements, and laboring vainly to reconcile discrepancies, is inclined to assent to this sweeping declaration; while the general reader, who accidentally discovers opposing testimony concerning important facts, is often compelled to feel the cooling shadows of doubt resting upon his mind when it is all aglow with the thoughts which the record of great and good actions creates.

The historian, however honest and truthful, laborious and skilful, is every moment liable to fall into errors of fact or opinion when relying upon the records or statements of others, or even when consulting the impressions of his own senses and experience. He can only hope, at the best, in producing his picture as a whole, to display general truths in form and color and expression, without essential errors, conscious that in minor details there are many almost invisible departures from the strict line of fact, and many false colors, scarcely discernible in the mass except by the eye of the subtle critic.

To form a correct judgment of the value of a record, it is important to comprehend the stand-point from which the historian views the field of his observation. If the influences of self-interest, partisanship, personal likes or dislikes, national or sectional prejudices, the pride of opinion, and the score of other causes which may give a bias to his judgment and feelings, form the surroundings of that observatory, we have a right to question the absolute truthfulness of his report of the sayings and doings of men.

The historian of the Great Rebellion which is now desolating a portion of our land, and is smiting with the rod of affliction once happy homes in every part of the Republic, will have a most difficult task. He will be compelled to search diligently for the nutritious grains of Truth in vast heaps of the dusty chaff of Error; and he will often find, to his dismay, that much of his cherished treasure is counterfeit. A thousand causes for suspecting falsehood, on every hand, exist; and even official documents will fail to give materials for an absolutely truthful picture.

When the Duke of Wellington was applied to, several years after the battle of Waterloo, for correct information concerning that event, by a person who was about to write its history, the great commander said, in substance, "No man is more incapable of giving you the required aid than myself. Of that battle I only *saw* what came within the limited range of my own vision: the remainder I *heard* from others. Take all the official reports and the descriptive writings on both sides, and, with the best judgment you possess, seek for the truth. You will more certainly find it by that method than by any other." Such will be the nature of the task of the historian of this Rebellion. Yet he will possess the advantage of assistance from a power almost unknown in such relations in the time of Wellington and Napoleon. I mean the PRESS. Its deportment is kingly, and its power sublime. Its ambassadors are virtually in every court and conclave, and its representatives receive the universal homage of the people. They are popular oracles in civil life; and in this war they have been welcome guests in every national camp, and courageous soldiers on every field of battle. The "Army Correspondent" forms a part of every military staff; and his unrestrained freedom of action in marches, in bivouacs, in reconnoissances, and in battles, gives him opportunities for the accurate observation of men and things around him. Our leading newspapers all over the land are filled with his records; and commanders of troops are amazed and gratified by the general accuracy of his delineations of passing events. A thousand things which the official reporter of a march, a battle, or a siege would never hint at, are noticed and described by him; and these "studies from nature" will add charm and value to the material from which the historian must select the forms and colors for his great picture.

The most honest, conscientious, and diligent "Army Correspondent" may be often deceived: so may the military commander and his subalterns. There may be incompetent and dishonest men among them: so there are in every pursuit of life. But it will be found, I think, that as a class they are most competent and truthful. I have studied the events of this war with great care and intense interest, and have had occasion, a hundred times, to compare the statements of "Army Correspondents," written immediately after the occurrences described, with the official despatches furnished soon afterward, and in most cases there has been a remarkable coincidence in the narratives of substantial facts. Like Froissart, they tell us of what their own eyes have seen and their own ears have heard; and, like him, they will deserve the thanks of posterity.

The brief campaign on the Virginia Peninsula, so graphically described in all of its essential features in the following pages by an "Army Correspondent," appears as one of the most remarkable on record; and in the history of the Great Rebellion it will loom up in Alpine grandeur above all others, in the displays of patient endurance, indomitable courage, splendid fighting, and skilful military movements. Its importance and greatness cannot now be estimated nor comprehended. It has been more written about already, and will be more written about hereafter, than any other distinct movement during the war. The magnitude of the forces engaged and of the stake at issue, invested that campaign with momentous interest from the beginning; and its apparent failure invites thorough analysis and exhaustive investigation. The time for that ordeal has not arrived. Much—now hidden in the bosom of official reticence—of the secret history of the inception and progress of that campaign must be learned before we can determine the proper places for the actors and the actions in the chronicles of the nation. Only in the light of a full revelation of all the facts, which a wise prudence, perhaps, now withholds, can a proper estimate of that campaign, as a military movement, be formed. Every thing done in the sunlight has been seen and studied by different observers, and by none with more apparent intelligence and vigilance than the author of this little volume. He has constructed a narrative, after personal observation and inquiry, which is rich in incidental knowledge and congruous in arrangement and proportion. Its value as an authentic record—so apparent to the eye of our present information—can be certified only by the tests of future revelations of truth.

B. J. L.

POUGHKEEPSIE, N.Y., October, 1862.

THE

SIEGE OF RICHMOND.

CHAPTER I.

PRELIMINARY.

A CORRESPONDENT leaving his home in the North to connect himself with an army advancing in the field, in the few days required to make the necessary journey, changes the whole course of his life. He leaves dwelling-houses, comforts, gentle fare, and pleasant friends, to find tents, coarse living, and cold and suspicious men. His occupation is changed, and so is his dress. Regular habits of daily life are of necessity broken in upon. At all hours of the night he may be roused from his bed on the ground, to commence a weary march, or collect the particulars of some desperate conflict. His life is no easy one. Clad in a suit of shabby clothing, carrying all his wealth in his haversack, he wanders about, observing here, questioning there, ever and anon writing, and compelled to be always on the look-out to avoid the retailers of false news.

His reception in the army, and treatment whilst there, depend solely upon his own conduct. Politeness and gentlemanly bearing, carefulness in conversation, and, above all, a strict adherence to the truth in all sent home to his newspaper, will always secure the confidence and friendship of military men. No class is more hospitable; none more easily offended. Honor seems to vie with anxiety for military distinction in every officer's mind; and the correspondent who appreciates this, and conducts himself as a true gentleman, will always find a welcome in every marquee in the army.

Before entering the lines of the army, it is necessary for the correspondent to procure a pass from the War Department at Washington. This is granted "by order of the Secretary of War," and signed by the "Military Supervisor of Army Intelligence." It is an elegantly printed letter-sheet, bearing the following words:—

"War Department, Washington City, May 13, 1862.

"Permission is given to A. B., a correspondent of the Philadelphia Press, to pass within the lines of the United States forces as a newspaper reporter, subject to the following conditions:—

"First.—That he is loyal to the Government of the United States.

"Second.—That he gives his parole of honor that he will faithfully observe the order of the War Department, and publish no intelligence contrary to the orders of the War Department, and will observe such rules and regulations as may be prescribed by the commanding general.

"By order of the Secretary of War.

"E. S. Sanford,
"*Military Supervisor.*"

"I accept this pass on the above conditions, and give the parole required. A. B."

The parole attached to this pass is signed in duplicate; one copy being filed among the archives of the War Department, the other remaining in the possession of the correspondent. Accompanying the pass, printed in ordinary type on an oblong slip of paper, is a warning from those in authority, giving hints about "contraband news:"—

Notice to the Correspondent.

"SIR:—You are hereby notified that the following are some of the items of intelligence which are deemed objectionable by the *War Department*, as tending to give aid and comfort to the enemy, and to injure the military operations of the United States Government, viz.:—The location or change of location of the head-quarters of generals; the names of generals, regiments, brigades, or divisions in the field, except when engagements have taken place; the number of regiments, brigades, divisions, batteries, or pieces of artillery, or the proportion of cavalry in service at any point; statements of the kind of arms or ammunition, or the number of days' rations served; the number of transports used for any movement; the description of any movement, until after its object shall have been accomplished or defeated; allusions to the objects of movements, or suggestions of future movements or attacks; the position or location of camps, pickets, or outposts; and pictures, representations, or maps of Federal fortifications or lines of defences.

"The only restriction in the description of battles or engagements will be upon such information as will indicate the strength of troops held in reserve, or the future movements of our armies. Accounts of skirmishes, cases of sickness, wounds, or death, may be forwarded by telegraph, or other medium, at any time, and the name of the regiment in which the cases occur be given, but not of the brigade or division.

"You are not to infer that the above items comprise all which are objectionable, but must use your judgment in withholding other improper information.

"Respectfully,

"E. S. Sanford,

"*Military Supervisor of Army Intelligence.*"

These restrictions of the War Department were very sweeping, and, had they been observed to the letter, much less news would have been sent North than was daily printed in its hundreds of newspapers. Correspondents often went to the very edge of the contraband, and perhaps in some cases overstepped it. A description could scarcely be written, without the writer's being unconsciously betrayed into what might be construed a violation of his parole,—it is so natural to put down the names of generals as commanding divisions or brigades, and to state the force engaged in battles. Still, the Department was quite lenient, and none of the correspondents were ever called to account for what they wrote home from Virginia.

The offer of the telegraph-line to send accounts of "skirmishes, cases of sickness, wounds, or death," to the North, was one, no doubt, generously made and intended for the public benefit. But so far as correspondents were concerned it was a sealed book; and so it was usually to all. Very few cases of sickness, wounds, or death ever could have been telegraphed home. The slow-moving, constantly delaying mail-bags carried all such news. The telegraph, whenever a correspondent inquired about it, was exclusively reserved for "official business."

Upon the first arrival at general head-quarters, the pass granted by the War Department was always shown, and its bearer would receive another, signed in duplicate, like the first, and with the two in his pocket the correspondent could pursue his calling without fear of molestation. This second pass, differing slightly from the first, read as follows:—

Pass, with parole appended.

"FORTRESS MONROE, April 17, 1862.

"Mr. A. B., an authorized correspondent of the Philadelphia Press newspaper, has permission to join the army of the Potomac, in the field near Fortress Monroe, to practise his vocation under such rules and regulations as the GENERAL COMMANDING, and the MILITARY SUPERVISOR OF ARMY INTELLIGENCE, may prescribe.

"By order of the SECRETARY OF WAR.

"E. S. SANFORD,

"*Military Supervisor of Army Intelligence.*"

Parole.

"I give my *word of honor* that I am a loyal citizen of the United States, and that in my discharge of the duties of a correspondent of the Philadelphia Press newspaper, and of any and every other newspaper, under the authority above accorded to me, I will not write, make, or transmit any intelligence, opinion, statement, drawing, or plan, whatsoever, that will give, or tend to give, *aid or comfort to the enemy*, or be injurious, or tend to be injurious, to the Federal cause, or the military operations of the United States Government.

"I make this promise with full knowledge of and free assent to all the penalties imposed by the 57th article of war, upon the imparting of direct or indirect intelligence to the enemy. A. B."

"HEAD-QUARTERS, ARMY OF THE POTOMAC, May 15, 1862.

[Here was printed the "notice to the correspondent," given above.]

"Approved, R. V. MARCY,
"*Chief of Staff*"

The fifty-seventh article of war threatens an ignominious death to all persons found giving intelligence of military plans or movements to the enemy.

The journey down Chesapeake Bay was a most pleasant one. The steamer Louisiana, a snug sea-boat of moderate speed, was the one upon which the author embarked. Every one who entered it at Baltimore had to show a pass, and his full name, residence, and occupation were taken by a young man who wrote them upon a long sheet of paper. He was part of the Baltimore provost-marshal's clerical force, and his object was to procure a complete list containing the names and residences of all leaving for the fortress, besides making a strict examination of the passes.

The Louisiana was one of a line permitted to be run by private owners for their profit, but which was paid a weekly or monthly stipend to carry all the passengers and freight that the Government chose to send, even if it excluded every thing else from the decks. Cattle, boxes of ammunition, and beef recently killed, were the usual freights on Government account. The line also carried the mails, and its owners were under bonds to make a daily trip each way. Nine-tenths of the passengers had Government orders for free transportation. The boats were usually much crowded; though generally there was no difficulty in procuring state-room accommodations. A fine table was always kept.

The majority of the passengers were army and navy officers and men, paymasters, and sutlers. Some of the officers and men had been just discharged from hospital, or had been home on furlough or the recruiting-service, and were on the way to their regiments. Others were newly-appointed officials, with "hay-seed still sticking to their collars," as the phrase goes. The paymasters and sutlers were bound on their usual journeys to the scene of their employment. The few civilians were occasional Congressmen and correspondents, anxious owners of vessels reported to have been condemned by the Government, and sight-seers. The great majority of those in civil life were on pious errands, to relieve the wounded, or search for and take North the bodies of soldiers who had given their lives as proof of devotion to their country's cause.

The boat was fast alongside the Government wharf at Fortress Monroe early on the next morning after leaving Baltimore, and the passengers, upon landing, found themselves under guard, and standing amid all sorts of military goods, awaiting the pleasure of the blue-coated sentries who held them in temporary confinement. The object of this was to prevent any one's straying away before the provost-marshal had seen and "sworn" him. Afterward the party were marched off to a little box-office in the Hygeia Hotel, and there each took the oath of allegiance. Having thus proven their loyalty, all were at liberty to go where they pleased.

The veteran General Wool was at that time in command at the fortress, and but a few days previously had captured Norfolk. Earnest attention was, of course, directed to the scenes presented by that recently liberated town, and hundreds of curiosity-hunters filled up every vessel which plied between Monroe and Norfolk. Fragments of the blown-up Merrimac had been fished out of the roadstead, and were upon exhibition in a dozen places around the fortress. The ancient quietness of Old Point Comfort had left it. Its fine hotel, for years kept as a fashionable watering-place for Southern families, was used as a hospital. Nearly every private residence—and before the war there were many of great beauty—had been converted into a Government storehouse. Huge piles of round-shot, boxes of ammunition, cannon, and other kinds of ordnance stores, filled every available square foot of ground. The ammunition, carefully protected from the weather, was of all descriptions; musket-cartridges, rifled shells, grape and canister, shrapnel, and all the species known to military men, but in naming which a civilian will always become bewildered.

The hotel and buildings are between the fortress and the sea, and back of the fortress is the destroyed village of Hampton, and the half-burned bridge across an estuary known as Hampton Creek. Three miles distant, across the water, nearly in the direction of the mouth of the bay, is a huge, ungainly mass, rising up from the sea, having the Stars and Stripes floating over it, and known all over the country as the "Rip Raps." Sewell's Point is the cape upon the left side of the mouth of Elizabeth River, and is within range of the Sawyer guns mounted on the Rip Raps. Newport News is a point of land at the mouth of James River, and may be called the cape bounding the western side of Hampton Bay, Old Point being its eastern limit. The Rip Raps were originally quicksands, and, being admirably situated for the site of a fort to defend the entrance of Chesapeake Bay, the attention of the Government was early directed to them. On their improvement since 1810, millions of dollars have been spent. These quicksands were very unstable; but the amount of stone poured upon them for half a century has been almost enough to rear an island, even if none had been there before. Now the work seems to be successfully progressing, and the occasional sinking and sliding which for years annoyed every contractor appears to occur very rarely. Within a few hundred yards of the beach at Newport's News is the wreck of the ill-fated frigate Cumberland, the history of whose strange destruction by the enemy's ungainly ram has taken its place among the romances of the war. The frigate lies careened over, the masts visible for a few feet below the tops, and every rope and ratlin as the attack of the Merrimac found them. Few sadder sights meet the eye than the ruins of this devoted vessel.

Between Fortress Monroe and General McClellan's head-quarters, in May last, the Government ran two mail-boats, by way of the York and Pamunky Rivers, so timed as to make a connection with the boats to and from Baltimore. Then, two most miserable boats were employed, though since the best and speediest of the Government transports have been placed upon the line. The I. F. Secor, upon which the author made his passage up the two rivers to Cumberland (at that time the head-quarters), was not only a very slow boat, but had a most unaccommodating set of officers. There was scarcely a seat upon it; and no one could procure a morsel to eat. The mail, thrown in a most promiscuous pile upon the upper deck, was left to guard itself, and, when a shower of rain threatened to drench it, all hands—captain, crew, and passengers—were called into service as a fatigue party, to throw it down-stairs into what professed to be a "ladies' saloon." This boat, and its accommodations and habits were evidently behind the age. Nearly all the passengers who had come down the bay went up the York River upon the mail-boat.

The lower part of York River, like that of almost every other Virginia seaboard stream, is very wide, and one may journey for miles without seeing land. Until the boat approached Yorktown, its course was far away from either shore; and the tediousness of a five hours' journey upon an uncomfortable steamboat, with nothing to be seen but a vast waste of waters, was almost insufferable. The dim sight, late in the afternoon, however, of the brown bluffs in the vicinity of Yorktown, soon relieved every passenger's gloom; and the arrival at the wharf, with the motley assemblage there of negroes, soldiers, and warlike munitions, all three of which seemed to be mixed up in an inseparable mass, turned every sad look to laughter. The army had left the town several days before, and a small garrison took charge of the United States property and joked with the poor negroes.

A few miles farther up is West Point, the head of the York River. Here two tortuous, though navigable, streams, the Pamunky (accent upon the first syllable) and the Mattapony (accent upon the last syllable), join their waters and form the York River. West Point is the terminus of the Richmond & York River Railroad, of which any one at all familiar with events in that locality must have often heard. For several days West Point had been a supply-post for the army; but their passage farther up the Peninsula had rendered it useless. Its neighborhood, too, had been the scene of a battle and Federal victory. Quite a fleet of vessels were at anchor in the harbor, although, so far as could be learned, no troops were stationed upon the shore.

From West Point the railroad runs up the northern bank of the Pamunky, and, crossing it at White House, passes due west to Richmond. This road was of great use to the Confederates in carrying their army to Yorktown. When Manassas was abandoned, and they discovered that General McClellan was landing upon the Peninsula, the railroad was used to its utmost capacity for the speedy transportation of troops to their new line of defence. When Yorktown was abandoned, all sorts of craft were employed to carry the soldiers up the river and place them at the earliest possible moment around Richmond. All along from West Point to White House this railroad and the telegraph-line accompanying it had been broken and cut in a hundred places. Ten miles above West Point there was a high, dangerous embankment, down which, during the haste to get to Yorktown, had crashed a train loaded with troops, many of them being drowned in the river.

Oyster-beds met the eye in every direction, in both the York and Pamunky Rivers. The numerous bends of both were the favorite haunts of these shell-fish. The Pamunky is one of the most crooked streams in the Union. From West Point to Cumberland in a direct line is ten miles; by the river it is thirty.

From Cumberland to White House is five miles; the river runs thirteen. On each bank, as the mail-boat passed up, were evidences of the recent evacuation by the Rebels. Burned boats lay on the shores, and pieces of wrecks were driven about by the tide. The few houses alongside the river all had little white flags upon them, to avert the fancied vengeance which ignorant Virginians feared would be wreaked upon their property. Deserted earth-works peeped out from the midst of trees and bushes. At one place was a barn filled with corn, which the enemy had endeavored to burn, but the quick advance of the Federal troops prevented it. Its sides were burst out and partly thrown down. Two miles below Cumberland the enemy had endeavored to obstruct the river by sinking old wrecks in the channel. The river-bed being of the softest sand, of course these obstructions had been moved about by wind and tide in all directions. One day the passage would be open, the next, closed; and the latter happened to be the case when the Secor endeavored to pass them. In the night she could not do it, and, almost within sight of the wharf at Cumberland, was compelled to cast anchor and wait until morning gave light and help. The result was that her passengers —though not without a fair share of grumbling—each had to pick out sleeping-places upon the decks, and pass the night upon them. Six o'clock the next morning the boat was moored to the wharf at Cumberland, and, going ashore, the author found the general headquarters, showed his War Department pass, procuring the second one, which has been quoted on a previous page, and from that time was regularly attached to the Army of the Potomac.

CHAPTER II.

THE ORGANIZATION OF THE ARMY OF THE POTOMAC.

BEFORE commencing the narrative of General McClellan's military movements, it would perhaps be well to devote a few pages to an explanation of the organization of his army, the duties of each branch of the service, and a description of the occupations and habits of his troops. With such previous knowledge, the military terms and movements will be better understood, the exact meaning of words and phrases which usually render military descriptions so incomprehensible to civilians being known. With a knowledge of the internal arrangement of the army and the feelings and sentiments of the soldiers, one can always hear of their achievements with a deeper feeling of interest.

Military Organization.

The army of the Potomac was commanded by George B. McClellan, of Pennsylvania, senior major-general in the regular service, his commission being dated May 14, 1861. The first subdivision of the army was into six parts, five of them called "provisional army corps;" the remaining one, containing a large proportion of cavalry, being considered an independent division. These were commanded by the six highest brigadier-generals in that army: Brigadier-General Edwin V. Sumner, of New York, and of the regular service, commissioned March 16, 1861, and Brigadier-Generals

Samuel P. Heintzelman, of Pennsylvania, Erasmus D. Keyes, of Maine, Fitz-John Porter, of the District of Columbia, and William B. Franklin, of Pennsylvania, all commissioned May 17, 1861; and George Stoneman, of New York, commissioned August 9, 1861, all holding rank in the volunteer service. General Stoneman was the commander of the independent division of cavalry, and was called the "chief of cavalry." These were the commander-in-chief's field-marshals,—the great generals of the army.*

The subordinate divisions were, first, of each corps into what were technically called "divisions," there being generally two, but sometimes three. These were commanded by brigadier-generals, and were numbered in each corps according to the seniority of the commander, being "first division," or "second," or "third." A division generally contained three brigades of infantry, a detachment of cavalry, and several batteries of artillery. A battery numbers six pieces; and both cavalry and artillery were always under the immediate orders of the commander of division. A brigade was commanded by a brigadier,—though, in consequence of promotions, casualties, and the constant mutations of military life, at least one-third of the brigades were commanded by their senior colonels. Four regiments of infantry were usually contained in a brigade.

The generals of division were all famed for bravery, military skill, and the confidence of their troops. They were Philip Kearney, of New Jersey, Joseph Hooker,

---

* In mentioning rank, the highest commission held by the officer during the author's stay on the Peninsula will be the one given, unless otherwise stated.

of California, Darius N. Couch, of Massachusetts, Israel B. Richardson, of Michigan, Henry W. Slocum, of New York, George W. Morell, of New York, George Stoneman, of New York (cavalry), William F. Smith, of Vermont, John Sedgwick, of Connecticut, Silas Casey, of Rhode Island, and George Sykes, of Maryland. George A. McCall, of Pennsylvania, whose force of Pennsylvania Reserves made an additional division, joined the army a few days previous to its march to the James River.

The generals of brigade were also brave and courageous officers. Of them the author remembers John H. Martindale, of New York, John F. Reynolds, of Pennsylvania, William F. Barry, of New York, George G. Meade, of Pennsylvania, Abram Duryea, of New York, Oliver O. Howard, of Maine, Daniel E. Sickels, of New York, Thomas Francis Meagher, of New York, Willis A. Gorman, of Minnesota, Daniel Butterfield, of New York, John Newton, of Virginia, Winfield S. Hancock, of Pennsylvania, William H. French, of the District of Columbia, William T. H. Brooks, of Ohio, and David B. Birney, of Pennsylvania.

The organization of regiments of cavalry and infantry, and of batteries, both in the regular and volunteer service, varied. For field and staff officers in cavalry, the regular service allowed to each regiment one colonel, one lieutenant-colonel, two majors (in one regiment three), one adjutant, one regimental quartermaster, one sergeant-major, and one quartermaster-sergeant. The company officers were ten captains, ten first and ten second lieutenants (in the regiment having three majors there were twelve of each). In the volunteer service there were always three majors, three sergeant-majors, and three quartermaster-sergeants, and there were twelve of each grade of company officers. In each of the old regiments of regular infantry there were one colonel, one lieutenant-colonel, two majors, one adjutant, one regimental quartermaster, one sergeant-major, and one quartermaster-sergeant, and ten of each grade of company-officers. The new regiments had sixteen of each grade of company officers, two sergeant-majors, and two quartermaster-sergeants. A volunteer infantry regiment was formed upon the plan of the old regiments, excepting that one major filled the place of two. A few volunteer regiments, however, followed the example of the new regiments. The batteries in the army of the Potomac were generally collected in regiments, and had field, staff, and company officers as the above-noticed exceptional regiment of regular cavalry. Still, each battery was always known and spoken of by the name of its captain.

Of regimental commanders whom the author met amid the dreary swamps and bloody fields of Virginia, there were Colonels Simmons, Gallagher, Magilton, Tucker, Woodbury, Gosline, and Miller, all killed whilst bravely fighting their country's battles. And of the living, Lieutenant-Colonel Hatch, a prisoner at Richmond, a courageous Jerseyman, who preferred being captured with his regiment to leaving it; and Colonels Henry L. Cake, one of the bravest of officers and kindest of men, Baxter, Owen, Morehead, Ballier, Davis, McCandless, and Irwin, of Pennsylvania, all eminent for military skill; Taylor, of New Jersey, and Bartlett and Howland, of New York, of whom no word of praise need be spoken; and Farnsworth and Averell, of the cavalry service, one of whom was a besom of destruction to rebel guerrillas, and the other acknowledged to be one of the most accomplished officers in the army. These were but a very few of those regimental leaders of the army upon whom its original enlistment, gradual instruction, and present efficiency almost solely depended.

The General Staff.

All the heads of different departments of service in the army not purely military, but still necessary for its daily existence, with their secretaries and clerks, and also all the aides-de-camp of the commander-in-chief, were embodied into one mass and known as the general staff. These always remained with General McClellan, —when at rest, forming a grand encampment, when on the march, a brilliant cavalcade of elegant horsemen. Brigadier-General R. V. Marcy was chief of staff, and through him all documents not coming officially from some of the departments, and all visitors, had to be presented to General McClellan. The subordinate officers of these departments were, of course, distributed throughout the army, the working of nearly all of them being brought home daily to every soldier. An explanation of the duties of each will not prove uninteresting.

The Aides-de-Camp.

These were gentlemen of the rank of colonel and below it, some of whom were chiefs of departments or assistants to higher officers, and the others, with no fixed duties, assistants to the commander, liable to be called upon at any moment to carry important despatches, or ride to battle-fields, or accompany the general on his constant journeys to all parts of the army, or attend at head-quarters to introduce visitors, pass letters, despatches, &c. through the chain of sentinels to General Marcy, the chief of staff. These gentlemen performed a hundred important duties of all descriptions, and perhaps were among the most useful and hardest-worked of the army. Among them were the English, French, and German dignitaries who have crossed the ocean to study an American war.

The Adjutant-General's Department.

The adjutant-general was the official dispenser of all military orders, and the receiver of every species of military report, document, suggestion, &c. requiring the notice of the commander. His office transacted a rather large business; nine-tenths of it, however, being routine work. Brigadier-General Seth Williams, of Maine, was the adjutant-general. Assistant adjutants-general of adequate rank were assigned to every corps, division, and brigade. All of these—and such is the case in most of the other departments—form an independent roll in the lists of the army, having its fixed duties and system of promotion. Every document intended for the perusal or approval of the commander had to ascend regularly from its starting-point through the line of adjutants, and be first read or approved by each general to whom any one of these adjutants was assigned. If any of them disapproved of it, its upward course was not in every case arrested, but its hopes of a final perusal or approval were much shaken. Having ascended to the top of the line, it was returned through the same course to the first holder. Every military paper is always signed "By order of General

A. B., C. D., Assistant Adjutant-General." The adjutants are the secretaries and clerks of the army, keeping all its records and accounts. Besides their civil duties, they have various military ones to perform, a description of which does not come within the scope of this work.

The Quartermaster's Department.

General Stewart Van Vliet, of New York, presided over this department, which took charge of all the transportation of the army and also supplied it with forage. All the army-wagons, public horses and mules, and vessels, were controlled by quartermasters. Persons entitled to transportation had it allowed them by weight, and means of carriage, upon both land and water, were always furnished upon application to the quartermasters. The department also carried all the army-supplies, taking them to the points ordered by the commissaries of subsistence. They did no loading or unloading, however, the simple carriage being the extent of their duties. Of forage they had complete charge, transporting it and delivering it to those entitled to draw it. Several thousand wagons, and the Richmond & York River Railroad, were employed for land-transportation; and steam-vessels, brigs, schooners, sloops, and barges, almost without number, brought the supplies. The Pamunky, from White House down, was alive with craft, and every Northern port had scores of vessels at its wharves, all controlled by the quartermaster's department of the army of the Potomac. Affairs both in it and the subsistence department were always excellently managed.

The Subsistence Department.

Colonel Henry F. Clark, of Pennsylvania, was the chief commissary of the army. His subordinates received all the supplies of provisions and clothing as they arrived at White House, had them unloaded from the transports, and, after transportation to the camps, delivered them at three or four great depots of supply, first to brigades and then to regiments. The subsistence department also sold at cost-prices to commissioned officers those articles of food provided by the United States, of which sales, however, a most rigid account was kept. Commissioned officers receive a commutation in money for their rations, and when in the field they have to purchase food of the commissaries. The Government provides a few staple articles not given to the men, which are sold to the officers.

The Medical Department.

The surgeon-general of the army was Dr. Charles S. Tripler, of New York, and his department had supreme control of the sick and wounded, medical stores, ambulances, and hospitals. A surgeon was attached to every brigade, and two to every regiment, and each regiment had a hospital steward, who acted as apothecary and general overseer of the regimental hospital. The medical department had complete sanitary control of the army; its duties in this being somewhat like those of Boards of Health and Quarantine. A few of the surgeons were learned men and experienced physicians; but the majority were scarcely competent for the responsible posts they filled. Emergencies such as battles or skirmishes were the great tests of medical ability and bravery, and these trials saw many lamentable failures. The only badly-managed department of General McClellan's army was the medical department.

The Pay Department.

There was no head of the pay department upon the general staff. Once in two months every paymaster came from Washington with his pay-rolls and money, and visited each regiment in his charge. Five or six regiments, and some batteries, would be the number paid by each paymaster. To arrange his accounts at home, go to the capital and pass through the official forms, draw his money, visit the army, return to Washington and settle his accounts, would occupy the entire two months. The paymaster's position was a most laborious and responsible one.

Engineers and Topographical Engineers.

These were the architects, surveyors, draughtsmen, and map-makers for the army. They planned, staked out, and superintended the digging of intrenchments and building of forts; surveyed and built roads and bridges; made maps of the country; sketched the enemy's positions; calculated distances for artillery when brought to bear upon masked or concealed positions of the enemy; constructed railroads; and performed all such duties,—duties which require great skill and thought. They were a useful body of men, doing an immense amount of work, and usually of a kind which was not rewarded by the praises constantly showered upon the more glittering achievements of their brethren who fought the battles. Yet their labor was almost all of the siege of Richmond. The army crossed the swamps upon their corduroy roads, and the water-courses upon their bridges. The troops protected themselves in the engineers' rifle-pits, or mounted the enemy's works by means of their ladders and fascines and sand-bags. The corps constructed numberless intrenchments and redoubts, all places from behind which artillery and infantry could use their arms with safety. They would run lines of works up to the enemy's pickets and compel them to retreat. A vast field which at dusk gave no sign of the Federal presence would at dawn be crossed by a frowning earth-work, filled with Federal troops and bristling with Federal cannon. The engineers were truly a most useful body of men.

The Inspection Department.

Colonel Sackett was chief inspector of the army, and various division-inspectors formed his corps. Their duties were at intervals to inspect the troops and report the condition of their arms and ammunition. A visit from the inspector always caused a general cleaning of every thing the soldier carried. A regimental inspection by the colonel took place every Sunday morning.

The Ordnance Department.

The chief of ordnance in the army of the Potomac was Colonel Charles P. Kingsbury, of New York. The duties of his department were almost similar to those of the subsistence department, relating, however, instead of to provisions and clothing, to arms and ammunition. The ordnance corps superintended the receipt from arsenals and depots at the North, and the delivery to the troops, of cannon, small arms, shot, shell, cartridges, mortars, sand-bags, accoutrements, and every thing which comes under the great head of ordnance. They supplied that which took away life; the commissaries, that which sustained it. This department was admirably managed.

The Provost-Marshal's Department.

This was the great police office and force of the army. Brigadier-General Andrew Porter, of Pennsylvania, was provost-marshal general. His force was made up principally of details of officers and men from cavalry regiments. The provost-guard extended all through the camps; picked up straggling soldiers and negroes, and if they had no passes sent them to the nearest division guard-house, from which the soldiers were sent to their regiments, and the negroes to the subsistence depots if they were wanted there, or, if not, they were kept until otherwise disposed of. The guard picked up all stray horses and mules, and returned them to the public herds; they traced out stolen property, and were generally the fortunate seizers of Rebel spies. They also took charge of all prisoners, who were always turned over to them by the captors. The provost-guard was a terror to evil-doers: the punishment inflicted upon them was always summary. A department like this is a necessity in every large army. Better order never was kept anywhere on the continent than in the army of the Potomac.

The Post-Office Department.

The post-office of the army was at general head-quarters, with sub-offices at the head-quarters of each division; and Mr. William B. Hazlett, of Pittsburg,

Pennsylvania, was the postmaster. Letters to the army were sent from all the Northern offices to Washington, assorted there, and tied up in bags directed to each regiment; then sent to Baltimore and carried down Chesapeake Bay and up the York and Pamunky Rivers to White House. From that place they were transported by railroad and wagon to the general post-office, from which they were sent to each division. Letters to the North were collected at division head-quarters and sent to the general post-office. Thence they went to Fortress Monroe, where they were assorted, an entire day being lost, during which they lay there. Afterward, by way of Baltimore, they were sent to their several addresses.

The post-office at head-quarters was a large tent, with a rail fence running across the middle of it to keep off the crowd, whose pressure was often too strong for more feeble barricades. The front was generally wide open, and at one side there was a bag for the deposit of letters. Back of the fence a long table stood, upon which the assorting was done, and upon each side and to the rear of the enclosed space there were rows of rude boxes, labelled with the names of generals and chiefs of departments. Upon the arrival of a mail, all the bags were thrown under a covering of stretched canvas in front of the tent, by the agent who brought them from White House, those for each division being immediately collected and sent to it. Upon the Richmond & York River Railroad there always seemed to be a war between sutlers and mail-carriers about the mail-car. Each brought his treasures up the river upon the mail-boat, and each was entitled to transportation, one car often being all allowed them. When a large sutler's stock and a heavy mail came up, the reader may judge of each one's efforts to be ahead of his opponent. The successful one, when his goods filled the car, of course thought it all right; whilst the other loudly complained of the deprivation of his fair share, and could see nothing but wrong in the transaction.

Considering that the army was such an itinerant, unsettled body, the affairs of the post-office were generally well managed.

The Printing-Office.

A small printing-office, with a complete assortment of types and paper, and a hand-press, always accompanied the general head-quarters. It was under the direction of the adjutant-general. All the general orders issued to the troops were printed by it in the shortest possible time. A travelling printing-office has, it seems, become a regular item in the organization of modern armies.

The Guides.

Certain persons, having the requisite knowledge, were always hired, during the marches and encampments, to explain localities, roads, plantations, and every natural or artificial feature of the country through which the army desired to pass. These were termed the "guides," and received most liberal pay. They formed no department, each one being separate and independent of the others, and most of them were closely watched. They were presumed to be able to give a history of the public and private career of every influential citizen in the neighborhood of the army. Where the residences of men able to do this accurately must have been before the war can be readily imagined.

The Balloon Corps.

This was an extra department, tried at first as an experiment, but soon, from its great usefulness, adopted as a recognized branch of the service. Its chief was Professor Lowe, who had two balloons of large size, ample arrangements for the manufacture of hydrogen, and complete apparatus for the speedy inflation of his delicate globes. These balloons ascended in all parts of the camp, and employed every moment of favorable weather in observations of the enemy's movements and positions. The topographical engineers and signal-men ascended in them to make sketches and estimate the numbers of troops and strength of earth-works and batteries. Officers of the day looked over the edge of the basket to learn the nature of the ground in front of the picket force they commanded. Many went up out of mere curiosity; but every one who saw the grand and universal view the balloon afforded had its sublimity deeply impressed upon his memory. The enemy had no balloon, and the ability the Union officers had of spying from safe distances into their most secret places gave them paroxysms of rage. They often brought out their artillery to shell the balloon, or shot musketry at it, or cried at it in derision. It was a most tantalizing thing to them to see the little ball and smaller car, standing one beneath the other in the air, a black speck or two in the car, too far distant to be injured, but not too far distant to note the minutest movements made by their troops. The balloon never ascended that scores of Rebels did not curse it.

When a balloon-ascension is made, a strong cord,

which varies in length from one thousand to two thousand feet, holds the frail instrument to the earth. A pulley-and-tackle arrangement worked by men below is the power employed to pull it down, and, this being secured by heavy weights, there is but slight danger of the balloon's escape. Colonel Lowe and his assistants very seldom ascended, officers and others having authority for the ascension being sent up by twos or threes at a time, and after a few minutes' stay hauled down.

Every one has seen a balloon in the air, and knows what appearance it presents; but very few have seen the earth from a balloon, and fewer still have viewed from it the encampments of two contending armies. A newspaper correspondent thus describes the sight, the ascension he writes of having been made near Gaines' Mills, seven miles east of Richmond:—

"When the balloon has ascended to the end of its tether, a grand view of both armies is unfolded. Within a circle of two miles in radius the sight is very perfect; beyond that the angle of vision becomes so nearly horizontal that woods, houses, and hills materially interfere with the view. The landscape has three marked objects upon it, which are the first to strike the eye. The Chickahominy, almost beneath one's feet, bordered by its dark-green swamps, runs like a thread from where it rises on the horizon, away off to the northwest, to where it blends with woods and hills in the southeast. The James River, in front, though distant, runs in a deep, crooked valley, and bears on its bosom hundreds of craft, that in the distance look like specks upon the blue waters. Richmond, covering a large portion of the western horizon, is, however, the principal sight. It appears to the balloonist as a confused medley of red, white, and black; and heavy brown fortifications stretching from the right to the left, with thick earth walls and plentifully sprinkled with cannon, surround it on all sides. The Capitol Square can scarcely be discerned, being too thickly surrounded by buildings. The white Capitol, however, is quite conspicuous, and, of course, the Stars and Bars float over the roof. Three church-spires, seemingly all in one spot, are the brightest part of the town, and catch the eye almost before the observer is aware he is looking at Richmond. But little else, however, can be distinguished,—although, for a general view of the town, nothing could be better than that from the balloon. The space between the Chickahominy and the fortifications around Richmond is almost filled with Rebel camps. A thousand cavalry horses were picketed in one field, and others were plentifully sprinkled all about. Wedge-tents, used by the officers, and little dog-tents, by the men, shone in every direction as the sun's rays struck them. Intrenchments and rifle-pits lined the front of their position, though very few guns were mounted. Several guns of heavy calibre are sprinkled along these earth-works. Rebel camps, however, are the most prominent of all the sights: they show in every direction, and the northern and western horizon seems to be their only boundary.

"Of our own position, as seen from the balloon, I must be silent. One thing, however, in the whole view, is most remarkable. Right through the centre of the picture runs a curved belt of dark-green and yellow, about a mile wide. Not a man, gun, tent, or wagon appears upon it. It is the line between the two armies. Over it, cannon-balls are thrown, and on its surface scouts and pickets hide from each other, but no military sign is to be seen upon it. Everywhere else, stretching as far as the eye can reach, are the thousand-and-one things incident to war; but this broad, quiet, deserted belt of land, so lonely, so sombre, varying only as it is swamp or field or stream, lies there so still that it almost inspires the beholder. Jupiter's belts, or Saturn's rings, never were a grander sight than this belt of land on which nothing like tent or gun appears."

Telegraphing from the balloon was an ordinary thing during the siege of Richmond. During the progress of the battle of Fair Oaks, the balloon was constantly in the air, a wire being run from it to the nearest telegraph-station. The telegraph-operator in the balloon writes the following account of it:—

"The telegraph has been called upon to perform a still more mysterious wonder. For some time past I have been ordered by Colonel Eckert (our superintendent of military telegraphs) to try a telegraphic experiment from a balloon. Saturday morning, when we heard that a great battle must be fought, Professor Lowe notified me that I should extend the wire to his balloon, and we would try it. In one hour we had brought the wire a mile and a half, and I was ready to ascend with the professor. The battle had commenced. When it had reached its zenith, Professor Lowe and myself, with the telegraph, had reached an altitude of two thousand feet. With the aid of good glasses, we were enabled to view the whole affair between these powerful contending armies. As the fight progressed, hasty observations were made by the professor, and given to me verbally, all of which I instantly forwarded to General McClellan and division-commanders, through the agency of the obedient field-instrument which stood by our side in the bottom of the car. Occasionally a masked Rebel battery would open upon our brave fellows. In such cases the occupants of the balloon would inform our artillerists of its position, and the next shot or two would, in every case, silence the masked and annoying customer. For hours, and until quite dark, we remained in the air, the telegraph keeping up constant communication with some point. From the balloon to Fortress Monroe—a distance of over one hundred miles—this wire worked beautifully. A number of messages were sent and received between these two points; and, had it not been for the tremendous rush of business on the wire, I should have telegraphed you directly from the balloon while the battle was raging. Sunday morning, at daybreak, we again ascended. Early in the morning the battle was renewed, and with more fierceness than the day before. Incessant firing of musketry and artillery was kept up until noon, when I had the extreme pleasure to announce by telegraph from the balloon that we could see the enemy retreating rapidly toward Richmond. At this time we could see firing on the James River, to the left of Richmond,—distance from the balloon (some said) fifteen miles. This fire was of short duration.

"The streets of Richmond in the morning presented a deserted appearance,—but very few people to be seen in them. During the afternoon and evening of Sunday nothing of interest transpired, beyond the removal of the Rebel dead and wounded, all of which we could distinctly see from the balloon. Every available machine that had wheels was brought into requisition for this purpose. From the scene of battle into the city of Richmond the road was literally lined with ambulances, wagons, and carts, conveying dead and wounded. About twilight we saw camp-fires innumerable around the city; smoke issued from all their hospitals and barracks; which showed us to a certainty that the main body of their army had fallen back to Richmond. Monday morning we made several ascensions, and found a small force near the last scene of action, and thousands of troops marching out from the city: so you may look momentarily for a report of another severe battle."

The Signal Corps.

One of the most important and, at the same time, most modest branches of the public service was the signal corps. It was an independent body, under the special and immediate control of the commander-in-chief, and was made up of details of officers and men from each brigade in the army. Major Myer presided over its operations. It constructed and worked the telegraph-lines, accompanied all reconnoissances, and was constantly on the alert for the transmission of intelligence to and from general and division head-quarters. All over the extensive field of work apportioned to General McClellan signal officers were found, each one closely watching the enemy's movements.

The officers and men composing the corps were originally selected by a military board which examined their qualifications. Candidates presented themselves to it, and were asked various questions, all of which were intended to test their quickness of memory, and their ability to learn and remember the dumb-motions required in the service. Good eyesight was also considered an essential requisite. It is astonishing to what proficiency some signal officers arrive. By the naked eye they can discern troops and batteries on the enemy's lines, where others entirely fail. They can sit in a room surrounded by hundreds and talk by means of the signal code, and that they were doing so could never be discovered. The ordinary motions of the arm, always used when people are not intentionally keeping themselves perfectly quiet, effectually conceal the three simple motions, combinations of which are employed to transmit information. Then, again, officers standing at great distances can converse by swinging their arms. It is truly wonderful; and the great results which have been brought about by the corps cause utter astonishment to both armies.

There are two systems of signalling used,—by telegraph and by flag. The telegraph was employed upon permanent lines, as between White House and head-quarters, or head-quarters and the division quarters of generals whose ground had been effectually gained from the enemy. Uncertain lines, which, though having a prospect of permanency, were nevertheless at any moment liable to be removed, were run by the patented insulated wire, which has so often astonished the troops, who invariably take it for some vile Secession invention. This is a small wire, insulated with gutta percha and covered with twisted cotton, the whole making a flexible cord about one-fourth of an inch in diameter. It is carried on a reel. A line five miles in length can be constructed and placed in working-order in two hours. The reel is run along the fields and roads, the attendants fastening the cord to trees or bushes at points where it might be accidentally disturbed. When a field is crossed, it lies on the ground, and is found to suffer no harm from the contact. Portable magneto-electric machines, invented by a gentleman named Beardsley, are used for the transmission of signals. These are light boxes about the size of a knapsack. Indeed, the whole telegraphic system of the army of the Potomac was of an itinerant character, and the bottled lightning ran about on horseback as rapidly as the operator who controlled it. The code used was the alphabetic dial-plate of the fire-alarm telegraphs of our large cities.

Flag signalling, however, was the form most generally used, and was the most dangerous. Each signal officer was provided with three square flags,—a white one with a red centre, a red one with a white centre, and a black one with a white centre. These colors had nothing to do with the signal code, however,—the different flags being employed for different kinds of weather and with different backgrounds, that one being used which will be most conspicuous at a distance. These flags transmitted signals by swings, and at night a torch was substituted for them.

The manner of their use can best be shown by illustration. Suppose part of the army makes an advance of several miles within the enemy's lines; a detail from the signal corps always accompanies it. When it leaves the permanent telegraph-station, an officer with his flags is stationed there; at the first turn of the road taken, another is placed, and so on at every point where bends in the road, or trees, or hills, or other obstructions, intervene, and prevent a direct view of the last flag. Every observation made, if it be thought necessary, is readily signalled to the permanent station. The commanding officer of the body of troops sent out tells the flagman with him the message to be conveyed, and the latter gives his flag the swings which correspond to it. The next in the chain observes and repeats, and so the message goes, with lightning-like velocity, back to head-quarters.

In battle, the signal corps is of the utmost advantage. The general commanding the forces engaged places himself on a convenient spot with his flagman.

High hills in the vicinity, out of danger, but excellent for viewing the enemy's movements, are selected, and flagmen placed upon them. Every thing done by the enemy is indicated. Smoke may hide an approaching column from those on whom it is quickly marching. Some of the signal officers, perched like hawks about the field, are sure to observe the advance, and the next instant the general knows it and has warned his subordinates of the threatened danger.

Batteries throwing shot and shell at an enemy concealed from them by intervening hills or woods have all their movements regulated by signals. Miles to the right or left, but in a position where the enemy can be seen, stands the signal-man with field-glass and telescope. One of the guns is fired, but the shell flies wide of the mark. "A little to the right," is signalled. The next shot is nearer, though still ineffective. The flags swing for "a little to the left." The third falls short. "Two hundred yards further," speeds over the line. The fourth strikes; and "a good shot" informs the artillerymen that their range is correct.

Signal duty, from the exposure of those engaged and their conspicuous flags, which are so many targets for the enemy's shot, is one of the most dangerous in the whole service. The bravest and coolest men are required to perform its duties. Sharp eyesight, knowledge of distances, and great judgment are equally necessary to make a good signal officer. The code employed is, of course, known only to those in the secret. Since the beginning of the war, it has been changed once, an alteration being rendered necessary from the desertion of an officer who communicated the former code to the enemy. Now, however, but little danger of the revelation of the secret is feared. The importance of the signal service may readily be conceived by any one who knows the great distances of opposing columns and the wide spread of an attacking army. A commanding general can be in but one place, and it is absolutely necessary that he should have the latest information of the condition of every part of his command. Every battle yet fought by the army of the Potomac has been regulated by signals. The advance, the retreat, the attack,—all are done by the command of a small flag which receives its impulse from a general who may be sitting in a tent a dozen miles away. Every discovery of the enemy's intentions, as shown by their conduct on the field of battle, was made by Major Myer's efficient corps. These men are among the most useful in the army; yet they never pull a trigger, and seldom draw a sword. They toil on at their dangerous task during all hours and through all weathers, and to their exertions are owing many brilliant victories achieved by the Union troops.

The foregoing is a brief view of the organization of the army of the Potomac, a marshalling which has been pronounced upon all sides to be most excellent. Confidence and courage were the characteristics of the military line, and nearly all the departments were managed in a most praiseworthy manner. In routine business the adjutant-general's office was somewhat dilatory, and a shadow was cast over all by the lack of an educated medical staff,—a fault which all deplored deeply.

CHAPTER III.

ENCAMPMENTS AND MARCHES.

BEFORE the army sat down to the siege of Richmond, it was rapidly marching toward the Chickahominy, only encamping when it was necessary to rest the troops or allow the advanced guard time to scour the country. After the siege was commenced, the troops were nearly all the time encamped,—movements made for attack, or defence, or picketing, or intrenching, not necessarily causing a change of the camping-ground.

The encampment of general head-quarters was the most regularly laid out and strictly guarded. Its ground-plan was a parallelogram, with the staff tents upon the long sides, and the commander-in-chief's tent upon one of the short sides, the guard tents being upon the other. At the commander-in-chief's side of this parallelogram a space a hundred feet square is marked out, constantly guarded by sentinels, and upon which no one is allowed to encroach. In the centre of this sacred spot are two large wall tents, each some twenty feet square, pitched alongside of each other, though with a slight intervening space. One of them is occupied by General McClellan, the other by General Marcy, the chief of staff. Both are furnished alike; each has a stove, camp-stools, and table, lounge, camp-bed, desk, and toilet-materials; and various wine-bottles standing about show the means used, even by major-generals, to beguile weary hours and entertain visitors.

In front of these tents a hundred-feet-wide street runs to the guard tents upon the opposite side of the camp. Upon each side of this street the staff tents are pitched, whose occupants decrease in rank according as they are more distant from the hundred-feet square. In these are found the provost-marshal general, the adjutant-general, the inspector-general, the heads of departments, the aids to the commander-in-chief, &c. A row back of these staff tents is devoted to under-officers and clerks, and a third row to servants. Outside of all the horses are picketed,—for every one in this camp rides,—and farther still is the baggage-train, so useful in moving all the paraphernalia. Each tent is like a small parlor, well furnished, and having every comfort and luxury one could expect. The officers occupying them are always about, chatting and talking, the business of many of them not requiring their attention more than one-fourth of the time. The clerks and aids, however, have more onerous duties, preparing every thing for those they assist, a simple reading or signing being usually all that is required of the superior officer. Amid the quiet and seclusion of this encampment the business of a great army was transacted.

In the march toward Richmond, as each corps, or, in some cases, each division of the army, was moving forward to gain a certain point, some at nearer, some at more remote periods of time, an encampment of troops, excepting at Cumberland, White House, and around Richmond, scarcely ever contained more than a single corps or division; the relative positions of the regiments always varying according to the nature of the ground. Grass or grain fields were always preferred for camping-grounds, and a ploughed field or one containing the long stalks and spongy soil left by the last year's corn-crop was never taken, except when nothing better could be had. Convenience to water was usually considered. In a division encampment the infantry brigades would, if it were possible, arrange themselves in a line side by side; but all ways and manners of forming the camp were forced upon them by hills, woods, and swamps. Necessity has sometimes placed regiments upon hill-sides so steep that a man could scarcely ascend them. On other occasions they were compelled to pitch their tents in the woods. No camp was ever placed in a swamp; it might have been on the borders of one, or swamps may have surrounded it, but the officers were too careful of the men ever to place them in the mud and mire where they would sicken and die.

In a brigade encampment the four regiments usually formed a square, two going to the front and the other two to the rear. The nature of the ground sometimes encroached upon this, too, rendering a change in the arrangement necessary. The brigadier-general would pitch his tents near his brigade, generally to the front of it, and the general of division selected a spot upon the outskirts of the division camp. The corps commander made his encampment at a point most convenient to all his troops. If his divisions were separated, it would perhaps be far distant from either, but still at the most eligible spot for both; if they were together, it would be with them.

Regimental encampments were easily formed and very convenient. Every regiment is divided into divisions each of two companies, and these would be ordered into line one behind the other, with intervals of thirty to fifty feet between them, the two companies of each division, provided there was room enough and the colonel wished it, being moved to the right and left to form a centre street of fifty or a hundred feet in width, running from front to rear of the camp. Standing as thus placed, the troops stacked arms and unslung knapsacks and pitched their tents in a row behind the stacks. Officers' tents were placed on the sides of the centre street, if it was wide enough; if it was not, or there happened to be no street, they were put on the outside of the encampment, each on a line with its occupant's company. The field and staff officers usually chose a place upon the edge of the camp, to the front, rear, or sides, and there their tents were pitched, forming the regimental head-quarters.

Each non-commissioned officer and private, although in winter he slept in warm barracks and huts, was furnished with a piece of water-proof canvas some five feet square, having buttons and button-holes arranged on its sides. Four of these, when buttoned together, made quite a large piece. This would be thrown over a musket or fence-rail supported by two sticks driven into the ground, and a fifth piece of canvas buttoned to one end of the rude tent thus formed effectually kept off the wind or rain. The other end was left open, and the lower edges of the canvas were secured all around by stakes stuck into the earth. Five men slept comfortably under one of these "dog-tents," as they were universally styled, only suffering inconvenience when a drenching thunder-storm set the whole camp afloat.

In addition to the field, staff, and soldiers' tents,

there were various others necessary for the transaction of the business of the regiment, which were placed upon the edge of the encampment. These were the surgeon's tent and the hospital steward's tent. The first was the office where patients called, were prescribed for, and given advice and medicines. The other was supposed to be the medical dispensary,—though it seldom really was; for a steward taken from the plough or work-bench, as nine-tenths of those in the army were, would scarcely be trusted to mix medicines, even for a quack. These tents were usually near the regimental head-quarters. Besides the above, there was always a large hospital tent to the rear of the camp, in which lay the sick who had been ordered into hospital. The commissary tent, under which the quartermaster-sergeant or regimental commissary kept his few days' supply of rations and served them out to the troops, was also to the rear of the camp.

Camps were named in a most arbitrary manner, and generally without recourse to system. General head-quarters on one occasion was called "Camp Lincoln." Then the army were earnestly working at the siege. But upon all other occasions its camp was named after different places in the neighborhood, such as "Tunstall's Station," or "Coal Harbor," or "New Bridge." Division and corps encampments were rarely named, and regimental camps were called after the various captains, or by numbers, or perhaps had no designation at all. No one was ever at a loss for a name; for "Camp, —— miles from Richmond," or, "Camp on the road to Richmond," always answered for an emergency.

In camp, the daily military duty was to mount guard, which was performed by each company in succession,—

one company's tour of guard duty being twenty-four hours. Mounting guard consisted in placing a chain of sentinels around the camp, policing all the streets, by removing dirt and garbage from them, and furnishing all the "details," as they were called,—squads of men, which might be required for cattle or head-quarter guards, or other purposes outside the regiment. Of course, the principal duty was the posting of sentinels, and this, when there were numerous points to be watched, required a great number of men. There is always a guard tent, or guard head-quarters, and the nearest sentinel to it is named "Guard Number One." The next is number two; and so on until the circuit of the camp is made and the starting-point is reached. A sentinel stands on his post for two hours, when he is relieved by another man. He is always instructed explicitly as to the particular duties of his position, which are always of the simplest character,—to prevent any one's passing a certain way, or entering a door, or to announce visitors to an officer, or to see that no one touches some piece of property he is guarding; duties which, to be correctly performed, require but little mental ability.

Some of the most amusing incidents of the war are those in which sentinels take the principal parts. No challenging ever took place in daytime; the countersign was given out at dusk, and then the strict watching commenced. Some sentinels were surly and gruff, others polite; but, generally, their assumed stoicism, or real awkwardness, was most ludicrous. Every one is instructed to salute a general or field officer, when such a one passed him, by presenting arms, but for a company officer shoulder arms was the custom. Some would present arms to all; some shoulder to all; and some would merely raise their hands to their caps,—the ordinary military salute. It was after dark, however, when the most laughable instances of sentinelship occurred. An officer lying in bed would suddenly have his attention called by a hasty challenge:—

"Halt! who comes there?"

"A friend, with the countersign."

"Advance, friend, with the countersign."

And then the "friend" would whisper the word to the sentinel, which, if correct, would pass him. This was the usual form of challenge and reply. But, if the "friend" did not happen to know the countersign, which was usually the case,—for until the army had fairly sat down before Richmond there was scarcely any one but straggling soldiers abroad after dark,—the form was somewhat altered:—

"Halt! who comes there?"

"A friend," or "a friend without the countersign."

"Stand, friend, where you are."

And the sentinel would at once call out the number of his post, which, if it happened to be far away from the guard head-quarters, would be echoed after him, one after the other, by the entire string, all the way to the guard tent.

"Corporal of the guard number ten!" shouts the sentinel.

"Corporal of the guard number ten!" is nine times echoed, in nine different ways, by nine styles of voices. Directly, carrying his musket with a precision which any soldier might envy, the corporal is seen solemnly marching along the line of posts to "guard number ten," to ascertain the trouble. The sentinel reports and the "friend" tells his story,—his case usually turning out to be that of a lost and straggling soldier who has unwittingly passed within hail of the guard. The corporal takes him to the officer of the guard, who disposes of him as he thinks proper.

Once the commander of a picket tour, by some mistake, did not receive the countersign. His men were posted upon a road, and the hour was much later than it was advisable to permit an unchallenged passage. Farther along the road some cavalry sentinels were pacing up and down, and, taking a musket from one of his soldiers, he walked toward them. Assuming the posture and appearance of a sentinel, he challenged the first one who approached him, who promptly answered, giving the countersign; and thus the officer procured it. When parts of regiments were detached upon distant service, they were sometimes overlooked in the delivery of the countersign.

The countersign for each night was selected by the aide-de-camp at general head-quarters who at that time happened to be on duty as staff officer of the day. It was sent to the head-quarters of corps, and from them through the different grades to the regiments, being given to each at about four in the afternoon. It was written upon a curiously-wrapped piece of paper. The officer of the guard in each regiment was furnished with it by the adjutant. Any one whose business took him through the camps after dark first procured the countersign; otherwise he would be halted and questioned at every twenty yards.

There are hundreds of anecdotes floating through the newspaper and periodical press of the country, whose wit is founded upon the mistakes or sharpness of sentinels. The two given below are new, and their truth can be vouched for.

The chaplain of a regiment once had a friend visiting him, who remained rather late, and started for his own regiment without taking the precaution of previously ascertaining the countersign. The chaplain bade him good-bye at his tent-door, immediately stepping into it. The other commenced his homeward walk, and had gone a few steps, when he was suddenly brought to a stand-still by a gruff challenge :—

"Halt! Who comes there?—WHO COMES THERE?"

"Me,—a friend of the chaplain."

"Have ye the counthersign?"

"No."

"Faith, an' if ye were a frind of the divil, and had no counthersign, ye couldn't pass here."

The other is told of a quartermaster, who came to the lines of his own regiment and was challenged. When he entered the colonel's marquee, he reported the following for the conversation. The sentinel was, of course, an Irishman.

"Halt! who comes there?"

"A friend, without the countersign."

"Well, an' what d'ye want?"

"Well, I am the quartermaster, and this is my regiment, and I want to get into it, but, not knowing the countersign, I suppose I shall have to go back where I came from and get it."

"Is that all? An', be jabers, what's to prevint my givin' the counthersign to ye?"

"Nothing, I suppose."

The Irishman whispered it to him; then, challenging

again, the quartermaster gave him the countersign and entered the lines.

Such ludicrous scenes as these are continually occurring; but nothing was more laughable than the string of echoing voices which would at dead of night roar out, "Corporal of the guard number ten!" or "Corporal of the guard number six!"

The usual military drill, whilst in camp, was two hours each favorable day at the bayonet exercise, one of the most healthy, graceful, and instructive exercises in the manual of arms. Other drills were usually dispensed with, as the men were considered to have attained enough perfection in them.

There was, of course, much leisure time, when the men were not called upon for any military duty. These spare moments were variously employed, according to each soldier's tastes. Many read, as there were an abundance of newspapers in camp, bundles of them being sent as donations from the North, and several first-class dailies from Philadelphia and New York being offered for sale upon the second day after publication, and bought up with avidity. Others wrote, all sending letters home to their friends, whose answers gave additional reading-matter. Numbers of the men kept diaries of their regiment's daily history. Some were artificers, and did the tailoring, shoe-mending, or carpentering for the rest. Then there was the never-failing supply of leaf tobacco found everywhere, which converted almost every smoker into a cigar-maker, and every chewer into a flourisher of the pestle. Nothing perhaps indicated the genuine life of a soldier better than a cigar-maker, with his workshop, wares, and customers. An old board was his table and the ground his chair; a Barlow, which for years had answered all the purposes of a case-knife, tooth-pick, and general knife, was his tool. Upon the board he prepared the tobacco, moistening it from a cup of water, and then, rolling it and cutting the ends, produced an elegant cigar of pure, unadulterated, Virginia tobacco. These cigars were sold at low rates to those uninitiated into the mysteries of the tobacconist's art, and, though somewhat rank from being so freshly made, were no doubt greatly enjoyed by their buyers.

The vast stores of tobacco left behind by the fleeing Virginians were most tempting to Northern dealers, who came South by scores to attempt their collection and transportation home. They all failed of their purpose. On land it could not be collected, because they had no teams, and, if they had, there would have been no means of transportation to Fortress Monroe. It would not be allowed on the mail-boats, and all the transports were engrossed with other duties. These dealers sometimes managed to get small stocks to the North, but they were seldom of sufficient value to repay the trouble.

If a paymaster had happened to visit the regiment a short time previously, then the troops would set aside nearly every thing else for what has been somewhere styled America's national game,—the game of "poker." A blanket thrown upon the ground extemporized a table, around which the parties seated themselves, with the spectators in a second row behind. The banker would produce an ear of corn, taking off the grains and selling them to the players. Timid parties made each one worth a penny, but bold ones would have it five or ten or twenty-five cents, some even going so high as a dollar. Then they played "going it blind" and "straddling" and "going better" and "bluffing," until some call to duty or a noisy quarrel ended the game, each man upon counting his grains usually finding himself worth neither more nor less than when the day's work was commenced. Playing "poker" was allowed in some regiments, excepting upon the Sabbath and late at night, when any one discovered at it was severely punished.

The men had a hundred devices to kill time and get amusement. They flocked in droves to all ox-killings and horse-burials. The shooting of a sick horse upon the borders of a camp was usually the signal for an hegira. A broken-down wagon or one fast in the mud, however, they viewed at a distance: they might be requested to help mend it or push it out of the mire. A dress parade or bayonet drill of another regiment drew large crowds, and ones, too, strongly inclined to criticism. When the army neared Richmond, the soldiers went in droves as far as they could to the front, to see the Rebels and watch their movements. Some of them, at a loss for other amusement, arranged lotteries of all kinds and descriptions; and among the most ingenious and profitable was one invented by an enterprising soldier of General Slocum's division. The man's nationality never could have been detected from either shape or voice or countenance; each belonged to a separate race; but he had enough shrewdness to discover that the Virginia statute-book legalized lotteries. His stock in trade was a dirty stocking-leg, one end sewed up and a running string through the other, a dozen numbered tickets, and a lot of cheap scissors, combs, and trinkets. "Only twenty-five cents a draw, and no blanks," was the generous announcement he made to the wondering group which surrounded him. If a bystander's curiosity overbore his caution, the lottery-dealer would take his twenty-five cents and allow him to poke finger and thumb into the filthy bag after a ticket, and then, scrutinizing it carefully to correctly ascertain the number, the dealer would pull out of a mysterious rent in his coat a pair of scissors, a knife, a comb, or a ring, or some other equally valuable article, and, presenting it to the ticket-holder, inform him that it was the "highest prize." One act of justice, however, which this man always did, is not usually found among those who deal in more valuable prizes. If the drawer of the "highest prize" did not happen to be satisfied with his supposed good fortune, the lottery-man, with the greatest possible frankness, would offer to exchange the money for the prize, and, if the tender was accepted, always did it, giving as his reason for such rare generosity, that there were plenty of other soldiers who would be glad of the chance to draw it. These lotteries gave great amusement to the troops, and, although arranged upon so petty a scale, were as earnestly sought after and argued about as if they were of the utmost importance.

When no amusement was offered,—no ox-killing, horse-funeral, or Rebel-shooting,—the soldiers lay under their little tents, or hunted cool places in the woods, where they would go in small parties, and talk, smoke, or read. This lounging in the woods once produced a most laughable result. The army had not yet reached the Chickahominy, but the enemy, as was occasionally the case in its march across the Peninsula from White House, was reported to be in great strength close at hand. A beautiful piece of woodland, cool and inviting, and jutting out into a field so as to make the cleared portion in the form of an L, interposed between one of the regiments and the part of the country where the enemy were said to be. Of course, numbers of soldiers were scattered through it. A body of troops who had been upon picket-duty came up to the edge of the wood upon the opposite branch of the L and fired their muskets into the air, making a terrible noise. Instantly there was a most inglorious scampering out of the woods, some in their great hurry tripping over the stumps and roots, and rolling out, heels-over-head. To a man, they reported that the enemy were attacking the camp; and some even declared that they saw Rebels. Those in the camp who knew the truth soon enlightened the others, and a laugh all around was the end of the matter.

The numerous religious associations of the North were most assiduous in sending tracts, books, and Sunday-school newspapers to the soldiers. The newspapers and books were much sought after and earnestly read, and so were the tracts, but not to so great an extent. More papers and little books, if sent, would find plenty of readers.

A Sunday in camp was spent in a way to make it as nearly as possible a day of rest. At ten in the morning was the inspection of arms and accoutrements by the regimental commanders. That over, there would be divine service, if the chaplain chose to hold it. The remainder of the day the men had to themselves. It was the policy in the army to give the men this day as one of perfect rest, if it could be done. The commander-in-chief adopted the plan at the earliest moment after he took command; and every officer is aware of its good sense. When the siege commenced, however, Sunday was, of necessity, almost ignored.

The food of the troops was, each day, one ration for every soldier. The different articles forming the ration, and their amount, are regulated by act of Congress. In the food given an army, too much sameness is always the great fault. It caused much dissatisfaction in the army of the Potomac. Though each soldier received as much as he could eat, yet day after day he would be compelled to take the four or five old things he had eaten for a year. It naturally caused discontent and grumbling.

These rations are always drawn from the subsistence department. Orders are sent by the general officers to each regiment, commanding that requisitions be made for one, two, three, or four days' rations, the number of days varying according to the length of contemplated marches and the supply on hand at the issuing-depots. These requisitions, after being approved by the commander of the brigade, are taken to the brigade-commissary, who delivers the food, which is carried to the regimental commissary tent and there issued to the various companies. The articles served to the troops are, for each day's ration, either salt pork, or salt beef or fresh beef, first one and then the other being issued (after the commencement of the siege, fresh beef was issued every day); pilot-bread; desiccated vegetables or beans; flour or corn-meal; coffee or tea; sugar, molasses, salt, vinegar, and pepper. Desiccated vegetables were thin plates composed of all sorts of vegetables, potatoes, turnips, carrots, beets, squashes, parsnips, &c., which were prepared by being first cut into small pieces, and then compressed by an enormous pressure into a hard, thin plate, entirely devoid of moisture. These were intended to be made into soup, but usually produced a substance of so sickening a character that the soldiers loathed it. Yet the surgeons considered it so very healthy that orders were issued forcing the men to eat. After the arrival of the army upon the James River, this mixture was discarded, and fresh vegetables issued in its stead.

In addition to the above, after the hard work of the siege had commenced, a ration of whiskey of one gill daily for each man was served out. From fifteen to twenty-five gallons, the amount varying with the number of soldiers, was each regiment's daily allowance. The delivery of a ration of whiskey to a company was irresistibly comic. The orders were, a half-gill morning and evening; and so soon as the whiskey-carrier—or, as he was universally called, the "jigger-boss"—came with the precious beverage, the whole company would flock around him, and, the captain superintending, each man received his allowance and drank it with extreme gusto, expressing his enjoyment in all sorts of lively ways. The troops were always on the look-out for whiskey, and in some cases they have paid smugglers as high as seven dollars a pint for it. When the commissary-wagon went around to the various companies in a regiment to deliver stores, there was always a universal cry for whiskey, and, if there happened to be none, the wagon and its attendants were saluted with groans. Whiskey seemed to be the object all were striving for; but the provost-guard did its duty so well that there was rarely any drunkenness in the army.*

* In such statements as the one contained in this last sentence, the author, of course, refers only to the time he was with the army.

Each company's cooking was superintended by one of its sergeants, who also drew its rations,—the four sergeants, in most cases, relieving each other at intervals. A detail of one or two men from the company assisted. These men would procure fire-wood, for which they had recourse to the neighboring worm fences, or, if fence-rail stealing was forbidden, they went to the woods and cut green timber. Trees a foot in diameter have often been felled to procure a half-dozen sticks of small-sized wood from the upper end; and a new tree was usually taken to supply the fire for preparing every meal. Pine and red and white cedar were the species of wood taken. The sticks, when carried to camp, were laid in a long, narrow pile and kindled. A cross-piece set upon two forked stakes, so soon as the fire was started, supported the four or five long black three-gallon camp-kettles in which each meal was cooked. One contained coffee or tea, another salt meat, a third fresh meat, a fourth bean soup or soup made from the desiccated vegetables, and the fifth—if there was a fifth—boiling water, or salt pork, or something else which the company had been fortunate enough to procure. The cooks worried over these kettles, roasting themselves and sometimes spoiling the food, until in their opinion each article was ready for eating. Then the sergeant would cry, with a loud voice, "Company A, fall in for soup," or, "Company B, hot coffee," or any other expression but the customary ones of breakfast, dinner, and supper, and the men, as hungry as wolves, would quickly fall into line, each with his tin cup and plate.

The coffee, soup, and meat were then served out, every one getting as much as he could eat. Previously to the announcement of the meal, sugar is generally stirred into the coffee-kettle, thus saving any trouble about teaspoons. The men eat in messes, sharing their victuals freely not only among themselves but with strangers. Extra plates could always be had by laying down as many pilot-crackers as were needed. Meat could be easily cut upon them, and the only way of eating them with any satisfaction was by first soaking them in coffee. The mess at a meal was usually the party who joined tent-cloths.

The food issued to the troops was very wholesome, but, as the same four or five articles were placed before them day after day, they would become surfeited, and, in the anxiety for a change, spend their money at sutlers' stores for unhealthy pies and cakes, mouldy crackers, and expensive sauces and spices. It was a common circumstance for a man to spend four or five dollars for a jar of mustard or catsup or Worcestershire sauce. There was always a great demand for these things, and prices ruled high. The sutlers' wagons and tents were filled with them. Sweet cakes, sodden pies, and candy were the great bane of the army. Such things were the staples of a sutler's stock, and from their sale he made his largest profits. Precept and example were used—uselessly, however—to prevail upon the troops to relinquish their unhealthy and expensive habits. They ate and sickened, and the sutler would thrive.

The cooking for each officer was done by his servant, who was either a negro or one of the soldiers, and he also purchased upon the officer's orders the requisite supplies of food from the commissaries.

Upon forming a new encampment, the search for

water was always the first exploration of the immediate neighborhood. Water for drinking, cooking, and washing was used by gallons, and every one interested in either started off to find it. Sometimes a hundred went, each with a canteen to bring back a drink for his friends. The soldier was always generous. The searching parties would go down into every hollow place, and trace up and down every stream, carefully scanning the banks on either side, to find all hidden springs. The Peninsula between White House and the Chickahominy was full of springs and brooks. The neighborhood of that river, however, was found to be different. Running through a swamp, of necessity every tributary stream would be absorbed long before it reached the main channel, and although there were hills in plenty bordering the swamp, yet scarcely a spring could be found. At an encampment, water was usually found in sufficient quantities to supply all. Sometimes it was taken from a single spring, sometimes from several, all of which had boxes or barrels sunk in them to keep out the dirt, and each one being guarded by a sentinel to keep thoughtless fellows from washing their clothes there. The kind of water procured was seldom very good. A fine white mud, in most cases, boiled up with it out of the spring, coloring it quite perceptibly and imparting a bad taste. The nearer Richmond, the worse was the water and the harder to get at. An adequate supply of water is every thing to an army; and one of the greatest of the soldier's troubles in Virginia was his inability to procure it good, clear, and cool.

The clothing of the troops was usually in pretty good condition, though stains and patches showed some rough usage. The suits worn during the siege had been the soldiers' constant wearing-apparel during the previous year, and in them the men had wintered opposite Manassas and besieged Yorktown. All had seen hard service; and yet, after passing through it, scarcely a man was ragged, and the rags were generally at the pantaloon-ends, where constant rubbing over the rough and sharp-edged shoes would soon wear the stoutest fabric into holes. The under-clothing and stockings were always good. The Government, through the agency of the Quartermaster's department, issues to each man twice a year what is styled a ration of clothing. If carefully preserved, this ration will be an ample supply, and in some cases more than the soldier will require: the value of any articles not drawn is placed to his credit on the pay-roll, but, if more than the allowance is drawn, the extra articles are charged to him and deducted from his next payment. The careless and improvident—those who when on marches throw away their clothing, thinking the loss of the pound or two left on the roadside materially lightens the burden they have to carry—are the ones who need and draw more than the Government ration, and, when the paymaster visits them, are always astonished at the amount which must be deducted.

The universal color for the uniforms of all arms of the service is a dark blue, with yellow cords on the seams for cavalry, and red for artillery. The Rebel uniform was generally an iron-gray, the color of the homespun cloth of which nearly all their clothes seemed to be made. Rebel field and company officers wore the same clothing as their men, stars upon the lappel indicating rank in the first, and bars upon the shoulders in the other. Federal and Confederate general officers seemed to dress with about equal taste and style, the uniforms being somewhat alike in shape.

"To police a camp"—a term of daily use in the army—is to send a party through it to collect all the dirt and garbage and burn or bury it. This was the great conservator of health, because upon the cleanliness of the camp depended very much the purity of the atmosphere the men were breathing. The commander of a regiment, so far as its internal affairs were concerned, always had the health of his troops in his own keeping. A careful man would superintend the cooking, and have all the remnants, whose decay otherwise impregnated the air with noxious gases, instantly removed. A slovenly officer was different. In his regiment the cooks regulated themselves, and, if any one threw out garbage, it lay where he threw it until by decaying it removed itself. Happily for the service, however, a colonel was very rarely found who was careless of the health and comfort of his men.

To personal cleanliness the troops were quite attentive, the lack of large streams interfering very slightly with the regularity of their ablutions. Every stream of any size was always filled with swimmers, and little brooks would be constantly lined with bathers. Every man in the army washed his own clothes, the Governmental provision for "two washerwomen to each company" not appearing to apply to the army of the Potomac. Of course there was some good washing done, and a great deal of very bad; but the strenuous efforts of all to learn the mystic art of combining soapsuds and friction in such proportions as to extract dirt deserved the highest commendation. Some earnest washers made themselves wash-boards, which they carried about, but no one was able to manufacture a tub. To nearly all, the muddy banks of some Virginia stream would be not only tub but wash-board, and, half kneeling, half sitting, they would for hours rub and scrub at a stubborn subject, rendered more intractable by their inadequate materials. Yet all managed to wear clean clothes, and have a stock on hand for an emergency.

Many of the officers and soldiers sickened from the unhealthy country in which they sojourned, and the exposure they necessarily encountered. These cases were mostly confined to a very few diseases. Rheumatism troubled some, but fevers were the almost universal maladies, typhus and typhoid holding the principal sway. Typhus is the proper name for camp-fever, ship-fever, jail-fever, and others arising among people of uncleanly habits when crowded together in unhealthy or confined places. It is the great scourge of military life; and one of our most respected medical writers has said that "it dogs the footsteps of retreating and discomfited armies and settles in their tents." It is strange, but none the less true, that defeat and low spirits have equally as much to do with causing typhus as dampness or dirt. A retreating army, or one which when lying in trenches or in camp constantly "feeleth that hope deferred which maketh the heart sick," always has the greater part of its sickness caused by typhus. Great nervous depression is its characteristic, and the patient frequently dies from the inability of his system to react. Typhoid is of the opposite type. Inflammation and delirium, with all the exhibitions of the wildest insanity, torment the poor soldier whose body is a prey to this terrible disease. He rushes to battle, commands an army, defeats the enemy, flies from the foe, shouts for help, drills his company, and clutches at some terrible imagination, all at the same moment. A hospital filled with typhoid and typhus patients is a harrowing sight. The dull, inanimate stupor of the one, and the fearful, uncontrollable excitement of the other, both appal us.

The gnawing of home-sickness, too, is a cause of illness in the army. Few will believe it, but many cases have been caused by this sad mental ailment. The most marked cases of this the author ever saw were at an army hospital at Quincy, Illinois. The surgeon pointed out two men who had been in the hospital there for months: home-sickness was their only trouble. It had unfitted them for every camp-duty; and, so weak that they could scarcely walk, and so depressed that they ruminated only upon home, home, they had been sent to the hospital. The surgeon stated that there was but one cure, and it would be almost instantaneous in its effect. If he could give them the joyful news that they were to be sent home, weakness, depression, all would leave them, and they would in a few days walk about, strong, healthy men. Another man had been sent to hospital with these two, and for the same cause; but his agony was too terrible: he succumbed to it, and his body now lies under a green sod upon the banks of the Mississippi.

Of course, many soldiers feigned sickness to avoid the disagreeable and dangerous duties of military life; and it depended upon the shrewdness and tact of the surgeons to hunt out these dissemblers. They generally were successful; and "shamming" became quite an unprofitable business. A surgeon of a year's experience of the constitutions and characters of the soldiers in the regiment to which he was attached, rarely was deceived by unsteady walking, whines, or groans.

A sick man in a regiment, so soon as discovered, would be reported "sick" by the surgeons and sent to the regimental hospital. If this hospital was in the camp, it would be the tent referred to upon a previous page of this chapter; but sometimes, especially when the army became settled, it was a deserted house near the camp. These hospitals in many cases were kept in a most slovenly manner, and a man or two from the regiment detailed to nurse the sick would take charge of them. General hospitals were also established at various points, to which sick were sent from these when they were too full, or when the malignity of the disease was such as to need careful treatment. White House was a general hospital; and so were Savage and Fair Oaks Stations, upon the Richmond & York River Railroad. From these large hospitals many patients were sent to the North for treatment. Very little comfort was found in any of these hospitals, and the soldiers' hatred for the whole of them was most intense.

Soldiers in camp usually appeared very well and very cheerful. Of course, under so hot a sun as the one which darted his rays upon Virginia, laziness throve amazingly. The troops, however, contentedly performed all required of them. "Poker" was the infallible time-killer, and, much to the disgust of the chaplains, was indulged in to an astonishing extent. The men always had a kind word for a visitor. Ignorance, however, of what was passing around them, and of things which were daily brought to their notice, strangely enough seemed to be universal among the common soldiers. Ask them the simplest questions, and they would answer negatively, or, Yankee-like, with another.

"What regiment do you belong to?"

"Thirty-first New York."

"Well, where's your brigadier-general's head-quarters?"

"I don't know; but look a-here, is there ary a sutler over your way?"

A private soldier seldom had more than two questions to ask a stranger,—where his regiment lay, and where was the nearest sutler. He scarcely ever answered any, because he did not know how.

About one-half of the regiments of the army had fine bands of music, enlisted before the law was passed prohibiting the future enlistment of regimental bands. Each band consisted of one principal musician, ranking as first lieutenant, twenty players, two enlisted with each company, and a drum-corps of ten boys, one from each company. There was always an abundance of music, especially upon the pleasant evenings, when every band in the army would play its sweetest notes. As Richmond was approached, however, band-playing was prohibited, as it indicated the Federal force and position to the enemy. Glee-clubs, some of them containing admirable singers, then were formed, each one enlivening the monotony of its neighborhood. The army always had an abundance of vocal and instrumental music, and it was one of the most useful enjoyments allowed the troops. It cheered them, and gave renewed health and spirits. Many a man owed his freedom from sickness to his regimental band or regimental glee-club. They were a better sanitary commission than the medical department.

A corps of pioneers, usually containing ten men, was also attached to every regiment. These men, on marches, cleared the roads of obstructions, and mended bridges and impassable places. In battle they were of great use,—opening passages, obstructing roads, breaking down bridges, and throwing every possible obstacle into the way of the enemy's advance. They worked hard, and often in most dangerous places. Better woodmen than the pioneers of the army, America never produced.

By military law, a sutler is allowed to each regiment, being appointed by the colonel. Many regiments, however, had no sutlers, they either having been sent away for malpractice, or the colonel refusing to name any. No position in the army could have been made more useful, and was at the same time more abused, than that of the sutler. Congress, at the solicitation of Hon. Henry Wilson, of Massachusetts, recently passed a law stating the list of articles sutlers would be permitted to sell, and prescribing the regulations under which they were to transact their business: so that the sutler acts as it were by legislative sanction. These men took their stocks of goods to White House by authority of clearances granted at some Northern port, and made oath that they only brought such articles as were allowed by law. When the sutler reached the camp, he erected his tent, and the United States guaranteed him payment for goods purchased by the troops to the amount of one-third of their pay. This he collected as the troops were paid, and, in case of a dispute, the account, verified by oath, could be collected from the paymaster.

If a regiment so decided, a tax of ten cents per month for each officer and soldier contained in it could be collected from the sutler. This would average some sixty or seventy dollars. When collected, the money is made up into a fund for the support of a band, the education of children born in the regiment, and to stock a library. It was very seldom collected in the volunteer service, though there was full authority for doing so.

Very few sutlers charged what may be called reasonable prices for their goods. Five times as much as the worth of an article was the usual charge for it. Even at this exorbitant rate they disposed of their stocks in an exceedingly short time. A sutler arriving at camp early in the morning with five thousand dollars' (at the selling-price) worth of goods, by noon will have sold three-fourths of it, and before sunset will have nothing left but that dead stock which is the loss of every store. Some sutlers brought their stocks, disposed of them, and then went North to invest their profits and purchase a second. Others remained constantly with the army, having wagons running back and forth to White House to transport the new supplies their assistants brought there.

These men, taking advantage of the monopoly they enjoyed, acted most unjustly toward the troops. There were a hundred little articles needed by the soldier and not furnished by the Government which he purchased of the sutler. There being no competition, he could not go from one to another and buy of the cheapest, but was forced to pay the price asked, and in many cases procure a most indifferent article. A few of these prices will astonish the cheap buyers and sellers of the North. Penny gingerbreads were from twenty-five to thirty cents a dozen. The poorest crackers brought twenty-five cents a pound. Four-cent sodden pies commanded twenty-five and thirty cents. Emery and sand-paper and sweet-oil, extensively used for cleansing muskets and accoutrements, sold for ten times their price in the North. Lemons, so poor that they would be dear if given away, were sixty cents a dozen. A pound of cooking-soda sold for thirty cents. Twenty cents was the lowest price for an eighth of a gill of ink. If a generous officer wished to "treat" a friend, he had to pay dearly for the privilege. Fifty cents paid for two glasses of porter or ale, provided he furnished his own glassware and drew his own cork. Forty cents would buy two glasses of beer. If he wished to take lighter stimulants and had a piece of ice to cool it, fifty cents would pay for two glasses of soda-water. Two mint-juleps were sold for a dollar and a half. A bottle of brandy cost from five to ten dollars; and then it was only sold to favored ones, who procured it after as much diplomacy and red tape as were required to secure a public appointment. None of these liquors were ever sold to the privates.

These high charges were nearly all profit. It costs but little more to take a stock of goods to the army than it does a country storekeeper to transport his from a commercial centre. One of these sutlers, whose prices endorsed the statement, told the author that from one-half to two-thirds more than Northern rates would amply pay for any sutler's risk and trouble. Two-thirds at least of the prices usually charged in the army were profit, and were transferred from the scant purse of the soldier to the greedy maw of the sutler. Such being the case, it was seldom that the sutlers had the good will of the troops. All sorts of difficulties were thrown in their way, and an accident happening to any one in the business was hailed with universal delight. A tariff of prices of articles sold should be established by law, and every sutler made to conform to it.

In their journeying to and from White House, the sutlers suffered some risk of capture by the enemy, —though, even considering this risk, an advance of seventy-five per cent. has been acknowledged by the more honest of them to give both insurance and profit. When Stewart's cavalry raid, on June 11, crossed the White House road, it encountered a heavily-laden sutler's wagon. The enemy took the horses, drank the liquors, carried off a lot of shoes the sutler had, and then spilled the remainder of his stock by the roadside.

The sutler who carried on his monopoly at General McClellan's head-quarters, afraid his wagon could not keep up with the others in the great march to the James River, threw every thing out as it drove along, a hundred soldiers scrambling after to pick up the broken pieces. Sutlers at White House were always in a most unenviable state of mind. All sorts of stories of reverses to the army in advance constantly reached them, and they were terribly afraid they would lose the trash they expected to sell at so high a rate. Stewart's raid capped the climax. After that the slightest rumor hurried them on board the boats, and, until the great destruction, their goods were daily afloat and ashore. The breaking up of the United States post at White House upon June 27 caused the financial ruin of nearly all. The sutlers were a wretched class of swindlers, and well deserved all their troubles.

Usually, each regiment kept its horses and wagons to the rear of its camp, but upon the approach of the Federal army to the enemy, the teams of a brigade or division were parked. A safe spot would be selected always, under shade if possible, and the wagons and horses were kept there in a mass. If the wagons were needed as a protection against threatened attacks of the enemy, they would be arranged in long rows in front of the Federal position, the horses being taken to the rear. Teamsters and ambulance-drivers were detailed from the companies for six months at a time, and received extra pay. The teamsters of the army were often very rude and brutal, cruel and rough to their horses, and always in a bad humor with every one. They were decidedly the most profane body of men in the whole army.

For forage the Government served out hay, oats, corn, and salt; but hay and oats could not half the time be had. Heavy contributions were levied upon the farms and inhabitants. From Ashland, north of Richmond, to White House east of it, and indeed in every direction, so far as foraging-parties dared to go, every bushel of grain, every ox or steer, horse or mule, was seized and confiscated. For twenty miles square, the country has been deprived of every thing which will sustain life. Corn shelled and on the ear, oats, and sometimes wheat, were brought into camp by wagon-loads, and, when they were exhausted, wheat and oat straw were cut from the growing fields and fed to the horses. Good pasture offered in many cases, and was always eagerly sought after and quickly cropped close to the ground: indeed, horses were often pastured in fields of standing wheat and oats.

With all the care and attention that could be given them, thousands of horses sickened and died. Corn when fed alone was their great bane, and although strenuous efforts were made to avoid it, yet when all other forage was exhausted it had to be fed to keep the animals from starving, and under its influence they soon sickened. There was sometimes much trouble in procuring adequate supplies of forage. Artillery horses, however, were always well fed and sleek-looking. As was proper, the stock of hay and oats was given them first, and very few ever died. To kill an artillery horse is in effect to disable a cannon: so all of them were kept in the best condition. Cavalry horses fared no better than regimental ones: both were treated alike.

It was the duty of the provost-guard to catch and send to the public herds every branded horse or mule found straying. They also did the same with animals having soldiers riding them without authority. Stray horses and mules were constant visitors at regimental encampments, and were taken possession of by the quartermaster. So many teams were disabled from the horses having died or sickened, that such voluntary gifts were unusually acceptable. The provost-guard seldom recovered them if they were good for any thing, as they could readily be passed off for old horses, especially if any were dead.

A brigade blacksmith-shop was established in every brigade wagon-park, and at it all the public and private horses of the brigade were shod. Mechanics also performed there any smith-work needed about the cannon or small arms.

Contrabands swarmed in all parts of the army, and roamed about the country in droves. Squads of runaways were gathered on all the marches, and at every halt where a plantation was camped upon, the negroes would be attracted by the music and tinsel and travel off with the Union army. The supply of contrabands far exceeded the demand. They were employed in the greatest numbers in the power of the authorities; but still hundreds, either from choice or necessity, prowled about, subsisting by charity and thieving, seen one day and disappearing the next, and some of them, no doubt, acting as spies for the enemy. The subsistence department gave employment to great numbers, and its officers generally gave a very poor report of the working-powers of the newly-liberated slaves. Many were taken for officers' servants and company cooks, but very often the runaways from one master became runaways from another. Of course, in many cases, the negroes worked well: if they did, they were always kept in their places, and good servants, being such a rarity, were well taken care of.

These negroes were a most amusing set of people, and the soldiers plagued them terribly to get more fun out of them. They would catch a little negro, and give him something to eat, and then ask him all sorts of absurd questions, such as, "What relation are you to Jeff Davis's coachman?" or, "What did General Johnston say to you when you saw him last?" Then they would ask the poor fellow if he was not a "Secesh," to which he would quickly answer, "No, sah," when some one would angrily start up, declare that he was, say that he had seen him talking to Rebels, and telling them that he was as big a Rebel as any of them; or, taking the subject in a different way, would argue Secession up and Union down, until the young African was completely befogged. This was a process through which nearly every negro boy entering the camps was made to pass. He would at first stoutly deny that he was a Rebel; but the truth became so strong from dozens of bystanders, who had all seen him in Richmond, or Secession was supported so well by its newly-found admirers, that the youngster would forget every thing in his fright at being found out, or his joy at discovering such good Rebels in the Union army, and at last confess "dat he were a Rebel, anyhow." Shouts of laughter, however, would soon bring him to his senses and good Union principles.

Old negroes never were treated in this way; but quite as much amusement was had from them by what may be called attempts at astonishing,—attempts which were usually successful. No richer scene ever was witnessed in the army than that which took place between a group of officers and an old gray-headed negro in a camp at Mechanicsville. The man had somehow introduced himself into the party, and happened to state,—

"Dar be right smart o' men round hyar, but I dunno 'bout dar bein' able for to take Richmond."

"Right smart of men!" said a colonel; "right smart of men! why, this is only a flea-bite to what's coming to eat up the Rebel army. Why, they're coming on all sides, just like locusts. Here's McClellan with half a million down around here" (waving his hand about him); "and there's Burnside down there, coming up from Carolina with a hundred thousand more; and General Banks up there, coming down with two hundred thousand more; and General Sigel, with two hundred thousand more; and General Fremont, with a hundred thousand more, all up there; and General McDowell out here, coming along with so many thousand that he can't count them; and every one of them will be here in less than a week!"

As the list of generals, with their imaginary armies, was run over, the old fellow opened his eyes wider and wider, expressing the most unfeigned astonishment; and when the colonel was through he gazed intently in his face and asked,—

"Got all dem men?"

Which was promptly answered, "Yes;" when he slowly rolled up his eyes, and, throwing out his arms, ejaculated,—

"Jesus an' de Lamb!"

That negro was the victim of the game of astonishment.

Wandering negroes were usually treated in this playful manner, it being very rarely that they were quarrelled with or in any way maltreated. Those in Government or private employ were never molested. The troops had a peculiar opinion about the race generally: they were in favor of freeing the slaves and of enlisting negro regiments, but they wanted none of these regiments to fight side by side with them. Send such soldiers to Port Royal or anywhere else but the army of the Potomac, and the troops would cheer them on with a will, but if negro regiments were brigaded with them they said they would almost mutiny. This was the universal sentiment, and the officers endorsed it,—excepting the mutiny. Their remedy they did not tell, but they were strenuously opposed to brigading whites and blacks together.

There were very few restrictions placed upon the soldiers whilst off duty. The principal one was against roaming outside of their camps. The stragglers were picked up and sent to the guard-houses by the provost-guard. Those holding passes, however, never had any trouble. A pass would state that its bearer was going to some camp, or house, or hospital, or wherever he might be sent, and had leave of absence for a certain length of time. They were granted by the captain of the soldier's company, and approved by its colonel. These secured their possessors within the prescribed limits of the journey, until the time had expired.

A restriction upon marauding also bound the army. Although foraging was ordered and carried on to the utmost extent, yet good discipline required that it should be by authorized persons. Any one going out and taking goods from friend or foe without having the authority to do so, was regarded as a common thief, and so punished. So were all persons who bought or took from the first party any thing which had been thus stolen, knowing it to have been wrongfully appropriated. Foraging was to be for the benefit of the whole army, and all things thus procured were to be placed in the public stores. Violations of this rule, if allowed, would have converted the army in time from a body of brave soldiers into an undisciplined horde of indiscriminate plunderers. Stealing from the poor, who, perhaps, had nothing to look forward to after their scant stock of food was exhausted, and who were usually defenceless widows living upon their acre of land in a wretched log hut, was also prohibited. To steal a chicken or an egg did very little good to any one, yet it took the last morsel out of the mouths of a hungry family. Upon large plantations belonging to Secessionists, no guards were ever placed, and but five mansion-houses were guarded during all the march across the peninsula. One was White House, at the time General McClellan's head-quarters; another was Dr. Gaines's house, employed as a prison for spies and doubtful inhabitants; another was Huger's, at the time General Hancock's head-quarters; a fourth was the large house at Savage Station employed for a hospital; and the fifth the residence of a Union man near Turkey Bend, whose owner had been long ago driven from his home on account of his opinions, and who went across the Peninsula with General McClellan to see once more the house which had not known him for over a year. All the other large houses, out of which every thing valuable had generally been removed by their fleeing occupants, were unguarded and left to be ransacked by the troops,—though what enjoyment it was to them to break furniture and crack window-glass, few had the good fortune to see. Mechanicsville was first battered to pieces by Federal and Rebel shells, and then had a greater part of the woodwork torn from the rickety houses to form floors for the soldiers' tents. The only tenable house in it, like every other one convenient to the army, was used as a hospital. The only property and plantations guarded were those known to be owned by Union men,—men like John M. Botts, who fought the monster until it defeated him, and then was imprisoned. These plantations, like the others, were deserted, but their owners were pining in Southern dungeons, not leading an enemy's forces; and even the troops, knowing upon whose property they were encamped, refrained from doing it any injury. The house of a former citizen of Maine was protected in this manner, and all felt a respect for its maltreated owner. Such protection even the most devoted advocate of confiscation will tolerate. Yet, in foraging, these men's property was taken when grain could not be procured elsewhere. It was their misfortune, for they lived in an enemy's country.

Upon the 29th of May, an officer was dishonorably dismissed for receiving stolen property, knowing it to have been stolen. A copy of the order dismissing him will show the court-martial procedure, and the punishment for such an offence:—

"General Orders, No. 132.

"I. Before a military commission, of which Colonel D. B. Sackett, Inspector-General United States Army, is President, convened by virtue of special orders No. 144, from these head-quarters, of May 10, 1862, was arraigned and tried Captain John Brown, Company H, 85th Regiment New York Volunteers, on the following charge and specification:—

"Charge—Receiving stolen goods, knowing the same to be stolen.

"Specification—In this, that he, Captain John Brown, Company H, 85th Regiment New York Volunteers, did purchase for the sum of ten dollars, from a marauder, a mule, and did receive and take the said mule into his own possession, knowing the same to have been stolen by the said marauder. This, on or about the 10th day of May, 1862, near Roper's Meeting-House, Va.

"Plea—Not guilty.

"After mature deliberation on the testimony adduced, the commission found the accused as follows:—

"Of the specification—guilty.

"Of the charge—guilty.

"And thereupon did sentence the said Captain John Brown, of Company H, 85th Regiment New York Volunteers, 'To be dishonorably dismissed from the service of the United States, and to be confined at hard labor for the term of three years in the Penitentiary of the District of Columbia, Washington City.'

"II. The proceedings and sentence in the case of Captain John Brown, 85th Regiment New York Volunteers, are confirmed. He accordingly ceases from this date to be an officer in the military service of the United States, and will be sent under guard to the United States Penitentiary for the District of Columbia, and delivered to the warden, with a copy of this order.

"III. The military commission, of which Colonel D. B. Sackett, Inspector-General, is President, is dissolved.

"By command of Major-General McClellan.

"S. Williams, *Adjutant-General.*"

The army had had so much drilling whilst lying in front of Washington, that, with the exception of the bayonet exercise, practice in the manual of arms and battalion drills were generally dispensed with. Dress parades at receptions and inspections were, of course, in vogue, but, with the exception of these parades on rare occasions, there was nothing to divert the attention of the troops from the siege. Unnecessary drill would needlessly fatigue them, and the battles and skirmishes they fought conclusively proved that they were sufficiently versed in military knowledge to be a fair match for the enemy. In like manner, no unnecessary labor was imposed upon them,—no grand reviews or objectless marches, no frequent changing of camps to suit the whims of generals. Firm opposition was always made to every such procedure by the higher officers with whom it lay to order marches and reviews, and the foolish projects were usually given up. Knowing, as the troops did, that they were carefully shielded from all unnecessary work, they performed the duties required of them, however arduous, with the greatest alacrity. The longest marches would be made, the hardest picket tours watched, and the most laborious wood-choppings performed, without a sound of dissent. The army was well disciplined, and its officers knew how to keep that discipline and the spirits of the men up to the highest pitch.

During May and June there were several visits of distinguished men to the army. Upon May 14, Secretaries Seward and Welles made a trip to Cumberland. They were most hospitably received by General McClellan, and as the troops were all encamped together, upon a vast plain, under his escort they passed on horseback through the camps. Each regiment was paraded, and cheered them,—an honor which they acknowledged by bows, and sometimes by a few words from Mr. Seward. The regular troops cheered them with great glee,—it being the first occasion of the kind upon which they were known to loosen their tongues, as they reserve all their shouts for the battle-field. The Secretaries went down the river on the following day, much pleased with their visit.

From the 8th to the 10th of June, the Spanish General Prim was the commander-in-chief's guest. Being an eminent military dignitary, he was, of course, honored with reviews of all arms of the service, and also with one of a section of a battery in action against the enemy. He spent his time very busily, visiting all parts of the army, and viewing the enemy's defences (Richmond was at that time besieged) from all points. He said that he was much gratified with the hospitality shown him, and paid the highest tributes to General McClellan's military genius.

Congressmen visited the army frequently, and always were shown the greatest consideration and given every facility for observation. Gentlemen without rank or official position, having the requisite passes, were treated politely, and given all information which could be given, to aid them in accomplishing the thousand errands which brought them to the battle-fields. Casual visitors might tell at home what stories they pleased: if they were gentlemen, they were received as such by an army of true soldiers; if they were not, their treatment was according to their merits.

In their opinions and feelings the troops were much like other men. They disliked negroes and Rebels, and were confident of defeating the enemy in every battle, and of capturing Richmond at an early date. Each officer and man had his plan for its seizure,—some good, some bad, and some most absurd. So prevalent was the fashion, that, rather than have no plan, a soldier would propose a nonsensical one. The troops had most decided opinions about every thing, even down to the exact amount of coffee a tin mug would hold. The army was the most inveterate set of arguers and boasters one need ever be thrown among. Their arguments, however, were usually a mixture of assertions and bets, and, with many, a contradiction was sure to bring the discussion to the great point of honor,—"Do you mean to say I lie?"—a course which ends all argument and commences something more serious.

For these reasons, military men, unless they had mixed much with other than military society, were not very pleasant companions to a civilian. They usually talked but one style,—the style *militaire;* and among ignorant subalterns it was in a strain of the most vulgar braggadocio. Such habits, growing upon them for the whole time they were in the army, of course, would produce jealousies and social schisms. It has done so in every army, and did so in this; and officers of the same State, or brigade, or regiment, would cling together and speak harshly of their brethren. The soldiers imitated their officers, of course. Army-jealousy is a terrible vice.

Amid all this Babel of opinion and argument, however, there was one sentiment in which the whole of the army, officers and men, agreed. All had the firmest confidence in their commander-in-chief, and expressed it upon every occasion in the plainest terms. The generals approved of his plans, and the troops, if he ordered it, would cheerfully incur the greatest perils. That confidence seemed as if it could not be shaken: every victory strengthened it; not a disaster impaired it. The enemy even breathed the infection, and, in their fear of McClellan, became bewildered in their movements, and expressed the most marked discontent with the conduct of the war.

In the army of the Potomac there were two species

of marching employed,—in "heavy marching-order," and in "light marching-order." The former meant that the troops were to carry all they possessed with them; the other was to march with only the musket, ammunition, haversack, and canteen, thus being in trim for working or fighting. Every order to march specified one or the other manner. For heavy marches, two or three hours' notice were usually given, so that time might be had for preparation; light marches, unless to picket, were generally to be commenced on the instant. Another style of order, always implying light marching-order, was sometimes made. This was "to be held in readiness to march at five minutes' notice." Such an order as this was given when an engagement was in progress or anticipated, and the soldiers stood in line behind their musket-stacks until the order was rescinded or they were marched off in accordance with it.

In a heavy march to a new camp, the generals of division and brigade would first arrange the order of the brigades and artillery in the line of march, and next the order of the regiments of each brigade. This would all be specified in the official order commanding the march, and every part of the whole would be able to, and usually did, fall into its proper place in the line, without confusion. The division general and staff preceded the division, and each brigadier and staff rode at the head of his brigade. Artillery rolled along in regular order—cannon, caisson, forge and ammunition wagon—to the end of their line. A regiment marched in the following manner: first the adjutant; then the pioneers; then the band and drum-corps; then the colonel and lieutenant-colonel; then the regiment, each man with his knapsack, haversack, canteen, and arms; and, bringing up the rear, the major, chaplain, and two surgeons, and, on foot, the hospital-knapsack-carrier. The colonel and adjutant sometimes exchanged places, however.

When these marches commenced, the men would be in regular military order, four abreast; but the first half-mile usually broke up all regularity. The men before they had walked that distance would become dispersed all over the road, some walking along the banks and others in the ditches: a squad straggling along the centre would be all the orderly part of the regiment. Some ran down into gullies to search for water, and others started off to see curiosities. Many on long marches became exhausted by fatigue, and lay down under the trees to rest. In warm weather these marches—if prolonged to six or eight miles—were most trying. The suffering for water was usually the greatest trouble,—men carrying such heavy burdens as the soldiers requiring a great deal, and good water in any quantity being rarely discovered. Several halts of an hour or half-hour each were made in these marches, to allow the men to unsling knapsacks and rest or search for water, and to give the stragglers time to come up. The wagon-trains of each regiment followed at the rear of the division in the same order as the regiments marched. Each regimental quartermaster and quartermaster-sergeant attended the teams of his regiment.

A march to battle would be made in light marching-order, the men four abreast, and generally on the double quick. The men were held under strict discipline during such marches. The march from the field, however, was far different. If a victory had been gained, the men would cheer and talk, and the officers imposed no restraint. If a defeat had been suffered, angry arguments about its cause would foreshadow the disaster long before they reached the camp. A march to picket was in light marching-order, and at common or quick time, and, when the picket tour was approached, it was conducted with great care and quietness. Homeward it was the same.

A march to chop wood or build roads and bridges would also be in light marching-order, at common or quick time, and—if the place to which the troops were going was not a dangerous one—without arms. Upon reaching the scene of labor, the command was usually given to an officer of engineers, who, through their company officers, directed the movements of the men. The march back to camp was as the one from it.

The general conduct of the troops upon these marches was such as could scarcely be found fault with. The burdens carried in heavy marches, and the discipline exercised in light ones, usually kept them to the road,—though, of course, in the former some would stray and visit the deserted houses in the fields. The inmates of every negro-hut were besought for "hoecakes;" and when the amazed woman would naturally say, "Why, bress de Lord! how can I gub one cake to all o' you?—dar, ye see dat I hab but one!"—some oily customer's reply would come, "Give it to me, aunty; I asked you first." Plaguing the negroes for "hoecakes" was usually the greatest extent of lawlessness when the troops were marching. No rapine or wanton destruction disgraced the marches of the army of the Potomac.

CHAPTER IV.

FROM CUMBERLAND TO WHITE HOUSE.

WHEN the Rebels evacuated Yorktown, a portion of their army retreated up the York and Pamunky Rivers,—partly on transports, and partly by swift marches along the roads bordering those streams. This body passed quickly up to and garrisoned White House and its vicinity. Their main body, however, retreated along the centre of the Peninsula,—the rear-guard giving the Union troops battle at West Point and Williamsburg,—and then passed into the Chickahominy valley, crossing that river on the numerous bridges below the Richmond & York River Railroad-crossing and strongly garrisoning all the passes.

A large body of General McClellan's troops did not take part in the siege of Yorktown. They remained on transports in the river, prepared at any moment to land and aid their comrades on the shore. Part of these, after the evacuation, landed, and fought the battle of West Point, and, continuing ashore, became the right wing of the army. General McClellan left strong garrisons at Ship Point, Yorktown, and West Point, so long as they were depots for landing supplies; but, after the marching of the troops had rendered these posts useless, the garrisons were removed.

Yorktown—occupied by the remnants of one of the most gallant regiments in the service, the Forty-fourth

New York Volunteers, the "Ellsworth Avengers"—was evacuated the latest of the three. Williamsburg, an inland town, whose heavy intrenchments witnessed some hot fighting before the Federal troops carried them, was for some time a military post of importance, and Colonel David Campbell, of the Fifth Pennsylvania Cavalry, was named as military governor. Passing events, however, soon deprived the town of its strategic value, and before the middle of May every Federal soldier had left it.

The main body of the Rebels retreated by West Point and Williamsburg to the Chickahominy valley, and General McClellan pressed strongly upon them so long as they continued in front of him. The battle of West Point was fought by Pennsylvania and New Jersey troops; and at Williamsburg Generals Sickels and Hooker by their brilliant charges gained high honors. Afterward, finding the intention of the Rebels to be to gain the Chickahominy and post themselves along it, the commander-in-chief conceived the plan of marching rapidly to White House, securing its good harbor and railroad as his means of landing and transporting supplies, and then, after passing across the Peninsula, of laying siege to Richmond. So, as swiftly as the rains and mud would allow, he brought his army up the roads before used by the body of Rebels who retreated to White House, and, on the 14th of May, rode with his staff into a vast plain at Cumberland,—a small village upon the Pamunky,—which he designated as the camp for the entire army.

His baggage-train, however, was not so fortunate. The road the general took, and upon which the train was to follow, forked at a place called New Kent Court-

House, two miles south of Cumberland. The wagon-masters brought their charge safely to New Kent, but, instead of taking the side of the fork leading toward Cumberland, they drove off the other way, directly for the enemy's pickets. Soon a force of Rebels, supported by a battery, advanced against them, and the entire train was thrown into confusion, when the timely advance of two regiments of regulars put the Rebels to flight. The wagons were afterward placed on the right road and proceeded to their destination. No damage was done to either army in this skirmish.

All the afternoon and evening of the 14th, troops from below were marching upon the vast plain and taking their allotted places in the encampment, and at dawn on the 15th, the commander-in-chief had all his soldiers within a circuit of four miles around him. Every division of the army was encamped upon that plain, and, by ascending a hill to the southeast, observers had a complete view of the largest encampment ever formed upon the continent. It was upon this hill that the artists of the pictorial newspaper press made their sketches, engravings from which were scattered so profusely over the country. But no engraving could ever present the grandeur of the sight, and one could only truly view the "Camp at Cumberland" from that high and barren hill. There never was such a scene presented afterward.

On all sides but the north there were tents,—high marquees for the officers, and low shelter-tents for the men. To the northward was the river with its gunboats, and, beyond, Manassas, with General McDowell's *corps d'armée*, and, farther still, Washington, with the great, earnest, rebellion-hating North looming up behind. That side of the hill needed no part of the army for its protection. In every other direction, though, there was a solid mass of tents and artillery and wagons, extending to a great distance. Twenty square miles were estimated to have been covered by that camp, and all over those twenty miles the eye would wander and view the vastness and power of the grand army. Its discipline and bravery, both before and since, have been proved on many a well-contested field. The camp was surrounded by a fringe of woods, which formed a fit bordering for such a scene. On but two other occasions—at White House and during the siege—was the army all encamped together, but in neither case was there any commanding spot from which the encampment could be viewed.

With the camp at Cumberland commences the military history of General McClellan's operations, as personally viewed by the author. At that point he joined the army, continuing with it until the 7th day of July. At Cumberland the march upon Richmond was really commenced. The *corps d'armée* were arranged into wings and centre, and Generals Stoneman, Philip St. George Cooke, and Emory, with their cavalry forces, were the advanced guard. General Keyes, with his corps, was on the extreme left, then General Heintzelman. General Sumner was in the centre, with General Fitz-John Porter adjoining, and General Franklin on the extreme right. The enemy were in force upon the Richmond side of the Chickahominy River, and had strong bodies advanced across it, but they made no demonstrations against the Federal army. General McClellan proceeded slowly and cautiously, abstaining from all offensive movements until the supply post at

White House was established and the whole army free to act in concert.

White House was peaceably evacuated by the enemy on the evening of May 10, and was immediately taken possession of by General Stoneman. Previously to their evacuation the Rebels burned the Richmond & York River Railroad bridge, a rude structure built upon piles and crossing the Pamunky, making a break in it just large enough to allow the Federal gunboats to pass through and ascend the river above. This destruction was thus a positive benefit to the Union cause, and at any rate could not have inflicted any injury, as the intention of the supply department was to use the railroad from White House to the Chickahominy, abandoning the section leading to West Point. The orders given to General Stoneman, when he occupied White House, were to hold it until the enemy appeared with stronger force, in which case he was to retreat. A transport, with supplies, sent up from Cumberland on Sunday, May 11, landed them, with every thing arranged for a hasty departure if danger appeared. The enemy did not come, however, and on May 12 several thousand infantry marched to the place, and formed an adequate garrison.

On the morning of Friday, May 16, the camp at Cumberland was broken up, and the army left for White House, five miles northwestward. Troops were constantly leaving Cumberland until Saturday, and Sunday morning saw the last teams of the United States army being slowly dragged from the once so thickly-peopled plain. A rain, which began on Thursday and continued all night, converted the roads into deep mud, and the marching troops and artillery cut them up terribly. This movement was most sadly delayed. Many of the teams had to be assisted along the whole distance by details of men, and it took nearly all of them thirty-six hours to pass between the two places. Virginia roads, after a rain-storm, are execrable.

The troops of Generals Franklin, Porter, and Sumner, upon their arrival at White House, encamped upon a piece of level ground extending along the Pamunky, and which had been planted with corn and clover. Generals Keyes and Heintzelman were to the south of them. Until his baggage-train arrived, General McClellan made the White House his head-quarters. Troops and teams were arriving from Friday until Sunday, and it was not until the afternoon of that day that every thing became settled and quiet. Monday morning, early, saw the vast army move again. The supply post had been established and had commenced operations, and the army was free to begin the earnest work before it. Generals Heintzelman and Keyes marched toward Bottom's Bridge, a crossing-place of the Chickahominy ten miles east-southeast of Richmond and thirteen west of White House. These generals commanded a force of forty thousand men of all arms of the service, and were well supplied with artillery. The main body left by roads crossing the Peninsula north of the railroad, though near it, and by noon on Monday, May 19, the entire army of the Potomac was on the direct road toward Richmond.

Before leaving White House, the commissary post and its operations, together with the condition and usefulness of the contrabands employed there, ought to be fully described. At the time the army left, the post was not in full operation; but the following week saw a port on a tortuous, scarcely-known river of Virginia, which was a fair rival of New York, Philadelphia, or Boston in the extent of its coastwise commerce. Steam and sail vessels continually arriving and departing, extensive wharves, with cargoes constantly unloading, crowds of negroes, carrying boxes, rolling barrels, dancing, singing, and joking, officers, armed with a little brief authority, giving orders with stentorian voices, and all the hubbub and confusion of a large port, were found at White House. It was a busy town, without a single warehouse in which to store its goods. Lines of railroad ran to the river-side, and beside them the commissary stores were piled, and, as they were needed by the army before Richmond, were loaded upon the cars and sent forward. All was under the superintendence of two most excellent officers. The quartermaster's department was presided over by Lieutenant-Colonel R. Ingalls, and the subsistence department by Captain G. Bell. Both were honest, hard-working men, and they conducted the business of the post admirably.

The Pamunky between Cumberland and White House is a crooked stream, bending about in all sorts of ways. This section, however, is the most pleasant portion of the river. A ride between its green banks, rolling and rich, skirted with beautiful hills and dotted all over with patches of dark woods, was most enchanting; and every bend enhanced its beauty. A few miles above Cumberland, bordering the northeast bank, were a series of islands, upon one of which were a few log huts, inhabited by half-breeds. This place was called Indian Town, and its inhabitants were said to be the last remnants of Powhatan's tribe. Near the huts there had been a ship-yard, and the half-burned ruins of a gunboat lay upon the river-bank and lined the shore below. Just above, at a point where its guns could sweep for miles both up and down the stream, was a Rebel earth-work, partly hidden by the trees, and with one end adjoining a house which claimed protection under one of the omnipresent white flags. Several traps for fish-catching were placed in eligible spots on either bank.

The approach to White House was one worthy the pencil. A beautiful curve of a mile in length, the outer side of which was a low bluff surmounted by trees, changed the course of the river. In the centre of this curve was the White House and its grounds, and above it were the wharves and landings. Land and water blended to produce the scene; and the life given it by the moving craft on the river and the toiling negroes on the shore rendered the whole most picturesque.

An unending stream of vessels passed both up and down the river. A fleet at Fortress Monroe fed the upward current, and another of anchored transports at White House received it. As the supplies were needed, the vessels containing them were brought to the wharves and unloaded by the negroes; and as soon as the cargo was discharged the vessel was sent off to a Northern port for another. Some of the transports—especially those containing ordnance stores—remained for months at anchor without being once disturbed. All kinds of craft were employed by the government,—brigs, schooners, sloops, canal-boats, barges, steamboats, and propellers,—every thing which could float, and whose owner could get the Government to employ it.

Some of the vessels chartered by the Government were the greatest oddities. The North seemed to have been ransacked to find all the queer, old, worn-out steamboats and broken-down barges and canal-boats. Steamboats which had, from age or debility, been discarded from Northern pleasure-lines, and which during 1861 suddenly disappeared from Northern bays and rivers, were all found plying up and down the York and Pamunky Rivers. Old tow-boats, familiar servants to the ship-owners of large cities, long, lank propellers, which neither nature nor art ever intended to be models either of speed or beauty, sprightly tugs, once frisking about in Northern harbors, all had been transferred to the Pamunky, where they puffed and labored and made the hills echo their shrill whistles.

Some vessels in Government employ were new and in excellent repair. By far the greater portion, however, were in bad condition, and were held at exorbitant prices,—prices promptly paid, and in many cases without adequate services rendered. Some were completely broken down,—leaky hulls and leaky boilers,—and others managed to get rid of doing any work. One owner is said to have gone up to White House to look after his vessel, when he was told by some one in the quartermaster's department,—

"The Government is going to discharge the boat."

"Why so?"

"Because the captain keeps dodging about and hiding among the big boats, and don't carry one cargo in six months."

Boats out of repair were condemned, and sent home

to be fixed up, the payment of charter-money being stopped in the mean while. Unless damage was caused by Government officials, the authorities never paid for its repair. The boats on the Pamunky were condemned by scores.

Coal was always furnished steam-vessels by the Government. Hundreds of barges from the Lehigh and Schuylkill regions of Pennsylvania came to White House loaded with fuel, and, when the stock on any boat was low, the captain procured an order to fill his bunkers, and, hauling alongside the nearest barge, took what was requisite. Contrabands were always furnished for coal-heavers, and the order having the number of tons taken marked upon it was a sufficient voucher for the captain of the coal-barge. This coal was bought by the Government, under some of the numerous contracts which were so famous during the summer of 1861. It was of all qualities,—a great deal of good, but still a great deal of bad.

Sail-vessels were generally chartered at prices very near the ruling ones in the freight-markets. They were employed to carry cargoes from Northern ports to White House, were paid fair freights, and the usual allowances for delays in unloading. When its cargo was discharged, the vessel usually sailed back to the North free of Government control. Still, in some instances the course taken with steam-vessels was followed in the case of the others, and as exorbitant prices paid to charter indifferent hulks as were ever paid the owners of dilapidated steamboats. Coal-boats were generally bought, being made into wharves when their cargoes were all out. All the landing-places at White House were old barges and canal-boats securely lashed together and laid side by side until they extended to deep water. Lumber was sent up from Fortress Monroe to cover them, and to make floors upon which the stores might be piled on shore.

All the labor of unloading stores or transferring them from one boat to another was performed by gangs of negroes. Twenty or thirty were placed under the charge of a sharp negro overseer, whose pay was generally regulated by the amount of work his gang performed. These negroes would commence at daylight and work until dark, every one arguing, ordering, singing, or shouting. A boat-load of negroes with no officer by was unbearable, and the overseer, whose supreme authority was most prominent in all his acts, generally led the rest in their noise by all sorts of unintelligible orders. Let an officer step on board, though, and all would be quiet, each man rolling his barrel or carrying his box, but keeping most careful watch over his tongue.

These negroes were paid good wages by the Government, and were fed with soldiers' rations. Each gang slept on a barge, and one of the number, exempted from other labor, did the cooking. The negro quarters were always a popular place of resort after nightfall for all who wished to be amused. Songs, dances, stump-speeches, and arguments, in which "words of learned length and thundering sound" were used without reference to grammar or dictionary, would be heard for hour after hour. A negro is an exhaustless wit; and these original Virginians, brim-full of every kind of fun, talked politics, discussed the war, gave characters to their former masters, and settled the fate of Richmond, nightly. But even humor often becomes listless; and theirs, as midnight approached, usually waned. Each weary fellow crept off to what he called his bed, the last one kicking over the candle. And until dawn Africa was quiet.

The usual statement of the officers of the subsistence department, as to their working-abilities, was that if free negroes from the Slave States could be exclusively employed they would wish no better help. Slaves who were runaways, or who had been emancipated by the advance of the Union troops, were very poor workmen. A Virginia negro never performs a quarter of a day's work on his master's plantation. If he is a house-servant, he is usually a favorite, and, of course, knows nothing of the really hard labor required on the transports. Field-hands plough, plant, and hoe corn, reap the crops, and husk the ears; but the greater part of them work when they please, and even then have no employment for a large part of the year. Even when wages are offered, the stimulus is not sufficient to overcome ancient habits of laziness. The department was always anxious to rid itself of these lazy runaways.

Parties of fugitives from all parts of Eastern Virginia came daily into the lines of the army. The majority flocked to White House to seek employment. Of course, they were taken if there was the slightest possible chance of giving them work, either there or at the issuing-depots on the railroad. These negroes had strange ideas of what they expected to find in the North. One of these numerous parties was asked,—

"Well, what made you leave your master? Wasn't he kind to you?"

"Oh, yes, massa, berry kind, berry kind."

"Well, didn't he give you enough to eat?"

"Oh, yes, plenty of dat; nuff to eat."

"Well, what made you leave him?"

"Why, de trufe am dat he made us work."

Another squad were questioned,—

"Well, what made you leave your homes?"

"Why, we'd heerd 'bout de Norf bein' such a nice place, so we tort dat we would go to um."

"Nice place! Why, how do you mean?"

"Well, we were told dat nobody did no work up dar."

The usual idea with all the runaway slaves was, that once out of the Confederacy and they would be free of work. Many a one who has had day-dreams, and night-dreams too, of living without work, has been terribly disappointed when he stepped upon the White House wharves. A free negro never has such ideas. He had to work too hard to support himself and family before he thought of leaving his home, ever to believe such rumors. No negro artificers or mechanics ever came into the Federal lines. They were always pressed into the Rebel service, where their skill in their various callings was employed to the utmost extent, and they were watched too closely to allow of desertion. The habits of the White House contrabands were a fruitful source of study, and gave amusement to every one there.

The army, however, was marching from the Pamunky, and leaving White House daily farther and farther in the rear,—a vast supply post, with hundreds of vessels and thousands of laborers.

CHAPTER V.

FROM WHITE HOUSE TO THE CHICKAHOMINY.

On Sunday afternoon, May 18, the main body of the army was quietly encamped behind and below White House, the majority of the regiments having been there since the day before. On Sunday morning, after inspection, divine service was held in many of them, the simplest and most impressive form of worship being the one selected. Upon such occasions, all the officers and men take part, singing the hymns, joining in the prayers, and listening attentively to the sermon. An hour and a half thus occupied always repays its expenditure. It directs the soldier's thoughts to different things from those he is accustomed to think of, turns away his attention from the bloody war before him, and makes him a better man and easier-ruled subordinate.

The Government has been most generous in its provisions for the religious welfare of the soldiers. Chaplains are appointed, one for each regiment, to be regularly-ordained clergymen of such religious belief as the majority of the troops in the regiment for which they are named. The Tract and Bible Societies of the North are allowed to send free through the mails huge bundles of newspapers, tracts, and books for distribution to the men. The great schism between Catholicism and Protestantism, by a master-stroke of policy, is prevented from raising its hydra-head in the army. Roman Catholic regiments have priests for their chaplains, and, in other regiments, where there were any number of Roman Catholics they were always allowed to join in the worship of the nearest regiment of their brethren, and receive the ministrations of its chaplain in their own. Religion in the army was well cared for, and many a soldier has doubtless been deeply thankful for it.

The morning being given to religious devotions, the men had Sunday afternoon to themselves; and at White House great numbers took the opportunity to enjoy a delicious bath in the Pamunky. The evening, however, was passed most pleasantly of all. As soon as the sun set, the bands all over the vast encampment assembled in front of the marquees of their regimental commanders, and each commenced playing. These bands before the war had been favorites in their native towns and cities, and had generally enlisted bodily into their respective regiments. Their members were no doubt excellent players then, but competition since with distinguished musicians from all parts of the North had given them a delicacy of touch and their instruments a sweetness of tone which made their music irresistibly charming. Fifty bands were playing at one time on that Sunday evening at White House, and a far-distant listener, though he could discern no single tune, heard a constant strain of the richest melody. The eve of the departure of the army for Richmond was well celebrated.

At three o'clock on the morning of Monday, May 19, the troops began moving from White House, and all the forenoon a constant stream poured along the roads toward Richmond. The left wing marched among the earliest, part advancing along the railroad, and part marching to the south of it and then pursuing a course parallel with it. The centre maintained a communication with the left, and it and the right wing passed to the north of the railroad and then marched westward. General Stoneman's advance, which had been posted some three miles west of White House, marched on Sunday afternoon. He drew in his force from the left, which then threw out its own advanced parties, and his forces afterward acted as advanced guard only to the centre and right. General Stoneman proceeded most cautiously, marching some six miles by Monday morning. This was a rapid advance for him. He had to beat up all the woods, search for masked batteries, throw out reconnoissances for miles to the right and left to discover lurking parties of the enemy and effectually clear every acre of ground he passed over. The main body marched without preparation for battle, depending on the exertions of the advanced guard. Some of the most widely-known officers of the army are the commanders of cavalry regiments in General Stoneman's division, and they gained a great part of their fame by the good service rendered whilst the army was marching upon the Peninsula, from Yorktown to the Chickahominy.

The army was at length fairly on the road to Richmond. At the time of its departure speculation was rife as to what would be the events as the troops neared the enemy's capital. Many were of opinion that Richmond would be evacuated. Others thought a fierce battle at an early date, with a Federal victory, would send the enemy out of the city they had been at so much pains to fortify. The majority, however, were of opinion, and justly so, that, having a superior force to the invading army, Richmond would be defended with a desperation worthy of a better cause. The real intentions of the enemy can be gleaned from their newspapers, and the official documents since made public. It was war,—unceasing, desolating war.

On May 14, the General Assembly of Virginia passed the following resolutions:—

"*Resolved*, by the General Assembly of Virginia, That the General Assembly hereby express its desire that the capital of the State be defended to the last extremity, if such defence be in accordance with the views of the President of the Confederate States; and that the President be assured that whatever destruction and loss of property of the State or individuals shall thereby result will be cheerfully submitted to.

"*Resolved*, That a committee of two on the part of the Senate, and three on the part of the House, be appointed to communicate the adoption of the foregoing resolution to the President."

The committee appointed in accordance with the second resolution communicated the next day with President Davis, and immediately reported the result of their interview to the General Assembly:—

"The joint committee respectfully report that their interview with the President was in the highest degree satisfactory, and his views, as communicated with entire frankness to the committee, were well calculated to inspire them with confidence and to reassure the public mind.

"After reading the resolutions, he desired us to say to the General Assembly that he had received the communication of those resolutions with feelings of lively gratification, and instructed us to assure the Houses that it would be the effort of his life to defend the soil of Virginia and to cover her capital.

"He further stated that he had never entertained the thought of withdrawing the army from Virginia and abandoning the State; that if in the course of events the capital should fall,—the necessity of which he did not see or anticipate,—that would be no reason for withdrawing the army from Virginia. The war could still be successfully maintained on Virginia soil for twenty years."

On the same day, Governor Letcher, echoing the resolutions of the General Assembly, issued the following proclamation:—

"The General Assembly of this commonwealth having resolved 'that the capital of the State shall be defended to the last extremity, if such defence is in accordance with the views of the President of the Confederate States,' and having declared that 'whatever destruction and loss of property of the State or individuals shall thereby result will be cheerfully submitted to,' and this action being warmly approved and seconded by the Executive: Therefore, I do hereby request all officers who are out of service from any cause, and all others who may be willing to unite in defending the capital of this State, to assemble this evening at the City Hall, at five o'clock, and proceed forthwith to organize a force to co-operate with the Tredegar Battalion, and any other force which may be detailed for the purpose indicated. The organization, upon being reported to the Executive, will be recognized and properly officered, as prescribed by law, and be subject to the orders of the Governor for local defence, under regulations to be hereafter prescribed.

"Prompt and efficient action is absolutely necessary. We have a gallant army in the field, upon whom we fully and confidently rely; but no effort should be spared which can contribute to the noble object. The capital of Virginia must not be surrendered. Virginians must rally to the rescue.

"JOHN LETCHER."

The meeting called in the proclamation assembled at the hour named, and appointed a committee to receive the names of recruits for the proposed organization. Several speeches were made. Joseph Mayo, the Mayor of Richmond, and a descendant of the founder of the city, among other things, said,—

"If the city of Richmond was ever surrendered to our enemies, it should not be by a descendant of its founder. He would sooner die than surrender our city; and if they wished a mayor who would surrender the city they must elect another in his place."

Governor Letcher also spoke, and, after a strain of the bitterest invective against the North, concluded by stating that "the city should never be surrendered by the President, by the mayor, or by himself." The meeting appeared to be enthusiastic in favor of the war, and of the defence of Richmond to the last.

The newspapers printed in the capital at that time advocated the destruction of the city rather than its surrender. The Richmond "Dispatch" said,—

"The next few days may decide the fate of Richmond. It is either to remain the capital of the Confederacy, or to be turned over to the Federal Government as a Yankee conquest. The capital is either to be secured or lost,—it may be feared not temporarily,—and with it Virginia. Then, if there is blood to be shed, let it be shed here: no soil of the Confederacy could drink it up more acceptably, and none would hold it more gratefully. Wife, family, and friends are nothing. Leave them all for one glorious hour to be devoted to the Republic. Life, death, and wounds are nothing, if we only be saved from the fate of a captured capital and a humiliated Confederacy. Let the Government act; let the people act. There is time yet.

"If fate comes to its worst, let the ruins of Richmond be its most lasting monument."

The "Dispatch," in another article, said,—

"We are proud of the spirit of our Governments, Confederate and State, relative to this question of holding and defending this State to the last. The army will not abandon the sacred soil of Virginia. That has been made the battle-ground, and on that must the enemy establish his superiority in a fair fight before it will be abandoned to him. The evacuation of the sea-coast positions and cities became a necessity. There was no avoiding it, in consequence of the immense advantage enjoyed by the enemy in his possession of the entire navy of the United States, and the material and mechanical skill for the rapid construction of iron-clad gunboats, while we had neither a navy nor the material and mechanical force to enable us to compete with him in any sense. It is true we had the Virginia [Merrimac]; but, besides her, nothing. Her destruction, and the questions it involves, suggest matters of debate which afford neither satisfaction nor benefit now to discuss. Our inability to meet the enemy on the water, as a general question, was clear and indisputable, and the withdrawal from the sea unavoidable.

"Second to Virginia is the defence of this city, for manifold reasons; and it is in keeping with the general purpose of both Governments that they should resolve to the uttermost to defend Richmond. All the means in the power of the State and the Confederacy are pledged to this; and we may be assured that the enemy will not be allowed to gratify the prominent desire of his heart,—to hector and domineer over the inhabitants of this far-famed and beautiful town,—until every means is exhausted.

"The President nobly takes the stand that, though Richmond should fall, there are plenty of battle-fields yet in Virginia to fight for the cause for twenty years. The sentiment is as truthful as patriotic. The Confederate Government assures us that the Old Dominion is not to be given up. God forbid that it should! It would be giving up much more than Virginia. The cause would be, indeed, itself wellnigh surrendered in that event. The Government is not only just, but wise, in its determination to stand by Virginia to the last.

"To lose Richmond is to lose Virginia; and to lose Virginia is to lose the key to the Southern Confederacy. Virginians, Marylanders, ye who have rallied to her defence, would it not be better to fall in her streets than to basely abandon them and view from the surrounding hills the humiliation of the capital of the Southern Confederacy? To die in her streets would be bliss to this, and to fall where tyrants strode would be to consecrate the spot anew and to wash it of every stain.

"The loss of Richmond, in Europe, would sound like the loss of Paris or London; and the moral effect will scarcely be less. Let us therefore avert the great disaster by a reliance on ourselves. It is better that Richmond should fall as the capital of the Confederacy, than that Richmond exist the depot of the hireling horde of the North. But Richmond can be defended, and saved from pollution. The fate of the capital of the Confederacy rests with the people."

At a later date, the editor of the "Dispatch" again wrote,—

"The Yankees, it appears, are so certain of soon being in possession of Richmond that they are already making preparations to start the old line of boats from Washington to Acquia Creek. These boats, having performed their mission in bombarding and burning the defenceless homesteads upon the banks of the Potomac and in kidnapping the negroes, are now to be transformed into messengers of peace, and in cementing by social and commercial intercourse the glorious Union with our murderers and conquerors. That interesting people seem to take it for granted that as soon as they have whipped us into submission we shall forget the past and be ready to make up and be as good friends as ever. As they advance into our country, they will inundate us once more with their wares and notions, their books and missionaries; the men now employed in cutting throats will be competing with each other for our custom, each one accusing the other of having been in the war, and swearing that he himself was always opposed to it; the ships which are ravaging our coast will come to our harbors laden with the products of Yankee industry, and go back with the teeming riches of our soil. Such, at least, is their expectation, founded on that knowledge of human nature which is derived exclusively from the study of their own character.

"We do not pretend to doubt that there are people in the South who would fulfil these expectations, but are sure that few of them are of native growth. There may be men from New England and from other countries who would hail with rapture the overthrow of the Southern capital, but they are a minority even of their own countrymen resident in the South. The great mass of them are loyal; and as to the native-born disloyalists, they are too few in number to deserve mention. Toryism is not in the South what it was in the Revolution. Then the Tories were powerful in numbers, and often respectable in character and position. Nor did they conceal their Toryism; for they were too strong to have reason for concealment. They proclaimed their sentiments boldly, and not only that, but fought us in the broad light of day. There are few Tories in Virginia. Whatever may have been the divisions of sentiment at the beginning of the war, the Yankee conduct of it has made us one people. Such a thing as union with them is hereafter an impossibility. If they conquer us, they must hold us by the strong arm; for all respect, all confidence, all love, has departed forever. They may force their hateful presence on our people; they may perfume our air with the balmy aroma of codfish, and make it musical with their nasal intonations; but they cannot recreate the Union. They might as well attempt to galvanize a dead body into life, and make it perform all the functions of healthy humanity.

"It will only be when the South is dead, physically and morally, that they can become masters of our country. Their empty vaporing and gasconading pass by as the idle wind. They may take our cities, but our immense territory remains, and not an inch of it will be theirs but the ground they stand on. They may plant their feet firmly, but it will be as a vessel plants its keel upon the waves, only to conquer that portion of it which it touches, and always to be at its mercy when it rises in its anger. Even their boastful menaces of the capture of Richmond are no better founded than their menaces uttered this time a year ago. They were just as exultant, and confident of the future, then as now. Their grand army brought telegraph-wires with them, to be extended as they advanced, hand-cuffs to be placed upon our limbs, and halters upon our necks; and they had arranged a programme for a magnificent ball in this city to celebrate the victory. They had even rented a large warehouse in Washington, wherein to deposit the host of prisoners who were to be taken at the battle of Manassas. The good Book advises those who put on their armor not to boast as those who take it off."

And on May 19 and 22 the same editor printed the following paragraphs:—

"The plan of the enemy has been fully unfolded by his press, as well as by his demonstrations at Yorktown immediately upon his advance there. He will essay to take this city by encroachment, with the protection of parallel lines. He will throw up dirt as soon as he reaches the proper point, and he will try to reach the heart of the city with the spade. If he is allowed to proceed in this way, he will most assuredly get here. His advance is not far from Richmond, and, if not molested, we shall soon see that he is flinging up dirt. But we do not apprehend that he will be allowed to go on undisturbed with this kind of strategy. He will never get to Richmond with that economy of bloodshed and life imagined by McClellan.

"The determination on the part of the people and their representatives to defend Richmond at any and all hazards, meets the unqualified approbation not only of all Virginians, but the people of the South. A Charleston paper, commenting on the resolve, says the words of Virginia's Governor and of the citizens of Richmond are those of earnest men. Her Legislature has resolved that the capital must never be given up. It is settled that neither the threat of bombardment, nor bombardment itself, is to induce a surrender, and that the honor of the Old Dominion must be preserved though her fair capital in ashes be the sacrifice. This, it is said, is also the determination of the President; and so we will cling to the hope that Richmond will be saved, or that, if it should fall, it will only be after a desperate struggle worthy the interests that are at stake."

The Richmond "Examiner," though fully as earnest

in its advocacy of the defence of Richmond, was neither so desperate nor so reckless as the "Dispatch." It fearlessly criticized the administration of the Confederate Government, and, in an editorial upon the progress of the war, roundly abuses President Davis for "telling his beads instead of fighting." Out of the city there appeared to be some despondency as to the condition of affairs at the capital. On May 15, the Memphis "Appeal" availed itself of its despondency to give its opinion of the Rebel Secretary of the Navy. Its editor writes:—

"We do not much like the aspect of affairs at Richmond as presented by telegraph. Four Federal gunboats are reported as having started up James River, and, so far as we are advised, there is no sufficient obstruction in that stream to prevent them from reaching the capital. Is Richmond to go the way of Nashville, New Orleans, and Norfolk? If so, the result may be attributed to the unnecessary destruction of the Merrimac, and the notorious incapacity of Mallory, whom Mr. Davis forced upon the country against the earnest and unanimous protest of the nation."

Every thing indicated the unanimous purpose to be to fight to the last.

Whilst the army was in camp at Cumberland and White House, and preparing for the march across the Peninsula, Richmond was threatened from a new quarter. The Merrimac had been blown up in the second week of May, and, the only obstacle to the ascent of the James River being thus removed, a strong gunboat-expedition was at once prepared, which, on May 16, sailed up the river. Commodore L. M. Goldsborough, a talented and experienced officer, commanded the squadron. His flag-ship was the steam-frigate Susquehanna, and he was acsompanied by a numerous fleet. Rebel batteries were found at several points upon the lower James River, but all, as far up as Jamestown, had been hurriedly deserted,—their cannon being mounted, and, in many cases, having the Rebel flag flying over them. These cannon were captured and sent to Fortress Monroe.

At Jamestown the commodore met the advanced division of his squadron, which had previously gone up the river, under the leadership of Commander John Rodgers. This division contained, among others, the gunboats Monitor, Galena, and Naugatuck, and on the previous day had fought a most gallant action with the celebrated earth-work known as Fort Darling. In their advance up the river, the gunboats had compelled the evacuation of all the Rebel batteries below the fort. Their officers also discovered that, a short distance above the fort, the channel had been effectually blockaded.

The action before Fort Darling was a most spirited one. The gunboats Galena, Monitor, Naugatuck, Aroostook, and Port Royal, on May 16 moved slowly up the river above City Point, getting aground several times, but meeting with no artificial impediments, until they neared Ward's Bluff, eight miles below Richmond, where they encountered a heavy battery (Fort Darling), and two separate barriers formed of piles, steamboats, and sail-vessels. These barriers extended along the river-bank, in front of the battery, and were secured with chains. They were intended to prevent the landing of an attacking party. As the gunboats passed up the narrow river, they were welcomed by a sharp fire of musketry from both banks, which in some cases resulted fatally. The stream at Fort Darling is but two hundred yards wide. The Galena, which led the fleet, ran within six hundred yards of the battery, as near the piles as it was deemed proper to go, where she let go her anchor, and at a quarter before eight, on the morning of May 17, opened upon the battery. The Monitor came up about an hour later, ran above the Galena, but found she could not elevate her guns sufficiently to strike the battery, which was upon a high bluff. She immediately dropped below the Galena, anchored, and opened fire.

The iron-coated Galena, at first, successfully resisted the steel-pointed balls from the enemy's rifled cannon, but at last it was found they were piercing her. Thirty of the shot struck her, and lodged in her armor, whilst two passed entirely through. A shell burst in the Galena during the engagement, which killed and wounded several of the crew. The Naugatuck resisted all the enemy's balls, but, upon the eighth discharge, her rifled gun burst, killing two men and wounding three. The Monitor stood three hours' fighting, without the least injury. The remaining vessels not being iron-clad, they did not enter into the engagement.

A few minutes past eleven o'clock, the Galena having expended all her ammunition, the gunboats drew off, and discontinued the action. There were thirteen killed, and fourteen wounded, on the Federal side. The aiming is reported to have been most accurately done by both parties, heavy shells pouring into the fort and rattling against the iron-clad gunboats. The enemy lost some killed and wounded, but there has been no means of ascertaining the number. The only official report of the action ever made public by them is the following brief despatch:—

"SIR:—We have engaged the enemy's five gunboats for two and a half hours. We fired the Galena (iron-clad). She has withdrawn, going down the river, accompanied by the three wooden vessels.

"Our loss in killed and wounded small.

"Respectfully, your obedient servant,

"E. FARRAND.

"Hon. S. R. MALLORY, *Secretary of the Navy.*

Commodore Goldsborough afterward kept gunboats continually plying up and down the James River, between Fortress Monroe and Fort Darling. No Rebel batteries appeared on the banks of the stream until August. Although in this contest the Galena proved not to be perfectly shot-proof, and the Naugatuck met with a misfortune, yet the result of the action was very favorable to the Union cause. The expedition opened the James River, drove away the enemy's artillerists formerly posted all along its banks, capturing numerous cannon, buoyed out a channel, tested the range and calibre of the guns of Fort Darling, and procured much valuable information of the strength and position of the enemy. It made a fearful inroad into the enemy's country, depriving them of almost the whole of their favorite river.

The news of the exploits upon the James River reached the army just as it was leaving White House early on the morning of May 19, and raised the spirits of the troops to the highest pitch. Generals Keyes and Heintzelman were on their march to Bottom's Bridge, and the remainder of the army, with General McClellan, that day advanced as far as Tunstall's Station, on the railroad, seventeen miles from Richmond. They encamped to the north of it. This march occupied four hours, and was directly westward, through a country abounding in beautiful scenery, although the land had been mostly worn out. The roads passed through much fine timber. This part of Virginia was rather rugged, with high, steep hills, and was almost universally covered with forest. The camp formed at the end of this march was named "The Camp near Tunstall's Station." The army which was united at White House had commenced to widen its front. The centre—General Sumner's corps—advanced along the railroad. The left wing, somewhat in advance, was to the south of the railroad, and the right wing slightly to the rear, spread out two or three miles north of it. The front, whilst the army was marching westward, presented a west-northwestern face.

The apparent slowness of the centre and right, however, was fully compensated by the alacrity of General Stoneman. On May 19, he advanced seven miles, reaching the Chickahominy at the railroad-bridge. This was a long trestle-work structure, and two spans of it had been burned. General Stoneman drove the enemy away from the neighborhood and took immediate possession, an engineer force being sent for to repair the bridge. General McClellan, whose activity knew no limits, rode from the camp at Tunstall's Station on the afternoon of the 19th, and made a reconnoissance of the bridge and its vicinity.

General Stoneman did not cross the Chickahominy: he had cleared a passage for the centre and left, and he was now to secure the way for the right wing. So, handing over possession of the bridge to Brigadier-General Naglee, commanding the advanced guard of General Keyes's corps on the left wing, on May 20 he marched six miles northwestward, to a place called Coal Harbor. This was the destination of the right wing, and was ten miles west of the camp near Tunstall's Station, which they did not leave until they had intelligence of the occupation of Coal Harbor by the advance. At Coal Harbor was found the first strong force of the enemy. Their pickets were driven beyond the place, and General Stoneman encamped there for the night. Whilst here, one of his cavalry regiments captured a large Rebel baggage-train, with forty mules and eighty oxen. About noon on the 20th, the right wing advanced five miles west of Tunstall's Station, encamping at dusk within five miles of Coal Harbor.

Upon leaving White House, the three bodies of the army diverged, and on May 20 were thus situated. The left wing had reached Bottom's Bridge and the railroad-bridge, having marched twelve miles in a day and a half. The centre, advancing first along the railroad and then in a line slightly north of it, had also arrived at the Chickahominy, and was in close communication with the left. It too had advanced twelve miles in a day and a half. The right wing was encamped three miles north of the centre, keeping up a connection with it, and had marched eleven miles since leaving White House.

The portion of the Chickahominy the army was approaching runs a course from northwest to southeast. At the Meadow Bridge, the crossing of the Virginia Central Railroad, the river is five miles north of Richmond; at the York River Railroad Bridge, which crosses twelve miles below, it is eleven miles east of Richmond. Bottom's Bridge is three-quarters of a mile below the railroad-bridge. Halfway between Meadow Bridge and the railroad-bridge is New Bridge, it being six miles east of Richmond. This bridge is the nearest point of the Chickahominy to Coal Harbor, which place is three miles northeast of it and sixteen miles from White House.

On the morning of May 21, the right wing commenced to march to Coal Harbor, encamping there about four o'clock in the afternoon. The roads were very crooked, and, the day being quite sultry, a great deal of time was necessarily consumed in this march. The course was still through a beautiful country, mostly woodland, and but little cultivated. Headquarters were moved to Coal Harbor on the same day. The right wing was thus six miles northwest of the centre, and had three miles farther to go to reach the Chickahominy.

On the 20th of May, General Naglee's brigade—the advanced guard of General Keyes's corps upon the left wing—crossed the railroad-bridge without opposition, and carefully examined the Chickahominy from that point to Bottom's Bridge. The general held his position across the river, and was at once strongly reinforced. On the evening of the 20th he encamped at a place called the "Chimneys," one and a half miles beyond the river. On the next day General Stoneman, on the right wing, advanced to New Bridge from Coal Harbor, meeting with no resistance from the enemy. He was thus but six miles from the capital. The policy of the Rebels seemed to be to allow the Federal troops to advance to the Chickahominy, and even to cross it, without disputing the way. The left wing of the Federal army on the 21st was firmly established at the Chimneys, within nine and a half miles of Richmond.

On May 22 an armed reconnoissance of two regiments of infantry, a company of cavalry, and a battery was sent out from Coal Harbor westward toward Mechanicsville. It advanced five miles, to within one mile of the village, when the enemy were discovered. This advanced position was held for four hours, when the expedition returned, having had a slight skirmish, in which one man was killed and one captured. Several spies—all negroes—were brought in by the reconnoissance.

New Bridge being an important crossing of the Chickahominy, it was fast becoming a place of great interest. The enemy were in strong force opposite the bridge, and it was determined to drive them away. So, on May 23, a detachment of the Second Artillery, under the direction of Major Robertson and Captain Fithall, mounted their guns on the high hills on the Federal side, and went briskly to work to shell the enemy out of their camps. The balloon made an ascension near one of the batteries, and, from its elevated position, a note was made of the effect of the different shots, which was communicated to those in charge of the battery. The enemy made no reply, but, after receiving the bombardment for a half-hour, suddenly broke camp, and left with their baggage-trains. The practice of the artillery was excellent.

This driving of the Rebels from the vicinity of New Bridge was followed the next day by a movement which completely surprised them. Four companies of the Fifth Louisiana regiment were picketing on their side of the bridge, and some distance to the rear of them a brigade was bivouacked. Part of the Fourth Michigan regiment, commanded by Colonel Woodbury, and a squadron of the Second Cavalry, led by Captain Gordon, crossed the stream a short distance above the bridge, and got between the picketing regiment and the brigade,—the Federal troops on the hills above New Bridge in the mean time making a diversion which attracted the enemy's attention. The first notice the Rebels had of the presence of the Yankees was the firing of a volley close behind them, which caused a serious panic. The Federal troops remained but a few minutes across the river, and, the brigade coming after them at double quick, they re-crossed, wading breast-deep in water. One man was killed and one wounded in the Fourth Michigan. The enemy lost seventy-five killed and wounded and twenty-one prisoners. This was one of the most daring expeditions of the siege, and so pleased General McClellan that he wrote in his official despatch of May 24 to the War Department at Washington, 'The Fourth Michigan regiment about finished the Louisiana Tigers.'

A Richmond newspaper, speaking of this expedition, says:—

"We must confess that in one instance, at least, the enemy has outgeneralled us unmistakably. Semmes's brigade, stationed on the Nine-Mile Road, were in hourly expectation of the enemy's appearance; and, to repel their advance, the Fifth Louisiana were thrown to the front,—but whether with proper available support remains unexplained. Somewhat indifferent, perhaps, two companies of this regiment were ordered to guard the bridge,—situated, we believe, on Garnett's farm,—with the remainder of the regiment in support with stacked arms. As anticipated, the foe made his appearance at the bridge; and a lively fire was opened, much to our apparent advantage; but, unconscious of trickery, the enemy suddenly appeared upon our flank, and, with great impetuosity, opened a heavy musketry-fire of great destructiveness and precision. Staggered at this unexpected and sudden manœuvre, the Fifth fell back in good order, but with much rapidity, successfully caring for their killed and wounded. That such a gallant and fine regiment as the Fifth should have been so roughly treated, remains unexplained, though upon all hands it is universally conceded that it followed from a disgraceful 'surprise.' The loss from this affair was extremely severe,—not less than fifty or sixty of the Fifth being rendered *hors de combat*."

On the 23d of May, part of the right wing advanced to the Chickahominy, and on the next day Mechanicsville was captured, the reconnoissance of May 22 having brought such information as would secure the Union troops from ambuscades or masked batteries. A portion of General Stoneman's command, with General Davidson's brigade, a part of General Franklin's corps, on May 23 advanced up the Chickahominy from New Bridge, which is four miles southeast of

Mechanicsville. At Ellison's Mills, a mile from the village, they encountered the enemy, who had four regiments of infantry and some cavalry and artillery. The Federal troops manœuvred to turn the enemy's flank, their artillery shelling the enemy, who briskly replied, whilst the Federal infantry outflanked them. Upon this being done, the Rebels retreated to the village, and at dusk took shelter behind its woods and houses. Both parties slept on their arms, and early next morning the cannon of both recommenced the action. The Federal troops manœuvred as before, and soon the enemy made a precipitate retreat, part going to Meadow Bridge, a mile and three-quarters to the northwest, and part rushing down the Mechanicsville turnpike and across its bridge. Both parties were followed by plenty of shells, and by noon every Rebel had crossed the river. The enemy carried off all their killed and wounded but one wounded man. The Federal loss was two killed and four wounded,—among the latter, Colonel Mason, of the Seventh Maine regiment. This was a brilliant victory for the Federal cause, and opened a large section of country. The Richmond "Dispatch" acknowledged it to have been a bad defeat. General McClellan paid Mechanicsville a visit immediately after its capture.

Whilst the right wing was so active, the left was by no means idle. On the 23d, General Naglee, with General Keyes's advanced guard, made a reconnoissance from his camp at the Chimneys, along the Quaker road, to within two miles of the James River, securing much valuable information. On the following day, the general received orders from the commander-in-chief, "if possible, to advance to the Seven Pines, or the forks of the direct road to Richmond, and the road turning to the right" (Nine-mile Road) "into the road leading from New Bridge to Richmond, and to hold that point if practicable." This would be a direct march along the Williamsburg road, westward from the Chimneys, toward Richmond. So, with his brigade, assisted by a cavalry regiment commanded by Colonel Gregg, and two batteries of Colonel Bailey's First New York Artillery, General Naglee proceeded to fulfil his instructions. He pushed his advance, not without considerable opposition, to the Seven Pines, encamping there on the night of the 24th. The forces which had opposed him proved to be five regiments of infantry, one of cavalry, and two batteries, commanded by General Stewart. General Naglee, when he engaged them, found that they made but a feeble resistance and soon retreated. On the 25th he advanced a mile and a half beyond the Seven Pines, and on the 26th a quarter of a mile farther. He was thus within four and three-quarter miles of Richmond. On the 27th he established his picket line, which ran north from the Williamsburg road, along which he had made his advance, two miles, to a house a mile and a half southwest of New Bridge, known as the "Old Tavern." From this point the line ran northeast to the Chickahominy, near New Bridge. This picket tour was three miles and a half long, and on May 28 was picketed by the whole of General Casey's division of General Keyes's corps. The position upon the Williamsburg road, to which General Naglee advanced, was the nearest point to Richmond attained by the left wing. It was only held until the 31st, when the enemy in the first day's fight of the Fair Oaks battle drove the Federal troops from it.

The Federal front upon the Williamsburg road after the battle was half a mile to the rear of General Naglee's former position.

On May 24 the general head-quarters were moved two miles west of Coal Harbor, the camp being called the "Camp near New Bridge," which bridge was nearly two miles south of it. Upon the next morning the remainder of the right wing moved westward to the Chickahominy, a short march of three miles taking them there.

Upon the evening of Sunday, May 25, the Federal position was as follows. The advance of the left wing was a mile and three-quarters beyond the Seven Pines, and held the country to the north. It was four and three-quarter miles from Richmond, and six and a quarter from where it crossed the Chickahominy. The main body of the left wing was at the Chimneys and the Seven Pines. For five or six miles above the railroad-bridge, the railroad and river run in very slightly-diverging lines, the river at New Bridge being but two miles north of the railroad. As the left wing advanced, General Sumner, with the centre, marched up the opposite bank of the river so as to be continually near it, and, upon the occupation of the Seven Pines and the country beyond them, he encamped upon a beautiful spot of ground just below New Bridge, and but three miles north of the extreme left. He, of course, at once set to work at building bridges, so as to maintain his communications, and in two or three days had built Grapevine and Sunderland bridges across the river opposite the camps of the two divisions composing his corps. The right wing, which was encamped behind fringes of woods on the borders of the Chickahominy, extended from the camp of the centre to Meadow

Bridge, a distance of six miles. General Stoneman had his cavalry force scouring the country for several miles back of the right wing, his object being to prevent the incursions of guerrillas upon the Federal rear and the roads to White House. The front presented to the enemy was the concave segment of a circle facing the southwest, one extremity being east of Richmond and the other north of it. It was upon this Sunday, when every thing was progressing so favorably in the army of the Potomac, that General Banks, pursued by General Jackson, was making his famous retreat up the Shenandoah valley and startling the entire North.

Pleased with his success, General McClellan upon that day issued the following general order:—

"HEAD-QUARTERS, ARMY OF THE POTOMAC, May 25, 1862.

"I. Upon advancing beyond the Chickahominy, the troops will go prepared for battle at a moment's notice, and will be entirely unencumbered, with the exception of ambulances. All vehicles will be left on the eastern side of the Chickahominy and carefully packed. The men will leave their knapsacks, packed, with the wagons, and will carry three days' rations. The arms will be put in perfect order before the troops march, and a careful inspection made of them, as well as of the cartridge-boxes, which, in all cases, will contain at least forty rounds; twenty additional rounds will be carried by the men in their pockets. Commanders of batteries will see that their limber and caisson boxes are filled to their utmost capacity.

"Commanders of army corps will devote their personal attention to the fulfilment of these orders, and will personally see that the proper arrangements are made for packing and properly guarding the trains and surplus baggage, taking all the steps necessary to insure their being brought promptly to the front when needed; they will also take steps to prevent the ambulances from interfering with the movement of any troops: they must follow in the rear of all the troops moving by the same road. Sufficient guards and staff officers will be detailed to carry out these orders.

"The ammunition-wagons will be in readiness to march to their respective brigades and batteries at a moment's warning, but will not cross the Chickahominy until they are sent for. All quartermasters and ordnance officers are to remain with their trains.

"II. In the approaching battle, the general commanding trusts that the troops will preserve the discipline which he has been so anxious to enforce and which they have so generally observed. He calls upon all the officers and soldiers to obey promptly and intelligently all orders they may receive: let them bear in mind that the army of the Potomac has never yet been checked, and let them preserve in battle perfect coolness and confidence, the sure forerunners of success. They must keep well together, throw away no shots, but aim carefully and low, and, above all things, rely upon the bayonet. Commanders of regiments are reminded of the great responsibility that rests upon them: upon their coolness, judgment, and discretion the destinies of their regiments and success of the day will depend.

"By command of Major-General McClellan.

"S. WILLIAMS, *Assistant Adjutant-General.*"

During all these marches and skirmishes, Rebel prisoners were continually captured, and the enemy also took many Federal soldiers. Men strayed beyond the lines, some when upon picket were entrapped, and in a hundred ways Union troops were taken and sent to the dungeons in Richmond. How they lived there the reader may judge from the following extracts from a letter written on the first days of May by one of the prisoners:—

"Our condition is most dark and dreary. There are only three windows in the room, and those on one end. The floor is always in a filthy condition. It having been used for a pork-warehouse (immediately before we were removed to it, however, for a slave-pen), the floor is perfectly saturated with grease. This makes it impossible to get it clean, and causes it to be coated with an amalgam of pork-fat and all kinds of dirt. In walking, this vile stuff adheres to the shoes, and we need a scraper more in walking here than you do in walking in the street. Then add to this the filth that comes from above. Almost four hundred men are on the two floors above us, and frequently, as it has now been the case for two days, their water-closets overflow and discharge their awful contents upon us. This comes down sometimes in torrents. Yesterday it poured down where a captain was lying with a broken leg. He had to be moved as quickly as possible, and has not been able to occupy his place since, on account of this stream of pollution flowing from above. A similar stream, with scarcely an intermission, has been now for two days pouring down into the cook-room, which is a room partitioned off in one corner of the one which we occupy. All our cooking is done in this room. You will say, 'How can you eat?' I answer, that I have scarcely thought of the matter in relation to eating. Our schooling has prepared us for it. You will wish to know what my food is. This I can soon tell you,—though I might give you a dietetic history which would painfully interest you. Our food, as furnished by the Southern Confederacy, consists in the morning of bread and meat; for dinner, meat and bread; for tea, meat and bread and bread and meat. This is all: and this is all we get unless we have money to send out for articles. Many times we cannot do this when we have the money, as we have not been able to do so now for three days. Therefore we have had no sugar, no coffee, no potatoes. All these articles are rarities, costing immensely. We have made out to supply ourselves comfortably well, by the blessing of a kind Providence.

"*May* 1.—It is May-day; but what a dreary one! dark and lowering without, and the floods which have continued all night still pour down upon us from the sinks above. We are the sewer for near four hundred men. There is not a foot in the cook-room, excepting under the stove, which is not covered with water. A hole has been cut in the ceiling, which lets most of the water down in one place, instead of sifting it down all over. Several holes in the plank of *this* floor have been cut this morning to allow the water standing on it to pass through into the basement, which has long since become an awful muck-hole. Thus, every thing is being prepared for disease when the warm weather shall come. The measles have already broken out among us.

"On the whole, we are in a most deplorable condition; and what very much aggravates this unbearable state is the sending home of the men and non-commissioned officers, while the officers are still held in custody. All the officers wear the most gloomy faces. Our fate is uncertain. So far as we can judge (being denied the papers entirely, one man being a few days ago gagged, and then made to keep time half a day at a time, in order to compel him to tell how a paper was got in), our army from the Rappahannock seems to be moving on this place. In this case we shall by no means be suffered to remain in Richmond, but will undoubtedly be sent South. You can imagine the undesirableness of this.

"*May* 2.—The rumor is that the officers are to be taken South. This is very probable. Report says we are to be taken to Salisbury, North Carolina. It may be interesting to you and others to know something about what are here called 'citizen prisoners.' They are Union men, citizens of the Southern States. I do not know whether this is the only depot for this kind of prisoners. But there are hundreds in this place. I know but few of them. Some act as cooks in the lower kitchen, and bring our meat and bread in to us. All these men are, in every respect, very worthy. There were three ministers among them. One has died. The cause of his sickness and death reveals the barbarism of the Rebels, and at the same time what the Union men suffer. This Mr. Webster—for such was his name—was a citizen of Fairfax county, and taken prisoner about a month before his death. He was taken with the following men, who were engaged in the peaceful occupations of life:—William S. Speer, aged fifty-two years; Isaac Wibert, sixty-five years; C. White; William Showers, seventy years old. These men were not in one instance permitted to go into their houses for money or clothing, or to bid their friends good-bye. They were marched with the army eight days, during which time they slept out-of-doors—it being in the month of January—and had but one meal per day.

When the age of these men is considered, the barbarism is unparalleled. But something worse than this follows. On the second day's march, Mr. Showers, who had reached his threescore years and ten, dropped dead on the road. The battalion halted not for a moment, and the officer in command forbade any attention whatever to be paid to the dead man, save to carry the body and place it by the wayside. There it was left. On the third day's march a negro dropped down dead, and his remains were served in the same way. The desolation wrought by these heartless Rebels is actually beyond description. I have seen men by scores taken to the prison, frequently followed by their wives and children until they were repulsed by the guards; and in one case the husband and wife kissed over the bayonet, the husband disappearing within the prison, while the wife went weeping away. I could write much more on this painful subject; but this will suffice to give you some idea of the state of things.

"*Evening, May* 2.—We have had a most terrible day. The floods from above continue. At one time, while writing this letter, the pipe from the upper closets burst, and discharged its contents within a few feet of our dining-table. Every man lit his pipe, and smoked for his life. The awful stench is still in the room. I do not write this to add to your affliction, but I have concluded you would like to know just how we are situated, and I am convinced, also, that the people of the North *ought* to know how their officers are treated. Many who have gone home have not given the true view. I have told the truth in this letter. You are at liberty to publish extracts from it. You must not permit my name to appear; for one man, for getting a letter through telling facts, was put into a criminal cell, and fed on bread and water for ten days. Many of the letters of the prisoners published at the North appear in the Southern papers."

The treatment received by prisoners captured subsequently to General McClellan's march to the Chickahominy was equally barbarous with that which they experienced before. William P. Haney, an intelligent orderly sergeant of the One-hundred-and-fourth Pennsylvania regiment, was captured at the battle of Malvern Hill in the beginning of July. The following is taken from his statement:—

"I was shown into that spacious mansion on the corner of Nineteenth and Cary Streets, known as Libby & Son's Warehouses. On inspection of the room, I found it contained about two hundred and fifty men, representing every department of our army,—soldiers, sutlers, teamsters, laborers, citizens, and negroes. The floor was covered with dirt, and the cracks filled with lice, the extermination of which occupied the time of the prisoners. It was with great difficulty that I could find space sufficient to stretch my limbs on, when bedtime came. This was the first time and place I ever played checquers with my nose through prison-bars, and it shall be the last.

"My term in this prison luckily proved to be a short one, as two days afterward we were all marched over to the Manchester side of the river, and from there to Bell Island, on the south side of the city of Richmond. This island contains about fifteen acres of land. The upper portion, about ten acres, is very high table-land, while the lower is low and flat, barren of trees, and with no spring or well upon it. On this latter part of the island we were encamped, in tents of every pattern and every color imaginable. Here, with naught but worn-out canvas to protect us from the scorching rays of the sun, we spent the remainder of our term of imprisonment, in hunger, and want of even the most common necessaries of life. Here, in the space of two hundred and fifty yards in diameter, were crowded together, at one time, forty-five hundred men. We were allowed only one hundred feet of the shore, where we could wash, and occasionally bathe. At first we were compelled to drink the dirty water of the river; but soon we found tolerably good water by digging five or six feet in the ground. Our food consisted of ten ounces of bread per day, six ounces of fresh meat every alternate day, with an occasional cup of soup. The bread was sour, and meat generally tainted before we got it, for the want of salt,—which article is as scarce in Secessia as hens' teeth. The only facility we had for buying any thing was from the quartermaster, who would occasionally bring over a boat-load of bread, pies, sugar, molasses, &c., which he readily disposed of, at prices ranging as follows:—bread, twenty-five cents per loaf of ten ounces; pies, fifty cents each; sugar, one dollar a pound; molasses, a dollar and a half a quart; eggs, one dollar per dozen; coffee, three dollars a pound; soap, home-made, at a dollar a pound; and other articles in proportion.

"United States Treasury notes, gold, silver, and even Northern bank-notes, of almost any description, are held in Richmond at nearly thirty-three per cent. premium. The fact is not known, nor believed, by their army in the field.

"Lieutenant Shay, from Alexandria, had charge of all the prisoners on the island, and treated us as well as prisoners of war could expect. The conscripts who stood guard over us were, with few exceptions, harmless creatures indeed. Their arms were of the poorest kind, some without bayonets, ramrods, and even locks. They were ignorant, and did not understand their business, as twenty-seven prisoners escaped from their lines; and, if kept there another week, one hundred more would have been missing from the island.

"Our cooking was done by a detail made from our own men. To kill time, the boys would practise carving bones for rings, bracelets, slides, &c., which, when well executed, would sell for high prices. Reading-matter was scarce. Few papers could be gotten, and they only by smuggling. The Richmond journals are a disgrace to the art,—poor in paper, miserable in print, and filled with abominable lies. They are rank on the questions at issue, and preach up the doctrine of no quarter to the Yankees. The 'Dispatch' wishes General McCall hung, and the black flag hung out. The city of Richmond is controlled entirely by refugee 'Plug-Uglies' from Baltimore. It wears a gloomy and deserted appearance, and appears to be inhabited only by the lowest class of society.

"When taken into the Rebel capital, by the Central Road, I noticed no fortifications save those immediately around the city. Their line of defence appeared very strong, but badly in want of artillery. Along an extent of nearly one mile I could count but five guns. These were heavy siege-guns, from thirty-two to sixty-four-pounders. These guns were not mounted, but lay upon the parapet diagonally with the line of intrenchments. It would be an easier task for an attacking force to storm the works than those upon the right of their line before Yorktown."

Sergeant Haney's statement of the scarcity of salt is corroborated by a proclamation of the Governor of Virginia intended to make some regulations as to its sale and price. This proclamation was made on the 19th of August.

It seems that the treatment of prisoners in all parts of the Confederacy is the same. Lieutenant Frank Parker, of Pennsylvania, who was confined in North Carolina, and was exchanged on July 23, tells a sad story of his sufferings.

"He was confined at Salisbury, North Carolina, in a cotton-mill, to which were attached six brick tenement houses, a frame barn, and three log huts, the whole surrounded by a board fence of ten feet in height. There were about one thousand prisoners, Northern Union soldiers, and Southern Union citizens from Kentucky, Maryland, Virginia, Tennessee, and North Carolina. The main building contained nine hundred souls, being an average of one man to every three feet of space, eight of whom only were allowed to be out at one time, for all purposes. The commandant of the post offered to allow the officers to parade the grounds attached to the buildings, under a double guard, the officers giving their parole not to attempt to escape or aid other Union prisoners in escaping, which offer was rejected by Lieutenant Parker and five others.

"Lieutenant Parker, and the five who rejected the

liberal offer, were then placed in a close room, ten feet by twenty, where they were subjected to many indignities, especially at the hands of Lieutenant Bradford, son of Governor Bradford, of Maryland, who has disavowed his disloyal son. This treatment they endured until the commandant of the post was changed, A. C. Godwin, formerly a California gambler and blackleg, taking charge, who brought from Richmond over two hundred Union prisoners, who were confined in this 'black hole.' Instead of their sufferings being ameliorated by the change, the tyranny was more insufferable than ever. This monster, Godwin, cut down the before scant rations of six ounces of musty, maggotty pork, and fourteen ounces of sour flour, which produced the death, from actual starvation, of some of the prisoners, after which the officers were compelled not only to feed themselves, but to furnish rations to the prisoners at their own expense. Godwin would not allow the officers to send outside for food, but started a sutler's store in the prison-enclosure, and charged them four hundred per cent. more than the price for which they could have purchased the same articles outside.

"On the 2d of July, a lieutenant died of typhoid fever, and the officers, having requested Godwin to allow them to give him a decent interment, were met with a flat refusal, he ordering a colored man to take him off in a cart and bury him in a tanyard, saying 'a negro slave was all the guard of honor an invader deserved.'"

Exchanged Union prisoners all tell the same tale of the barbarity of the enemy's Government and the cruelty of its officers. Northern men would blush for shame did the Federal Government impose upon the captured Rebels one-tenth of the horrors of Southern dungeons.

For two or three days General McClellan had been meditating a blow against the enemy, which, in the end, proved entirely successful. Two railroads pass out of Richmond toward the North,—the Virginia Central Railroad, crossing the Chickahominy at Meadow Bridge, and running north fourteen miles to Hanover Court-House, and then west five miles to Ashland, where it crosses the other railroad; and the Richmond, Fredericksburg & Potomac Railroad, which passes out of the capital toward the northwest, crossing the numerous brooks forming the head-waters of the Chickahominy, six miles above Meadow Bridge, and gradually curving around in its course until it comes to Ashland. The former of these roads, after leaving the Ashland junction, goes west to Lynchburg; the other running north to Acquia Creek upon the Potomac River. Ashland is twenty miles north-northwest of Richmond; Hanover Court-House is nineteen miles north. The two villages are five miles apart. A turnpike, crossing the river at Mechanicsville, connects Richmond with Hanover Court-House. The blow meditated was the destruction of both railroads at the junction, the absence from the enemy's left of General Jackson, who was in the Shenandoah Valley, favoring the enterprise. On the 26th of May a cavalry reconnoissance was sent out to test its practicability. This detachment passed up to Hanover Court-House, cutting the Central Railroad in three places, but meeting with no resistance. It returned in the afternoon, and, upon the favorable report made by its commanding officer, it was determined to send out a strong expedition to complete the destruction.

The night of the 26th of May and the morning of the 27th were rainy, and the roads were converted into the foulest mire. After a night's rain, however, the clouds cleared away at ten o'clock of the morning of the 27th, and the sun came out. At three A.M., General Porter's corps, which had been selected for the expedition, were routed out of their tents, and at four General Morell's division started in the midst of the rain, at a quick march, along the road to Hanover Court-House. General Stoneman's division was held as a reserve, ready to march at an instant's notice, and followed General Morell to within six miles of Hanover Court-House, halting there to await the result of the expedition. General Sykes's division, the remainder of General Porter's corps, advanced, as an additional supporting column, before daybreak on the morning of the 28th, but halted several miles from the Court-House.

General Morell's division marched through the rain and mud, the troops wrapping themselves in their water-proof blankets, and carefully guarding their muskets from the wet, until they were some four miles south of Hanover Court-House. Here the advanced guard, composed of the Twenty-fifth New York regiment, Colonel Johnson, some cavalry, and two guns, discovered the pickets of the enemy, who skirmished with the Federal scouts, but at the same time fell back. The enemy, from their movements, evidently thought the small force in sight was the entire Union strength, and, to convince them of the contrary, General Butterfield, one of the brigade commanders, ordered the Eighty-third Pennsylvania, Colonel McLane, and the

Seventeenth New York, Colonel Lansing, to pass into a wood on the left of the road and to outflank the enemy. In a few moments the two regiments had passed diagonally forward through the wood and were drawn up in line of battle in a wheat-field to the left of the Rebels. The Sixteenth Michigan, Colonel Stockton, and the Twelfth New York, Colonel Weeks, marched through the wood a few moments after, and formed to the rear of the others as a supporting party. This movement, entirely unanticipated, took the enemy completely by surprise, and, after a few volleys, their infantry broke and fled. The artillerists continuing to work their guns, a charge was ordered, which drove them away. The enemy were completely routed, the Federal troops pursuing them for a long distance along the road to Hanover Court-House. All their guns were captured, proving to be twelve-pounder smoothbore howitzers, belonging to a celebrated battery from New Orleans, known as Latham's battery. This initiatory repulse seemed to confuse the enemy, for they fled beyond Hanover Court-House, pursued by the Federal cavalry, who gathered prisoners at every step. General Morell's troops advanced briskly to the Court-House, and, finding it deserted, halted there for a brief interval. Whilst here, the Twenty-second Massachusetts, Colonel Grove, took up several hundred feet of the Virginia Central Railroad, afterward moving westward along it toward Ashland. There being indications of an enemy in large force in the neighborhood, a strong force was ordered forward to Colonel Grove's assistance.

At this moment the signal officers discovered and at once reported to General Porter, who was upon the field, that the enemy were advancing from Richmond up the railroad to attack the Federal rear, it no doubt being their intention to get General Morell between two fires and destroy his troops at leisure. General Martindale, a brigade commander, stationed the Second Maine regiment, Colonel Roberts, in line of battle facing the rear, and extending from the railroad to the turnpike upon which the Federal advance had been made, the two roads being but a short distance apart. Along and between these two roads it was expected that the enemy's forces would advance. The Forty-fourth New York, Colonel Stryker, and Martin's battery, supported the Maine regiment. The Twenty-fifth New York was afterward added to the supports.

The enemy soon appeared before this hastily-formed rear-guard, and Martin's battery opened upon them. The Forty-fourth New York being upon the Federal left, it was ordered to march into a piece of woods upon that side and clear it of Rebel skirmishers, in order to protect a hospital which was upon that flank, though some distance to the rear. The regiment started; but an attempt of the enemy to turn the Federal right caused it to be recalled,—when it returned to its first position and vigorously engaged the enemy. The three regiments and battery all fought with the greatest earnestness, pouring volleys and shells into the enemy with terrible effect. The Rebels were much stronger than their opponents, having six regiments of infantry, besides cannon. They appeared to be anxious to turn the Federal right flank, and directed almost all their attention to the Second Maine regiment, which was upon that flank, its right resting upon a wood. Having so much greater numbers to contend against, soon exhausted the regiment's ammunition; and, this being reported, the Twenty-fifth New York was ordered to relieve the gallant Maine regiment, which filed off to the left in order to allow the Twenty-fifth, which was to the rear, to march forward. This movement, for some reason, exposed the remaining regiment of the rear-guard to a fire upon the flank, from which it suffered severely, and which, for a few moments, could not be resisted. Still, beyond killing and wounding the troops, the enemy made no impression; the handful of troops stood as firmly as a rock,—no one faltering, no one ceasing for an instant the quick firing of his musket.

Whilst these brave troops were successfully checking the advance of an enemy double their number, the other brigades of General Morell's division, who had been in advance along the railroad, were quickly returning to their aid. They formed in line in the wheat-field, near the spot where the first engagement took place, and, pursuing almost the same manœuvres as in that contest, took the enemy a second time in flank. The Eighty-third Pennsylvania, Sixteenth Michigan, and Ninth Massachusetts, Colonel Cass, fiercely attacked the enemy's left flank; whilst the Sixty-second Pennsylvania, Colonel Black, beat up a small wood upon their right. The Twelfth and Fourteenth New York regiments advanced to the aid of the Federal rear-guard, attacking the enemy in front, and Colonel Berdan's sharp-shooters, posted upon all sides, with unerring aim picked off Rebel after Rebel. Nor was this all. Griffin's battery came galloping down from Hanover Court-House to the assistance of Martin's, and was ready for action and briskly shelling the enemy in a moment. These sudden advances upon all sides, totally unanticipated by the Rebels, who thought their every shot would cause the heroic rear-guard to fly, were too much. Fire in front and to the right and left, with murderous shells from twelve swiftly-worked cannon, was an attack too hot to be borne. They wavered and broke, and fled from the field, throwing away muskets, colors, and even parts of their clothing, in their anxiety to run the faster, and, rushing pell-mell into a dense forest, quickly disappeared.

The enemy's attack upon the Federal rear having been repulsed and defeated, attention was at once turned to the foe in advance. Strangely enough, not a regiment could be found, and the Federal troops advanced along the line of the Central Railroad, beyond Hanover Court-House and toward Ashland, destroying the road, but meeting no enemy. The Fifth and Sixth regiments of regular cavalry proceeded to Ashland and burned a bridge, five hundred feet long, over the South Anna Creek, one of the tributaries of the Pamunky, which river flows within a mile of Hanover Court-House. This bridge was upon the line of the Richmond, Fredericksburg & Potomac Railroad. The cavalry also destroyed an immense amount of commissary and quartermaster's supplies, which were stored at Ashland. A railroad-train was also captured and burned.

The results of this expedition were highly favorable to the Federal cause. Besides the immense destruction of stores, communication on both the railroads was effectually broken up, and was kept so during all the subsequent siege. Six hundred and twenty prisoners, several cannon, and numerous small arms were captured. The Federal loss was fifty-three killed, and two hundred and ninety-six wounded and missing. The enemy's loss, in killed, wounded, and prisoners, was fifteen hundred.

Ashland and Hanover Court-House are both most insignificant villages, mere railway-stations, but, like all other localities in Virginia, each one has a place in history. Before the war, Ashland had a hotel, at which passengers between Richmond and Washington stopped for meals. It also had a celebrated race-course. It was the birthplace of Henry Clay. Hanover Court-House, though one of the oldest county seats in Virginia, can scarcely boast twenty houses. In the elder days, its court-rooms were the scenes of many of Patrick Henry's forensic triumphs.

The Rebels engaged in these battles were from North Carolina and Georgia, with one Louisiana battery. On the afternoon of the 28th of May, the captured prisoners were sent down past Mechanicsville, on their way to White House. They were a sorry-looking set of men, and most of them were clothed in gray homespun. The majority seemed rather glad to have been captured. One German, from the manner of his walk and the grin on his face, was evidently going North to search for the heart he could not find in the Southern country. "There goes a good Union man," cried a bystander. "Yes, me a Union man," answered the German, amid the cheers of the surrounding crowd. There were numerous company officers in the party, and one field officer,—a major. With a very few exceptions, the Federal troops treated the prisoners with politeness. But few reproached or tantalized them, and they were at once stopped by their better-bred companions.

General McClellan rode to Hanover Court-House on the morning of May 28, and highly commended the gallantry of General Morell's division. During all of that afternoon, and also upon the next day, the troops of General Porter's corps were marching back to their camp, which they had left amid the rain and mud to go upon the expedition which resulted so successfully. General Stoneman also brought his troops back to the vicinity of Mechanicsville, leaving scouts in the country which he evacuated. After the 29th, Meadow Bridge was the extreme right of the army of the Potomac.

The frequent skirmishes and actions of the last days of May, all resulting favorably to the Federal troops, with their rapid advance to and successful crossing of the Chickahominy, began to make the enemy uneasy. Their troops were becoming dissatisfied, and the people at home began finding fault. Their newspapers were outspoken, and the following, from the "Richmond Enquirer," will show the temper of those who were anxious spectators of disaster after disaster:—

"We are now looking to General Johnston with great interest, and not without some solicitude. He has just beautifully executed some very judicious retreats. We are now anxious to see him display the more positive qualities of a military commander. The time has come when retreat is no longer strategy, but disaster. It must therefore give place to battle. We have no idea that Johnston contemplates a retreat. We are perfectly satisfied that he does not. We verily believe that, if he did contemplate one, he would find himself unable to execute it. The temper of the army would deny it. The men are weary of toilsome and destructive marches and the privations necessarily attending them, and almost clamor to be led against the enemy. The march from Manassas, and then from the Rapidan, and next from Williamsburg, thinned our ranks more than many battles would have done. The campaign has ripened for the battle, and the battle is at hand. We need now at the head of the army the clarion-call, and the battle shall be bold and enthusiastic."

At forty minutes after six on the morning of May 30, General Halleck entered Corinth. Federal success seemed to be looming up on every side. The troops before Richmond were in the highest spirits, eager for anticipated victories. The enemy during all the time from May 26 to May 30 were unusually quiet, and apparently lying idle in their camps. Thus was the condition of affairs upon the dark, rainy night of May 30, which proved to be the eve of one of the bloodiest battles of the war.

CHAPTER VI.

THE PENINSULA.

From the time it left Yorktown, every step trodden by the Federal army was upon classic ground. Williamsburg was the ancient capital of Virginia. Hanover and New Kent counties were the roaming-places for Powhatan's famous tribe of Indians, and the Chickahominy Swamp the scene of John Smith's capture by them. Its vicinity doubtless witnessed Pocahontas's heroic exploit, the treaty between the red and white man, and Smith's final release. It was here that the Englishman Rolfe wooed and won the sable princess; and her descendants, known as the "first families of Virginia," live upon all parts of the Peninsula. The old house upon whose site "White House" was built was the residence of Mrs. Washington. Coal Harbor, or its vicinity, in Hanover county, gave birth to Patrick Henry, and Ashland, in the same county, to Henry Clay. Chief-Justice Marshall lived all his private life in Richmond, and General Washington has ridden or walked over the whole neighborhood of the capital. Every inch of soil is famous as the residence of some patriot or hero whose ashes now lie in his honored grave. The ground was all sacred, and upon it two vast armies fought to decide one of the most momentous questions which ever agitated the world.

The soil upon the Pamunky River differs materially from that upon the James. The ground in the Pamunky Valley, and indeed all across the ridge to the Chickahominy, is sandy, changing easily into dust or mud. It is almost white in color. The valley of the James has the same soil, though with a large proportion of clay, and it changes into mud just as readily as that upon the Pamunky. The earth upon the Peninsula seems to have the greatest affinity for water, attracting it even when there is no rain, and when there is, changing in two or three hours into a vast mud-puddle a foot deep. This attribute of the soil was one of the greatest impediments to military movements. Men could scarcely walk through the deep, thick, sticky mire, and drawing artillery and wagons through such a mixture was an impossibility. This mud came and went in the shortest possible time. Three hours of rain would convert the entire country into mire; three hours of dry weather made half of it disappear.

To one accustomed to the thrifty farms and scientific agriculture of the North, Virginia farming presented few attractions. Corn, wheat, oats, and tobacco were usually raised, and the majority of the houses had small gardens. Virginia farms were always immense plantations, at least three-fourths being woodland. It was the policy of the large land-owners, for political or personal reasons, to buy out the small ones and drive them away. A dozen men would thus become the owners of a whole county. Wheat and oats were sown broadcast, never drilled; and the fields were just ripening when the advance of the Union army compelled the land-owners of Secession proclivities to leave their homes. These crops were all seized by the Federal troops for forage. Corn is planted one grain to a hill, and the hills and rows are each from four to five feet apart. The stalks are never cut as in the North, the ears being pulled from the top, and the stalks left standing until the plough turns them under the surface. Ten bushels to the acre is the average yield of a Virginia cornfield.

Rotation of crops is not resorted to, and the soil did not seem ever to have been nourished by fertilizers. Every fifteen or twenty years the old farm wears out, and a new one is cleared from the woods. Fields in every stage of exhaustion were presented on all sides. In the woods there was very little of the original forest remaining, the timber being principally of the second growth springing up on the exhausted fields of farms which were abandoned years ago. It was very sad to witness all these evidences of sloth and waste; their causes have been Virginia's customs for centuries. If this war, by introducing new inhabitants or new ideas, renders the Northern system of farming prevalent in the Old Dominion, all the desolation it has caused there will have been amply atoned.

Very few streams, either large or small, run to the three large rivers of the Peninsula. Springs were unusually scarce, and every stream had its contents discolored by Virginia mud. The slightest rains dislodged this mud in immense quantities, and the running water of the streams always did it. The water, therefore, was always marred. The James River for a great part of the year is the color of light coffee. Such liquids were almost loathsome to Northerners, used to cold, sparkling water in every brook, and accustomed to finding springs under the roots of almost every tree. In a rain the first hour sufficed to saturate the ground, and then every gully became a roaring cataract. The water from a thunder-storm would pour off through every opening, carrying bushels of mud with it, tearing up fences and fields, bursting through woods, and reaching the first stream, over whose bed it would rush in the wildest confusion. By the time the clouds of a storm had cleared away, its surplus water would all have run down from the high grounds, and could be heard roaring through the valleys as it drove its onward course to the swamps.

Virginia has two species of rains,—the usual northeasters of the Atlantic seaboard, and thunder-storms. The latter were the ones which deluged the camps, caused the freshets, and carried off bridges. They generally came in a series, one following another from all points of the compass for six hours at a time. Northern thunder and lightning seldom reached the sublimity shown in these almost daily scourges. Constant peals and flashes for ten minutes at a time were not infrequent, and the torrents of rain usually soaked through every thing. Tent-cloth, however, stood the test without yielding, when the water, foiled above, often made its attacks from beneath, running in torrents under the edge of the canvas and along the ground. During a night thunder-storm, it was a common thing for a soldier to wrap himself up in his water-proof blanket and have a small brook purling on each side of him. Such invasions were made by Virginia storms upon Union troops. Each storm, however, cooled the air, and, with all its inconveniences, was welcomed.

The effect of these rains upon the roads was most horrible. During and for several hours after the storm, most of them were converted into an impassable mire.

After the deluge, a day or two was required to insure safe travelling, and usually, long before that time had elapsed, another rain would put them into as bad a condition as before. Of course, from these impediments, military movements were constantly delayed. A broken wagon in a miry road necessitated the construction of a new passage around the obstruction through the adjoining fields or woods. Such labor required time, and, of course, every thing had to be delayed until it was performed. The miserable roads of the Peninsula are to blame for half the time spent by the army upon it.

A Virginia road was generally made with but slight reference to the points between which it was intended to run. It turned and twisted almost as badly as the rivers. Usually passing through the woods, no sheep or cow path ever was laid out with less idea of the laws regulating straight lines. These roads were made a hundred years ago, and their courses have not been altered since. In a country of horsemen, where a half-dozen donkey-carts and one or two carriages are all the vehicles in a county, very wide roads are not needed. These were exceedingly narrow, and in many places had to be widened to allow a passage for Federal artillery and wagons. The roads often ran between steep banks and sometimes in gullies. Nowhere but upon the level ground could two wagons pass. Some of the roads were styled "turnpikes," and upon them were the remnants of gates and toll-houses. These, however, were just like the rest,—quite as narrow and crooked and as easily converted into mud. The Old Dominion seemed sadly in want of instruction in the art of road-making; and General McClellan has left there some evidences of Northern skill in that business which will give it. Woodbury bridge and its approaches, Grapevine bridge, the road to Savage Station from Woodbury bridge, and the one across White Oak Swamp, are monuments of free Northern labor which it is to be hoped Rebel vandalism never will deface.

The climate of Virginia was not near so changeable as that of States farther North. The air seemed most favorable for those afflicted with throat and lung affections. The soldiers seldom took cold; such troubles were almost forgotten. The rays of the sun were most powerful, and could scarcely be borne. Under the shade of the trees or tents, however, a cool breeze generally tempered the extreme heat and rendered the day somewhat pleasant. Early morning and evening were always cool; but in the neighborhood of the swamps a dense fog rose up at dusk, obscuring every thing and making the air damp and disagreeable. There were few dull, cloudy days without rain. It was either clear, with those fleecy clouds which always chase each other across the heavens on sunshiny days, or else rainy; and changes from the one to the other were always quickly made.

The swamps usually occupied every lowland and the borders of all the large streams. They could generally be crossed with the aid of boards. The smaller swamps were passed by stepping from one "tussock," or small clump of grass and roots, to another. The water in these swamps mostly lay stagnant, the storms—except in extraordinary cases—failing to produce more impression than to cause it to rise a foot or two. Scarcely any current was ever perceptible in the swamps, and the streams which ran into them were all swallowed up on the border. Such places as these must have caused a great amount of sickness in the armies encamped around them; and, from the forms of disease prevalent in the Federal hospitals, the miasm from the swamps no doubt was the cause in the great majority of cases. Encamping beside them was always unpleasant,—a chorus of thousands of frogs, of all styles of croak, being music by day and lullaby at night. It was most painful, and pleased no one but some stray Frenchmen who had enlisted, and who caught and ate their favorite animal by hundreds.

The surface of the country was generally rolling. It sloped gradually upwards from the Pamunky, and was broken into gorges and valleys for the passage of every small stream. On the Chickahominy the land was very high, running down in very steep slopes to the borders of the swamp, thus forming on both sides a range of lofty hills. Three-fourths of the surface was wooded, but little of the primitive forest, however, remaining. These old pieces of woods were found to be filled with oak, beech, elm, ash, hickory, and cedar, and were usually free from undergrowth. Land once cultivated, but deserted, bore second-growth timber of all ages. This was pine and cedar exclusively, and was sparsely grown, also without underbrush. Virginia has inexhaustible supplies of timber for every purpose to which it could be applied. Walnut, cherry, locust, and chestnut were occasionally met with, though usually they were single trees standing alone in the fields, having been planted there, or allowed to remain in the general clearing of the woods when the land was first reclaimed.

The universal opinion of all observers of Virginia's agriculture was that the soil was not half cultivated, and what was done was in such an awkward manner that it was much more expensive than it would ever have been made by a Northern man. The adoption of Northern habits of farming, and the cutting up of the large plantations into small farms, were considered by all as two great means of amelioration. Hundreds of tillers of sterile soils in the North looked with sorrow upon the riches allowed to waste in Virginia. They saw her natural advantages, her facilities for navigation, the ease with which a market could be reached, and the really good soil and favorable climate; and, knowing so well the remedy which in a few years would make each field the garden-spot its first settlers found it, they almost wept over the desolation caused in a time of profound peace by the narrow policy of a few lordly land-owners. It is to be trusted that Virginia will be regenerated. An infusion of energy and free labor can easily do it.

The people the army found in Virginia seemed to be an entirely different race from that living in the North,—one which had degenerated in intellect, energy, and every thing which makes up the character of true manhood. A state of war may have changed the aspect of society and driven off the higher classes, but those left as the inhabitants of the Peninsula—from whom one was to make up his estimate of the people of the State—were certainly as debased and degraded as the poor negroes who surrounded them. Still, in all their abject misery they were kind and hospitable. They lived in their cabins,—for only the wealthy land-owners had houses,—were visited by our troops, and treated every one as well as they were able. Very little beauty was vouchsafed to the females, and the habits of all were such as to astonish sober, steady-going

Northerners. Every able-bodied man was in the Rebel army, and, of course, but few males were left in the country. If a cabin was visited, a strange sight was seen. An old man generally lolled on the door-step, with uncombed hair and grizzled beard, invariably smoking. The old lady, with a negro-turban on her head, and a pipe in her mouth, wandered about, grunting and grumbling,—not the slightest motherly appearance being traced in the sharp features and bony form of the ever-restless body. The young people were but little like young people of the North. The boys chopped wood and built fires, and the girls did the house-work and cooking, but neither were usefully employed a tithe of the day. The clothing for all was made of the cheaper kind of goods, being usually purchased at Richmond for very high prices. Crinoline of enormous proportions adorned all the younger females,—its entire absence from the dress of the older ones making a most ludicrous contrast. The males—grandsire, father, and son—were all clad in that sad-colored mixture known as "homespun."

These Virginians never conversed in a sprightly manner. Their talking was always a drawl. The blacks and poor whites spoke exactly alike, using the same phrases and expressions and seeming to have the same ideas. When one's back is turned, and a Virginian's voice is heard, the greatest linguists cannot tell whether it comes out of the mouth of a white man or a black one. "Thar," "whar," "befo'," "sah," "right smart," "powerful weak," "a heap," *et id omne genus*, are used alike by all colors; and unless a Virginian be of high cultivation, his language is on an exact level with that used by the slave whom he drives.

A talented Virginian, however, who is of good family, —and the talents appear to have been given only to that class,—cannot be excelled in beauty of expression and justice in the choice of language.

There is a great difference between the people of the North and of this region in the matter of energy. A Northern man is never contented: he always wants more,—is always pushing ahead. A Virginian, so he can have his allowance of whiskey and be at liberty to swear at the Abolitionists, is satisfied to live on as he has from his boyhood, cultivating his single acre and pasturing his single cow. He never wants to be richer or better. He never wishes to leave his clearing to see the world, or to desert his log cabin, even though it be to inhabit a fine mansion. He chooses his political idol, follows him through all the turnings and twistings of the political pathway, until one or the other, the patron or his client, is laid in the grave. He never changes his church or his religion. The gray-headed clergyman at whose altar he worships in manhood pressed his infant head at the baptismal font. He swears the same oaths, sings the same songs, and tells the same stories that he did twenty years ago. And his children after him, should not this war make a most marked alteration in Virginian society, will do as he has done, and be as perfectly satisfied with their course as he has been with his.

The opinions of all were usually in favor of Secession; and even the presence of the Federal army could scarcely repress the expression of treasonable sentiments. A few families, scattered sparsely throughout the country, favored the Union cause, and had suffered the severest hardships and privations from the Rebel authorities. By these, Union soldiers were always regarded as true friends; by the others they were only wanted so long as they paid extravagant prices for milk and strawberries. Some of the wives wished the war over, to have their husbands back and reduce the starvation-prices they had to pay for all they bought. Others, however, held out,—wishing untold horrors to the Federal troops and terrible destruction to the North. The women were, by all odds, far worse rebels than the men. They sent information to the enemy, trumped up false charges against the troops, of which investigation would at once prove the untruth, and made all sorts of traps to catch unwary officers. They were a sorry set of jades, and a disgrace to their sex.

Southern newspapers "fired the Southern heart," daily, with all sorts of misstatements. These had circulated extensively through all the Peninsula up to the time of the advance of the Union army. When reprinted at the North, the absurdity of the stories in them was plain: Virginia Secessionists, however, regarded them as truths, and treasured up every one as daily evidences of the increasing prosperity of the Confederacy.

Almost every man of Secession feelings who had any thing to lose by the advance of the army proclaimed himself a Union man. Such tricks, however, were soon discovered. An indiscreet expression, or a leaky negro, would easily betray all; and it was excellent practice at dissimulation which helped Mr. Rebel safely through the gauntlet he ran. A perjured Union man was always harshly treated. There was a respect shown for those who boldly expressed their opinions and strove to take no unfair advantage; but the poor traitor whose Union disguise had been dragged from him was always regarded as the vilest of men.

The women did most of their injury by their bad wishes and their endeavors to entrap Union officers. They would "wish that the rain would come down ever so fast down thar on the swamp," and "wish that Beauregard *would* come," or "General McClellan fall sick, or get shot, or the Yankees get beaten." They had plenty of unfriendly wishes, and plenty of unfriendly snares. The anecdote of Mrs. Mills and the two Federal officers, in which each played upon the other, the lady relying upon the approach of Stewart's cavalry at the time it made the raid to White House and around the army, although it has been extensively circulated, will bear repetition. Being a friend of both officers, and at the camp of their regiment when they swiftly rode into it and told their story, the author can vouch for its truth. Mrs. Mills's house was five miles east of Mechanicsville, and situated on a road along which Stewart and his force marched a few moments after the Federal officers left. The anecdote is the following:—

"Quartermaster S—— and Commissary Zack B——, of one of the regiments, are both of them very good fellows, and also very brave soldiers when either of their departments of transportation or supply are brought into conflict with the enemy. Each one mounts a mettled steed, and can control him with a grace which even General McClellan might envy. This morning they started out in company to forage for the officers' mess. Well provided with money to meet the exorbitant demands of the egg and strawberry hucksters of the section of country to which they were going, they gayly vaulted into their saddles, and, bidding good-bye to their friends, briskly trotted off on the road toward Oakland. Having reached there, they turned off on the White House road, and, after a short ride, stopped at a small house by the roadside to inquire what articles they had for sale. B—— was the spokesman, and, at his summons, out came a blooming damsel of eighteen summers to answer the inquiry.

"'Have you any eggs, or butter, or milk, or any thing of the sort, to sell?'

"'Whereabouts do you come from?'

"'About four miles from here. We belong to the Union army.'

"'You do, eh? Well, I don't allow a Yankee to come within twenty yards of me, much less to speak to me.'

"The officers opened their eyes at this desperate declaration, and, riding into the yard, the commissary continued:—

"'Say, look a-here: don't you know that such folks as you are the only kind of meat we have down in our camp?'

"'Yes indeed,' broke in fair Secessia: 'I've heard that much about you.'

"'Well, I suppose you have; and it's all true. Why, at the battle of Fair Oaks the Yankees ate eight hundred just such looking Rebels as you; and it took ever so many soldiers to guard the three thousand dead ones, and keep them off.'

"At this barbarous speech, which might have provoked most terrible results, if the young lady's flashing eyes were any index of her state of mind, the parents appeared, and, gently checking her, accosted the Union officers, and said they had nothing to sell. The father seemed somewhat amused at his daughter's spirit, and explained:—

"'That ere gal's got a beau in the Confederate army, don't you see, and, you know, that's a good reason for her being so much opposed to the Yankees. Just you make an offer to capture her, and see if she don't haul down her colors.'

"But the officers were not accustomed to doing such unmanly things, and, finding they could procure no eatables at this place, they withdrew to the road and continued their journey. Going a short distance along a road which turned off to the left, they stopped at a house where a lady lived whose husband was in the Rebel army. Mrs. Mills received them in a most bewitchingly friendly manner, spread out a glorious dinner, and offered to sell them oceans of milk and bushels of cherries. With a pleasant smile, so different from the excitable lass they had just left, she invited them into the house, setting chairs for their accommodation, and, after some pressing, made them consent to unsaddle their horses and turn them out to graze. Nothing could exceed the politeness of Mrs. Mills. She was so glad they had come, and so fearful that their long ride under a scorching sun might have fatigued them. And were they not hungry? Wouldn't they allow her to set out something for them to eat, to stay their stomachs until dinner? She was so sorry their camp was so distant; for nothing would delight her more than to send them strawberries and milk and cherries, and every thing which her garden could furnish. She thought the Union soldiers were such nice gentlemen,—so gallant and brave, and so considerate toward the poor Virginians who had lost their all in this sorrowful war. And couldn't they stay to dinner, and allow her to treat them with true Virginia hospitality?

"Such a loving reception, extended by the wife of a Rebel soldier to two perfect strangers, was so very unlike other earthly things, and so very like the concluding chapters of the 'yellow-kivered,' that it astonished the two officers. The commissary looked at the quartermaster, and the quartermaster, thinking that he detected a wink of B——'s eye, returned it, and both together they entered the house. With many thanks and protestations that nothing was further from their intention than to give trouble, they took seats on the chairs set out for them, and, whilst the lady bustled about in the preparation of dinner, had time to look about them.

"They were in a cleanly, well-kept Virginia log house, with old-fashioned furniture, and were evidently partaking the hospitalities of a lady of cultivated manners and excellent understanding. Their ride had been a long one, and the brush they had previously undergone so contrasted with this kind treatment that their hearts were almost melted in gratitude toward their fair benefactress. A few moments sufficed for the preparation of the meal, and the lady, placing chairs at the table, invited them to be seated.

"Of course, nothing on that humble board could, in her estimation, suit the epicurean palates of two such gallant officers of the Union army. Her bread she was afraid was too heavy and her butter too soft. Her milk had soured, and she was almost ashamed to tell it, but the very last piece of fresh meat had been eaten that very morning, and she had nothing but ham to offer the gentlemen, but then the ham had been her father's own raising, and she knew they would like it. Perhaps they would taste some of her early cherries and strawberries, and asparagus, too; but no, the cherries were under- and the strawberries over-ripe, and that good-for-nothing wench that did the cooking had left the asparagus too long on the fire, and it was boiled all to pieces. She knew the gentlemen wouldn't like it. And her potatoes, too, she had taken such pains with them, and just to think how sodden they were! Oh, it was awful!

"'My dear madam,' broke in the polite quartermaster, 'pray don't apologize any more. The meal is excellent; I hardly ever sat down to a better. Have you, Zack?'

"'No, indeed,' said Zack: 'why, at home I never had any thing like it. Salt pork and small potatoes are all we get up in our country.'

"The lady was terribly afraid that the gentlemen were not being suited, and that they really thought her dinner a poor one; 'but then, you know,' she added. with a smile, 'I am doing my best, and if I could do better I would.'

"'Of course,' said the quartermaster.

"'Of course,' echoed the commissary.

"'And if my butter is soft it is not my fault, is it?'

"'Oh, certainly not,' exclaimed both in concert.

"The lady was so bewitching that for two hours the officers sat at her table, eating and talking. The quartermaster made the apologies, and the commissary adroitly put the questions. The fair Rebel no doubt thought that she had effectually caught the two simple-hearted gentlemen who sat meekly before her, and, glorying in the triumph which another hour would bring, was slightly unguarded.

"'I believe, madam, that your husband is in the Confederate army,' said B——; 'you must be very lonely without him.'

"'Oh, no, not with such good company as you are; and then, besides, I hear from him every two or three days, and he tells me all that is going on. Only a day or two ago I had word from him.'

"The quartermaster treasured this up, and the commissary, looking ten times more simple-hearted than previously, ejaculated, 'How very nice!'

"'Yes, and he says that Beauregard's army, or a good part of it at least, is at Richmond, and that soon the Yankees will be driven away from about here, and then he can come and see me whenever he wants to.'

"The quartermaster took a mouthful of water, and the commissary said, 'Indeed!'

"After a pause the quartermaster asked, 'But, madam, suppose your husband should be shot: how would you take it?'

"Oh, never you mind her,' broke in B——: 'she knows very well that if he's killed I will come down here and marry her.'

"'You Northern gentlemen are so kind!' said the lady. 'Why, I never did see a finer set of fellows,—and every one unmarried, too. How very strange!'

"'Not strange at all,' replied the quartermaster, 'because only single men come to war: the married ones stay at home to take care of their wives.'

"The lady thought a moment, and said, 'I wish that

was the case with us. I was so sorry to lose my husband, and he was so sorry to go. Only the other day he was here, and some rough men came along and forced him to leave.'

"'Don't cry about it,' said kind-hearted Zack, as the lady's tears began to come; 'you know very well I'll make it all right for you if he's taken prisoner.'

"'Will you?'

"'Oh, yes. You see, my friend here is a quartermaster, and his sister knows a young man that was present at General McClellan's wedding, and I, too, frequently write letters to the general, and he will do any thing for me. Why, only the other day I sent him a letter, asking him for a barrel of whiskey, putting "commissary" after my name, so that he would know it was me, and he sent it to me right away.'

"'Did he?'

"'Yes; and there's no end to the boxes of crackers and barrels of pork and barrels of sugar and coffee and boxes of candles he sends me for myself and my regiment, and when his wagons—you know he keeps three or four—are doing something else, why, my friend, the quartermaster here, jumps aboard of his and drives over, and, handing the servant a piece of paper from me, comes back with lots of them. Why, the general will do any thing for me.'

"The lady thought she had found a friend, indeed, and gave him her husband's name and regiment. Zack took the name down, and said if the gentleman was captured he would send him over to her 'as soon as he could.'

"They sat talking for some moments, each one becoming more interested in the other, until the quartermaster espied a Federal horseman galloping along the road in front of the house. His manner was excited, and the lady, suddenly turning toward the door, muttered, 'Have they found out so soon what our friends are about?' Neither of the officers changed countenance,—as they were fully prepared for what was coming, and had not ridden three miles outside of the Federal lines to be gulled by any female manœuvres. The commissary continued talking, and, after a moment, the quartermaster went out, and, leading the horses to a point where the lady could not see his movements, briskly saddled them. When he finished, he re-entered the house, and joined in the conversation as if nothing had happened.

"'But, Mrs. Mills,' said he, after a moment's small talk, 'haven't you any milk or butter you could sell us? I almost forgot it, but we came here to buy something for the starving fellows in camp.'

"Had he seen the 'starving fellows in camp' about this time, perhaps he would not have talked so placidly of them. The telegraph-line had signalled danger to them, and with it came the order to prepare for a fight. 'Where is the quartermaster?' 'Where is the commissary?' were heard on all sides. They had been gone since early morning, and here, at four o'clock, they had not returned. 'The enemy advancing in force,' had been signalled from the very direction in which they had gone, and their long absence was almost a sure indication that they had been captured. Heavy bets were staked upon it. 'I bet two and a half to one,' said a colonel. 'Take it,' cried a major: 'they've got fast horses, and can go a streak.' Every one was anxious.

"But, with minds free from anxiety, the two officers still stayed with Mrs. Mills, procuring all sorts of dainties, and filling their bags and baskets with them. They rose finally, however, saying they must be going, and the commissary took out his pocket-book to pay for the articles they had bought. He flourished its contents pretty considerably, and the lady higgled about the change, and couldn't calculate, and had no dimes or quarters, and must go up-stairs for some small money. B—— didn't object, but winked to his friend, who brought up the horses, and they both mounted.

"'Mrs. Mills,' he shouted, 'I have the right money; here it is.'

"Down-stairs came the lady, and sought to engage them in conversation again. She reluctantly took the money, and, finding that they would go, was at a loss for further means of detention. But hospitality came to her aid, and she asked them to dinner next day. Of course they consented, and, thanking her, arranged what dainties were to be provided. Two minutes more settled that point, and, as they bade her good-bye, a shadow passed over her countenance. They walked their horses leisurely to the road, and, giving one look behind them, each one clapped the spur into his horse's side, and, with lightning speed, they galloped off. Five minutes afterward a Confederate troop came riding by,—some stopping at the house to search for Unionists. An hour after, and the two officers had reported to their commander the important news they had gleaned from Mrs. Mills's unguarded conversation, and, with their companions, sat comfortably around the mess-table, quietly eating the lady's berries and drinking her milk."

The ill feeling generally held toward them by the inhabitants, of course, did not improve the opinions the soldiers freely expressed of all Virginians; and when knavery was commenced by one side it was adopted and continued by the other. The people charged extravagant prices for all they sold, demanding payment in gold or Confederate notes: they would scarcely look at a Federal Treasury or Northern bank-note. Soldiers who had gold generally seized the articles wanted, cut down the price one-half, and, laying down the money, walked away. Others had a different plan. They accepted the offer to take Confederate notes, and presented the lithographed copies sold in Northern cities and hawked about by the sutlers at five cents apiece. With such money, it mattered little what price was paid for any thing. The people freely took these notes, praising their newness and good looks, and in some cases, when the genuine and copy were offered side by side, preferred the copy. These counterfeits were much better-looking than the originals, and were passed away in the army by hundreds.

The style of living of Virginians differed, as they were divided into the higher and lower classes. The latter were the "mean whites," who owned no slaves, and generally less than a half-dozen acres of land. Their lordly neighbors looked down upon their poverty and ignorance with a contempt which was no doubt fully reciprocated; but still they tilled their little farms, lived in their log huts, ate their meals, smoked their pipes, and were content.

The log huts of this lower class are so poor, and so unusual at the North, that a just description will scarcely be believed. They were set about the country without reference either to beauty or convenience. They are built of round hewn timber, joined at the corners, with the chinks filled in with mortar or clay. Never more than one story high, that one is so low that a tall man has to stoop in entering the door. Some logs thrown across above form the ceiling of the room and the floor of the loft, and a ladder of the rudest description, leading through a hatch, is the grand staircase. These huts have usually one room; a two-roomed hut is a rarity. Sometimes the ground is the floor, the poverty of the owner preventing the purchase of floor-boards. A large fireplace, built also of logs, and a log chimney, finish the building; whilst a shed, sloping the rain off from the door-yard only to run back again when it has fallen to the ground, is balcony, portico, and awning for the residence. Poor and restricted as these buildings may seem, yet they are homes for some one, and, as such, are no doubt as much beloved as the finest houses in the land. Large families of children are often reared in them, and many a distinguished Virginian first saw the light in one of these buildings. Old Hanover county, in Virginia, has always been proud of her Henrys,—her Patrick Henry, and her Henry Clay. One was born in a miserable hut whose ruins stand hard by the road from Coal Harbor to New Bridge; the other drew his first breath at Ashland, where, five years since, stood just such a hut as has been described.

Sometimes a change was seen in the almost universal order of things. A poor farmer would keep his house and lot in good order, and become an example to his less thrifty neighbors. One instance of this deserves to be noted. About a mile from Woodbury Bridge was the home of one of these deserving men. He lived in a rather comfortable log cabin in the centre of a twenty-acre field. Out-houses were scattered about irregularly, but all embosomed in vines and shrubbery, which betokened the careful habits of the wife. The principal part of the field was an orchard, containing some of the finest peach and apple trees. Cows grazed contentedly beneath them, apparently ignorant of the war which raged around this little oasis. In a fenced enclosure, garden-vegetables were raised, and seemed to have been well cared for. The owner of this property must have come from the North. There were so many little arrangements about the buildings and grounds that one never sees in Virginia, but which are so common in the North,—so many comforts and conveniences, and such a civilized way of building gates and fences,—that, if the man was not a Northerner, he was at least a strange specimen of a Virginian.

The field had all been cleared from the centre of a vast wood; yet every stump had been pulled out, and the land, even under the trees of the orchard, ploughed and cultivated to its greatest capacity. Two roads ran along, one on either side of the property, and a lane through the field, fenced by its owner, connected them. General McClellan gave this man a guard for his property, and granted him that protection which the white flag waving over the roof of his house claimed.

It is most gratifying to find such thrift in one of the lower class, when all around him live in wretchedness. Cleanliness and comfort seem to be usurped by the rich. Only those who have their tens and hundreds of slaves can boast a well-stocked plantation. This man was not one of these. Not a negro was near his house, and very likely he was too poor to own one. Every day's labor taken to keep that garden-spot fertile and productive must have been the work of his own hands; and where a single white man is found who violates the universal rule of sloth which hangs like a pall over Virginia's prospects, he should have his virtues given to the world.

The higher classes, of course, had plenty of money and owned thousands of broad acres; but their style of living was scarcely what would be expected of such great and showy people. Their mansion-houses, grand beside the wretched log huts of their neighbors, were generally tawdry, uncomfortable, and out of repair. The present owners rarely built them: it was usually done by the parents or grandparents. All of them, therefore, presented an air of antiquity which was most unseemly. The grounds surrounding them were seldom carefully laid out. A grove of oaks or elms was the front, and, behind, negro-huts, sheds, and shanties were planted around with a total disregard of all the rules of order. In these mansion-houses the "first families" lived, surrounded by their slaves and their plantations. Exclusiveness was their great vice. No intercourse was ever had with poor people; such were left to talk with the negroes. With an overseer to superintend the plantation, they lived in sloth, the negroes doing all the work, their masters and mistresses seldom watching how it was done. The usual means resorted to by such people to pass time were in great vogue in Virginia. Fox-hunts, pigeon-shootings, and such amusements, were very popular. Years ago in their idleness they invented the doctrine of State Rights and commenced its discussion. At a later day it changed to Secession. Then came high-running politics, and finally military musters and drills, until the iron rule of the majority, against the protest of vast numbers of her citizens, thrust Virginia from the Union and began her ruin and degradation. But this is wandering from the subject.

A description of some of the mansion-houses which in the progress of the war have become celebrated will suffice as a type of all.

Mr. Toler's House, at Cumberland.

This was a two-story frame building, having a porch in front, and was almost entirely imbedded in foliage. Brick chimneys were built at each end, and the house was surmounted by a high-peaked roof. Mr. Toler, the owner, was a Secessionist, though one holding peculiar opinions. He firmly believed that foreign intervention would end the war. It was upon this man's extensive plantation that the Federal army encamped whilst at Cumberland. Upon the approach of the Union troops, Mr. Toler's negroes, with the exception of a few women and children, all disappeared. They were doubtless among the commissary gangs at White House. This house was much decayed, and was a poor representative of Virginia mansions.

White House.

This, though one of the smallest and most insignificant of all the great manor-houses, from the historical associations connected with it was by far the most celebrated. It was built upon the site of a white house much larger and more pretentious, and which years ago had been removed to make way for the present structure. This first house—the real "White House"—was the one in which Mrs. Custis had lived, and at which General Washington visited her. The second house, far from being a *white* one, was painted a sort of pink color. The Lee family are the owners of the property,—A. S. Lee, of the Confederate army, son of its present commander-in-chief, Robert E. Lee, having, previous to the commencement of the war, resided there with his mother. The house was plainly built, in the form of a centre building and wings, its entire front being about forty feet and its depth twenty. It was two stories high, with a peaked roof, and porches ornamented the main building. Inside there were main halls, and a staircase occupying the centre, and a room on each floor in each wing. Two attics were under the roof. The whole structure was of frame. A building such as White House could be erected at the North for one thousand or fifteen hundred dollars. The grounds around the house were simply a grass-field, in which grew several large trees. There seemed to be no flowers. The house was fifty yards back of the river, and the negro-huts and garden were on the bank of the stream below.

When General Stoneman's troops occupied White House on the evening of May 10, the guard placed to protect the mansion found a paper pinned to the wall of the main corridor, upon which was written, in a lady's hand, the following words:—

"Northern soldiers who profess to reverence Washington, forbear to desecrate the home of his first married life,—the property of his wife, now owned by her descendants.

"A grand-daughter of Mrs. Washington."

This was written by Mrs. Robert E. Lee; and below it, upon the wall, one of the guard wrote an answer:—

"A Northern officer has protected your property in sight of the enemy, and at the request of your overseer."

White House was used as a hospital in June, and upon June 27 was set fire to by some Vandal and needlessly burned. The destruction of the railroad-depot at that time made did not call for the destruction of the house, and those who had charge of the United States property disavow the act. Some one beyond their control kindled the flames.

Dr. Gaines's House.

This was the largest of all the houses in the vicinity of Richmond. It was some six miles east-northeast of the capital, and had a hill beside it from which a view could be had for miles along the Chickahominy Valley. The house is celebrated as being fought around during the whole of the battles of June 27, the first of the series which rendered the flank movement to the James River so bloody. The house was a large square one, two stories in height, partly frame and partly stone. There was no architectural beauty about it, but every one envied its owner the noble grove of oaks which sloped down at its back toward the Chickahominy. A cool, refreshing breeze always came beneath their broad limbs, and fanned the weary wayfarer who stepped under them for rest. The owner of the house was a rampant Secessionist, and was kept under guard in his own dwelling.

Hogan's House.

This was a mansion of frame, built like Dr. Gaines's residence, but on a smaller scale. It was a mile north of the other. Usually the head-quarters of some of the Federal generals, "Hogan's House" became the heading of numerous orders. An enormous oak stood in front of it, at about two hundred yards' distance, on a lane which led out to the road. This tree was faultless. It was almost a perfect sphere, and covered with foliage which was without break or imperfection. It was the cynosure of all eyes; and thousands of dollars would have been willingly spent by Federal officers to have had that tree before their homes in the North. It gave a glory to Hogan's house greater than could be imparted by all the generals in the world.

Oakland.

This celebrated mansion was seven miles north of Richmond, and was a fine two-story brick and frame building, surrounded with elegantly laid-out grounds and well-cultivated gardens. It was the residence of "George W. Richardson, attorney-at-law," as he had it painted over the front basement-window. This man, evidently not over thirty-five years of age, had been a year absent from his home, being a colonel in the Rebel army, and commanding a Virginia regiment. He was a bachelor, having, in the year 1855, been disappointed in love through the aversion of his intended's parents.

The colonel's house was well furnished, and had been hurriedly deserted by his foolish family upon the day of the first reconnoissance to Mechanicsville. One side of the basement was the kitchen, the other the law-office, in which there was a valuable law library and numerous private papers. Above the kitchen was the dining-room, and over the office the parlor. The second story and the half-story above it were used for bed-rooms. The negroes, of whom there were six or seven, were rambling around as usual, and an old, sour-looking graybeard was pointed out as the overseer. Little chickens played around the house, and behind it were acres of garden-land, upon which every species of vegetable were being raised. The house and grounds were well kept, and the rural beauty of the place far exceeded that of any other mansion which the army passed.

Colonel Richardson was evidently a man of note in Virginia politics. He had been a Whig; and one of the addresses of the Whig committee of 1859, sent to every prominent Whig in the State during the Goggin-Letcher campaign of that year, was lying on the floor. For the instruction of politicians of the present day, it is reproduced here:—

"RICHMOND, April 18, 1859.

"DEAR SIR:—I am instructed, as Chairman of the Opposition State Central Committee, to correspond with our political friends in each county and town in the State upon the subject of the organization of our forces for the fourth Thursday in May. The committee would know what steps have been taken in your county to this end. Have your committees been appointed for the precincts or magisterial districts, to circulate documents, reason with voters, and bring them to the polls?—steps deemed indispensably necessary.

"The signs everywhere are most auspicious. We think that if we can make our vote what it was in 1855 for Governor, such is the depressed and disorganized state of the Democracy, our success is sure. Our aggregate vote was then 73,354: that of your county was 553. Can you not, by engaging the co-operation of discreet and influential men in every neighborhood, in seeing voters and urging them to attend the polls, and by circulating documents and spreading information generally, increase the vote you then gave?

"Let us hear as early as possible what you are doing and expect to do. Send here for documents if you need more, and direct how we shall send them to you.

"Very respectfully, yours,
"R. T. DANIEL, *Chairman.*"

It seems that Virginia politicians are not a whit more modest than those of a colder climate. Among Colonel Richardson's papers was the following business-like announcement of an aspirant for official honors:—

'TO THE VOTERS OF HANOVER COUNTY.

"FELLOW-CITIZENS:—It will devolve upon you at the ensuing spring election, in May next, to elect a commonwealth's attorney for the county of Hanover. I take this opportunity to announce myself a candidate for said office, and respectfully solicit your support for the same.

"WILLIAM R. WINN."

There was also among his papers a letter urging him to withdraw his opposition to Judge Dabney, who was running for attorney-general; and another, written when he was raising his Secession regiment, declining a staff appointment because it cost too much to get an outfit. Here is the letter:—

"COLONEL RICHARDSON.

"DEAR SIR:—With much reluctance I am constrained to decline the honorable post which you have so kindly tendered me in the staff. I was in Richmond yesterday, and ascertained that it would cost me the sum of one hundred and eight dollars to equip myself, which sum my circumstances at present will not justify me thus to expend. With many thanks for your kindness,

"I am, respectfully, yours, &c.,

"EDWIN T. SHELTON."

Colonel Richardson's greatest trait, however, was his love-making, and several soldiers carried off love-letters as trophies, in which the lovers poured out their whole souls in perfect rhapsodies of affection. One lady, though, utterly refused all his advances. His house was used by the Union troops for a hospital.

A Rebel General's Head-Quarters.

Opposite Mechanicsville, some distance to the right of the road leading to Richmond, and mounted on a commanding hill, was an elegant mansion. Embosomed in shrubbery, with an ornamented portico and tastefully-decorated grounds, it was a marked object on a horizon which showed nothing elsewhere but log huts, woods, cannon, and Rebels. Being so prominent, of course hundreds of officers and soldiers watched it, and they saw all that passed there. It was evidently the quarters of some Rebel general, and he, too, one high in command. Prancing horses stood pawing at the gate-post. Orderlies were lounging about, and aids constantly coming and going with messages. Every day a retinue started off from it and disappeared among some of the many neighboring woods, returning afterward, though sometimes at long intervals. Fleet horsemen came and went, and lazy sentinels walked the rounds, keeping off the vulgar crowd.

Who the great man was who kept such a fine house, and commanded the services of so many, was a subject of earnest speculation. Field-glasses did not bring the house and its occupants near enough to discern features, and so the question could not be decided. If the occupant really was what he seemed, he showed great taste in the choice of his residence; and a correct appreciation of the beautiful is said to be an unfailing indication of a great mind. His house was two stories high, with an ornamented porch surrounding it. A cornice, such as is universal in the North, though seldom seen in Virginia, surmounted the walls. The building was of frame, painted white. Shrubbery of every description was planted about in great profusion. The grounds were laid out partly as lawn and partly as garden, and, though shut to the common herd, were filled with Rebel officers. The spot upon which this house was situated was one of the most beautiful upon the Peninsula.

Hopewell Baptist Church.

Church-architecture in Virginia is of the simplest description. The Hopewell Baptist Church is near Tunstall's Station, on the Richmond & York River Railroad. It is a modest little building, about twenty-five feet square and fifteen feet high, built of frame, painted white, and kept very clean. A road is some few yards distant, and the church-door faces it. Inside, the building did not present quite so favorable an appearance as outside. There was a small gallery, capable of seating some thirty persons. This gallery had a separate entrance from the outside, and was not connected with the floor of the church. Opposite the gallery was the pulpit, the rostrum standing upon a small platform a step above the floor. The entire church would perhaps seat a hundred persons comfortably.

A large folio Bible, bearing the imprint of "Thomas, Cowperthwait & Co., Philadelphia, 1850," and having "Hopewell Church" written opposite, lay upon the rostrum. A New York edition of the Baptist collection of hymns was on a table before the pulpit, and in the table-drawer were the records of the church. A little desk alongside contained a few Bibles and Testaments and about twenty little books,—the Sunday-school library. All of these were printed in New York or Philadelphia, many of them having been issued by the American Sunday-School Union. The only blot upon the whole scene was the twenty or thirty square, wooden spittoons, filled with tobacco-quids, which were upon the floor.

One of the most peculiar consequences of the relations of master and slave is that, before a slave can associate himself with any religious congregation, the written consent of the owner must first be obtained. Several of these papers were among the records of Hopewell Church, and, as they are curiosities, copies of a few are given:—

"Introduced by Charles Canby, a highly respectable servant of the Retreat Farm, is Lavinia, Patsey Jr., Patsey Sr., and Arena, as asking permission to be baptized; which lease I grant to any, a regularly-ordained Baptist preacher.

"WM. P. BRAXTON, Agt.

"For DR. C. C. COOKE and MISS ANN C. DAVIS.

"June 21st, 1856."

"Martha has my permission to unite with the Baptist Church. SAM'L WEBB."

"My man Luke and woman Katy have applied to me for permission to join the 'Church.' They have my full consent to do so, hoping it may make them better servants.

"W. H. MASON.

"TO THE MINISTER AT HOPEWELL CHURCH."

"TO THE PASTOR OF HOPEWELL CHURCH:

"SIR:—My servant-woman Caty has this morning asked me to let her join the Baptist Church at Hopewell. Should the pastor of that church think her prepared, I have no objection to her doing so.

"I am, respectfully, yours,

"HENRY WEBB."

A report of the Dover Baptist Association, which was also among the records, stated that J. F. Parkinson was pastor of the church, and that he had seventeen white and one hundred and ninety colored members under his care. This clergyman had charge of other churches in the neighborhood, and seems to have been an itinerant. The Sunday-school was reported "flourishing," there being fourteen teachers and seventy scholars. The church appeared to be in excellent condition, and, had not an advance of the army caused its members to desert it, perhaps it would have continued throughout the war a place of God's worship, filled by a pious membership, and dispensing the blessings of the gospel where they are most needed,—among the poor negroes.

A Virginia Store.

Near Coal Harbor there was a store which had been deserted by its proprietors. It was a log building, a story and a half high, with two rooms on the ground-floor, and no cellar. The building—which was old and dilapidated—was set upon four piles, one at each corner. Inside, a pale fence ran across one of the rooms, somewhat in the style of a Northern counter. Some shelves were fastened to the walls, and boxes and barrels lay around, but no merchandise could be seen. The other room seemed to have been a stable, as it was divided into stalls. Inside the store and about the door lay scattered the account-books and papers of the concern, and also parts of a copy of the Statutes of Virginia. This store—from the character of these papers—seemed to have been engaged in a peculiar kind of business; a business never transacted at stores in the Northern States. Nine-tenths of the merchandise sold was whiskey; and, from the prices, the article generally sold must have been of the most villanous character. If other Virginia stores were any thing like this one, people need be at no loss to account for the cause of that mania which took the State out of the Union. One page of the day-book (page 1240), dated "June 8," but having no year written upon it, was picked up by a soldier. It contained thirty-seven entries, of which thirty-one were for rum and whiskey. Credit was in each case given, even for a drink. One man gave a note, at four months, for a debt of one dollar and seventeen cents. Whiskey was sold at seventy cents a gallon, and rum at a dollar. A drink cost four cents (cheaper than at most places in the North). Liquor was, in many cases, sold upon orders: indeed, there was not a single order found among the papers of the concern which did not in some way refer to the article. One bill, and six orders, picked up from the ground one after the other, all referred to whiskey. The bill shows how much the whiskey cost:—

"Messrs. Paisley and Brown, Bought of Wilson Williams, January 8, 1861, one barrel rectified whiskey, 43 gallons, at 24c., $10.32.

This stuff, bought at twenty-four cents, was retailed at seventy,—quite a small profit. The six orders were rich specimens both of chirography and orthography, and are given below:—

"March 8, 1857.

"Mr. Brown you will Pleas send me 1 gallon of whiskey.

"Respectfully yourse,

"ELIJAH KELLEY."

"Mr. Brown & Paisley, you will send me one lb. of coffee & 1 of shugar, & five lbs. of six penny nails, & a quart of corn whisky, and much oblige

"WM. B. GOODLY.

"March 12, 1857."

"Mr. Brown, you will pleas send me half gallon of brandy.

"Yourse, Respectfully,

"ELIJAH KELLEY."

"June the 6, 1856.

"Mr. Brown, you will please send me a half pound of candles and a quart of common whiskey and a half gallon

16

of molases. I have sent you 25 cents to pay for the candles and whiskey; the molases you will please charge.

"MARGRET K. BIRATT."

"Mr. Pirsley and Brown will please send by the bearer six lbs. of sugar, 2 lbs. coffee, 1 lb. of candles, 1 quart of best whiskey, 1 pair of lines, and one plug of tobaco.

"W. F. ROBINEAU.

"May the 27, 1859."

"Mr. Brown, plese send me for pounds of brown shugar, 2 pounds of wrise, 1 pound of crackers, for which I send you the money.

"You will plese send 3 pounds of lard, 2 yards of your best yellow cotton, 1 bottle of whiskey that you sell at 60 cts. per gallon; plese send a bill, I will settle in a corse of a fortnight.

"JAMES S. KELLEY.

"Sept. 19th, 1859."

The Virginia slave code requires that all slaves found wandering, or engaged in any business at a distance from their homes, without a written permission, shall be seized as fugitives. Several of these slave-passes lay on the ground, of which the following was by far the most elaborate:—

"The bearer of this, Joe, belonging to Mr. Joseph Pauly, of this county, has permission to sell, for my woman Betsey, two and a half dozen chickens, in the city of Richmond, and in the county of Hanover and Henrico, as he may deem best.

"WM. C. SMITH.

"EASTERN VIEW, HANOVER, August 24, 1855."

This store, exhibiting the vice and ignorance of Virginians, was within twelve miles of the Rebel capital.

If a community is judged by its mode of domestic life, Hanover county, Virginia, must be a very poor place.

The Lager-Beer Saloon at Mechanicsville.

Lager, pretzels, old cheese, brown bread, and sour-krout, seem to have had as many admirers among the *ton* of Richmond as elsewhere. At Mechanicsville there was a large-sized lager-beer saloon and garden. Counters, taps, kegs, and glasses flourished in the house, and fine York River oyster-shells lay in a pile in the back yard. The garden was some ten acres of oak, cleared of the undergrowth, and rural chairs and tables were scattered around. The turnpike from Richmond to Hanover Court-House ran by the house, crossing the river a half-mile distant, at a most beautiful spot, and, after winding among the hills, entering the capital from the North. From the city to this saloon was a favorite drive, and every convenience was had there which Virginia chivalry could need. The beer sold at this place came from Philadelphia breweries, and the glassware and furniture were also of Northern manufacture.

A Virginia Mill.

Ellison's Mill, at which point the Federal troops first met the enemy upon their advance to capture Mechanicsville, stands upon a road leading up the left bank of the Chickahominy, and is a mile below the village. It is a grist-mill. In the North people are used to large mills, with all the modern conveniences for cleaning the grain, bolting the flour, and facilitating the storage and transportation of the manufactured article. Until Ellison's Mill was examined, the author never knew that grain could be ground by so small an amount of machinery.

The building was of frame, two-thirds of its height being the peaked roof surmounting all Virginia houses. It was set on piles, and the wheel was alongside, uncovered, as likewise were the minor wheels and axles which conducted the power to the building. The wheel was ten feet in diameter, and driven by water conducted over it by one of the old-fashioned troughs. Two or three cogged wheels served to alter the direction of the power from vertical to horizontal, to regulate it, and to conduct it to the mill-stones inside. The floor of the mill was of broad boards, with all sorts of chinks and knot-holes. On a raised platform at the back stood a single pair of mill-stones, a crane for removing the upper one when necessary being fastened into the wall. The machinery here was of the rudest and simplest description. The grain, without any previous preparation, was led between the stones, and afterward fell through a constantly-shaken sieve of bolting-cloth into a bin, out of which it was taken and given to customers. There was no means of separating wheat from bran, or of granulating the flour, or of separating the products of the different cereals. Everything —wheat, oats, rye, corn, barley, and whatever else was brought for grinding—went between the same pair of stones, and its product fell into the same bin; and half the flour sold from this mill, no doubt, was a mixture of all the grain grown on Virginia's soil. The poorest machinery and most unskilful arrangement, necessarily insuring the poorest product, seems to be the rule in all Southern industrial manufactories. After the war, perhaps, a new era in manufactures, commerce, and patriotism will commence.

The style of architecture in Virginia was scarcely worthy an age of semi-civilization. For a people with so great a history and such large pretensions, it was deplorable. But little genius has been evinced in the Old Dominion in its latter days. All has been a mass of laziness, sloth, and ignorance, which the desolations of war could scarcely make worse. An infusion of energy is sadly needed in every Virginia community, and the sooner it is given the better will it be for its prosperity.

CHAPTER VII.

THE BATTLE OF FAIR OAKS.

It is no easy task to describe a great battle,—especially one of which such contradictory accounts are given as of the battle of Fair Oaks. Spectators viewing limited portions of the field for a short time give their descriptions; and soldiers who have fought in the strife and survived it sit down afterward and write their impressions. All tell the truth as they saw it or heard it, but to reconcile their narratives is almost impossible. Then, when the official reports are made known to the world, they usually lack what is most needed,—a comprehensive description of what they profess to report. The materials from which the history of a battle is written are usually most uncertain and unreliable; and the subsequent narrative of the battle of Fair Oaks is given to the reader with many misgivings,—though if it has errors they are errors derived from the materials which the author has been compelled to use, and, if it is incomplete, the early date after the conflict at which it is written is his apology.

This celebrated battle has two names. In the North it is known as the "Battle of Fair Oaks," receiving that name from a cluster of beautiful oak-trees some six and a half miles from Richmond, and a short distance south of the Richmond & York River Railroad. In the South it is called the "Battle of the Seven

Pines," a cluster of pine-trees near a frame house a mile southeast of Fair Oaks, and the spot to which the enemy drove the Federal forces upon May 31. The name of Fair Oaks is fast usurping the place of the other, however, and will doubtless in time become the universal designation.

The battle-field of Fair Oaks was upon a very flat country, mostly swampy, and nearly all covered with forest. The railroad ran in an east and west line through it. South of the railroad, and distant but a half-mile, was the Williamsburg road, which was parallel with the other. The Seven Pines were upon this road; and another, called the "Nine-Mile Road," started from the first, opposite the Seven Pines, and ran a mile northwest to the railroad, crossing it near Fair Oaks, and continuing beyond, a mile and a half in the same direction, to a house but a short distance from New Bridge,—known as the "Old Tavern." The peculiar name this road bears is given it because the Seven Pines are nine miles from Richmond if this road be travelled to the Old Tavern, and then one running from New Bridge, past the tavern, to the capital, be taken for the remainder of the journey. To the westward, the direction of Richmond, the woods were very dense, and along the edge had been felled to obstruct the passage of troops. Thick forests also ran along the Federal left to the south of the Williamsburg road. These forests and their "abatis," the felled portion, entirely obstructed the view of an approaching enemy.

It will be remembered that on the 26th of May part of General Keyes's corps was advanced along the Williamsburg road to within four and three-quarter miles of Richmond, and a mile and three-quarters beyond the Seven Pines, the enemy retreating before it. Upon the morning of the 31st, General Keyes's forces were all in that vicinity. General Heintzelman was at the Seven Pines. General Sumner was upon the other side of the Chickahominy, near New Bridge, and by road four and a half miles distant from General Keyes. He had built Grapevine and Sunderland bridges, and was prepared at any moment to cross to the assistance of the left wing. These three corps were all the Federal troops that were engaged in the battle of Fair Oaks, and they numbered in all some fifty-four thousand men, of whom some forty-six thousand were in the battle. The force of the enemy in position numbered about sixty-four thousand. There were four divisions of their army, each one corresponding to a Federal *corps d'armée,* and were commanded by Major-Generals Smith, Longstreet, Hill, and Huger. Forty-eight thousand of them fought in the contest.

At about four o'clock on the afternoon of May 30, there commenced a series of the heaviest thunder-storms which had visited that section of country for a long period. Incessantly until midnight the rain fell in torrents, and it was accompanied by the severest thunder and lightning. The 31st day of May was dark and lowering, with a short space of sunshine at noon; June 1, however, was a bright, clear day. This deluge filled all the streams, and by noon on the 31st had changed the slow-motioned Chickahominy into a roaring torrent. Upon this rise in the river the Rebel commander relied; for he says in his official report that "heavy and protracted rains during the afternoon and night, by swelling the streams of the Chickahominy, increased the probability of our having to deal with no other troops than those of Keyes." General Sumner was separated from his friends at Seven Pines by that swollen river. The object of the attack the enemy were premeditating was to cut off the Federal left wing, speeches to that effect being made to their troops before they were marched to the battle-field. Stating this to have been his intention, the Rebel commander-in-chief begins his official report with the following paragraph:—

"Before the 30th of May, I had ascertained, from trusty scouts, that Keyes's corps was encamped on this side of the Chickahominy, near the Williamsburg road. On that day Major-General D. B. Hill reported a strong body immediately in his front. On receiving this report, I determined to attack them next morning, hoping to be able to defeat Keyes's corps completely, in its advanced position, before it could be reinforced."

The enemy did not appear to be aware that General Heintzelman was across the river and in a position to support General Keyes.

The disposition of General Keyes's corps upon the morning of May 31 was one scarcely calculated to resist an attack. A rifle-pit and a redoubt were constructed, three-quarters of a mile in advance of the Seven Pines, and there was an abatis one-quarter of a mile in front of them. Parties of men were laboring upon these works on the morning of the 31st. General Casey's division, numbering five thousand troops, was encamped near the redoubt, and in advance of it, pickets being thrown out some distance to the front. A half-mile to the rear of General Casey, General Couch's division was encamped. He had eight thousand men.

For several days previously—indeed, almost constantly since the advance of the 26th—there had been skirmishing between the Federal and Rebel pickets, and in each case a regiment, or a part of a regiment, would be ordered out to support the pickets and end the skirmish. This force was usually adequate to the work, and was strong enough to compel the enemy to retire. Upon the 29th of May, the enemy were driven back, with a number killed and wounded, the casualties upon the Federal side being two killed and two wounded, one of the former being Major Kelly, of the Ninety-sixth New York regiment. Upon the next day the enemy's attacks were equally as well repulsed, six of their dead being left upon the ground. Upon the 31st, Lieutenant Washington, an aid of the Rebel General Johnston, was captured by the Federal pickets.

The Rebel commander's plan of attack was an excellent one. It was intended to force General Casey's position early on the morning of the 31st. To do this, Major-General Hill, with sixteen thousand men, was to advance along the Williamsburg road, Major-General Longstreet, who had the direction of operations upon the enemy's right wing, supporting him with sixteen thousand more. Major-General Huger, with his division of an equal number, was to move down the Charles City road (a road running southeast from Richmond and passing three miles south of Seven Pines), in order to attack in flank the Federal troops who might be engaged with Generals Hill and Longstreet, unless he found in front force enough to occupy his division. Major-General Smith, with sixteen thousand more men, from the Rebel centre, was to march to the north of the Federal troops, along the road leading from Richmond to the Old Tavern, thus turning the Federal right flank and covering the Rebel left. This plan of attack, had it been fully carried out, would have completely overwhelmed the handful of troops in General Casey's command. It, however, failed in several important points.

It was the intention that all the enemy's columns should move at daybreak; but the same cause upon which they relied as an insurmountable obstacle to the passage of Federal reinforcements across the Chickahominy—the rain-storms of the afternoon and evening of the 30th—retarded their own movements. Generals Hill and Longstreet were in position upon the Williamsburg road early enough to have attacked the Federal camp by eight o'clock upon the morning of the 31st, and General Smith had his division posted upon the road to Old Tavern at the same time, and could also have attacked at the same hour. But, for some reason, General Huger did not attain his post upon the Charles City road. The commander of the body of troops forming the left wing—General Longstreet—was unwilling to make a partial attack, instead of the combined movement which had been planned, and refrained from giving the order to advance until General Huger was in position. Hour after hour, from eight in the morning, he waited for his assistant, but no word came from him; and about half-past eleven he resolved to make the attack without General Huger. That general did not make his appearance at any time during the battle, and his division was not engaged in it. Several miles to the rear, inextricably mixed up in swamps, his immovable artillery blocking the passage, he spent the day, his troops raging with the thought that the elements forbade their sharing in the anticipated plunder of the captured Federal camps.

Just at the commencement of the action, General Johnston, the Rebel commander-in-chief, arrived upon the ground and took command of the troops. He posted himself with General Smith's division upon the road to Old Tavern, in his report of the battle giving as his reason for choosing that position, "that I might be on a part of the field where I could observe and be ready to meet any counter-movement which the enemy's general might make against our centre or left." At half-past eleven o'clock General Hill disposed his division in line of battle extending on both sides of the Williamsburg road, and sent out artillery and numerous skirmishers in front. General Longstreet placed his troops in line immediately behind General Hill, and this mass of thirty-two thousand men at once began moving toward the thick wood which had hidden them from the Federal pickets.

General Casey's division does not appear to have had much knowledge of the immense force which was marching to attack them, and grave charges of having been surprised have been brought against the general. In such a case, it is best to let him speak for himself. In his report he says,—

"On the morning of the 31st May my pickets toward the right of my line succeeded in capturing Lieutenant Washington, an aid of General Johnston of the Rebel service. This circumstance, in connection with the fact that Colonel Hunt—my general officer of the day—had reported to me that his outer pickets had heard cars running nearly all night on the Richmond end of the railroad, led me to exercise increased vigilance. Between eleven and twelve o'clock, a mounted vedette was sent in from the advanced pickets to report that a body of the enemy was in sight, approaching on the Richmond road. I immediately ordered the One-hundred-and-third regiment Pennsylvania Volunteers to advance to the front for the purpose of supporting the pickets. It was soon afterward reported to me by a mounted vedette that the enemy were advancing in force; and, about the same time, two shells were thrown over my camp. I was led to believe that a serious attack was contemplated, and immediately ordered the division under arms, the men at work on the abatis and rifle-pits to be recalled and to join their regiments, the artillery to be harnessed up at once, and made my dispositions to repel the enemy. Whilst these were in progress, the pickets commenced firing."

General Naglee, who commanded the first brigade of General Casey's division, says in his report,—

"Two shells thrown into our camp first announced the hostile intentions of the enemy. No alarm was felt by any one; for it was seldom that twenty-four hours passed that we did not exchange similar salutations. Soon after, it was reported that an attack was impending, the usual orders were issued, and within half an hour the troops moved to positions that were assigned to them by General Casey."

Spratt's battery of four guns was posted to the north of the Williamsburg road, in an open field, and but a short distance from the wood behind which the enemy were advancing. The Rebel skirmishers came through the wood just at noon, and on the instant the Federal pickets commenced firing. The vast body of advancing troops being hidden by the wood, the attack was mistaken for one of those skirmishes which had constantly been fought for three or four days previously, and but one regiment, the One-hundred-and-third Pennsylvania, was ordered out to support the pickets. It marched quickly along the Williamsburg road to the edge of the wood, thinking that a handful of skirmishers would be its only opponents, and almost stumbled upon the Rebel troops advancing in line of battle. On the instant they fired a murderous volley from thousands of muskets at the surprised regiment, and one-fifth of its number fell killed and wounded. The remaining soldiers were unable to reply,—the surprise was too great; and, despite all the efforts of its officers, the regiment broke shortly, and, completely demoralized, retreated along the road it came, being joined on the way by a great many sick. This mass of stragglers, as they passed along through General Casey's camp and to General Couch's, in the rear, conveyed an exaggerated idea of surprise and defeat. The conduct of the One-hundred-and-third Pennsylvania has been much censured, and, scarcely knowing the overwhelming disadvantages under which it fought, people at home have spoken harshly of it. This is unjust. No regiment in the army, under the circumstances, could have done better. Sent forward, as its soldiers supposed, to check the advance of a few straggling skirmishers, thirty-two thousand Rebels, whose line of battle extended far to the right and left, suddenly rush upon it, and, in the midst of the surprise, thousands of them fire a deadly volley at it. The rout was excusable. Upon such a surprise, veterans would have hastily retreated.

This handful of opponents being disposed of, on came the thirty-two thousand, anxious to engage General Casey's six thousand spread out in line of battle in front of the rifle-pit and redoubt. Spratt's battery, and Regan's, Bates's, and Fitch's, which were behind it, commenced the action at once, and Spratt's was supported by the One-hundredth New York regiment, standing in the Williamsburg road to the left of it, the Ninety-second New York to the rear, and three companies of the Eleventh Maine, numbering ninety-three men, and eight companies of the One-hundred-and-fourth Pennsylvania, in the field to the right. These troops were all from General Casey's division, and, as soon as the enemy were clear of the wood, were ordered to charge. Colonel Davis, of the One-hundred-and-fourth Pennsylvania, thus describes it:—

"The regiments sprang forward toward the enemy with a tremendous yell. In our way was a high worm-fence, which cut our former line of battle; but the boys sprang over it into the same enclosure with the enemy, where we formed, and renewed the fight. The battle now raged with great fury, and the firing was much hotter than before. Spratt's battery, during this time, had kept up a lively fire in the same direction."

The artillery-practice was excellent, and the guns were worked with a speed which only the excitement of a great battle could give. At first each battery threw what are called "spherical case shot," a deadly missile, consisting of a clotted mass of seventy-six musket-balls, with a charge of powder in the centre, which is ignited by a fuse in the same manner as a shell. The ball first acts as a solid shot, ploughing its way through masses of men, and then, exploding, hurls forward a shower of musket-balls, each one as deadly as if discharged from a rifle. The four Federal batteries threw from sixty to eighty of these shot in a minute, aimed at every part of the advancing Rebel line, each shot telling with frightful effect.

The enemy, however, marched steadily on, and hurled a perfect tempest of musket-balls upon the batteries and their supporting regiments. Still the cannon worked as swiftly, pouring their deadly shot into the dense masses of the foe. The Federal missiles tore their ranks wide open, making frightful gaps filled with falling dead and wounded men. Still they came steadily on, closing every gap, and minding the terrible hail of the guns no more than if they had been shooting blank cartridges. When they were within four hundred yards of Spratt's battery, the Federal infantry opened fire, and the artillerists changed their case shot to canister. These missiles were as murderous as the others. Hundreds of the enemy fell before the fire of those terrible cannon, but still all the gaps were closed, and they marched on, hurling musket-balls upon the Union troops,—doing it all with an order and discipline which were admirable.

Still the canister tore through their lines, and still they steadily advanced, through the field, over the high worm-fence, through the field again, and up to the muzzles of the Federal cannon. When the brave artillerists delivered their last fire, the enemy were but twenty yards distant. The commander of the battery ordered it to retire; but, all the horses of one of the pieces being killed or wounded, that gun could not be saved. The four supporting regiments had lost hundreds of men, and, as the overwhelming force of the enemy came down upon them, they fell back with some disorder to the rifle-pits and redoubt. In this contest the colonel of the One-hundredth New York was killed, and Colonel Davis badly and his major mortally wounded. This was the first reception given to the thirty-two thousand by General Casey's handful of men.

Those of the division who survived were now together, and they made a second stand at the redoubt. Two batteries, Bates's and Fitch's, were in position. The Federal line still extended from the Williamsburg road northward. The enemy, upon capturing the deserted cannon, halted a few moments, and brought forward four batteries, which opened upon the Union troops. The Federal guns replied, and the enemy again began their advance. They came on as steadily as before, sending before them showers of musket-balls. The Rebel artillery worked swiftly, and so did the Federal, and every infantry soldier in both armies loaded and fired as quickly as he could. The noise was overpowering, and the scene—the dead, the wounded men groaning, the fierce battle raging, and over all a pall of the whitest smoke—was so awful that few can realize its horrors. Still the enemy's line advanced, storming the redoubt, and, after a short, fierce contest, capturing it. The guns of Bates's battery had to be left in the redoubt, and were taken; Fitch's battery was saved. Almost cut to pieces, every regiment having suffered fearfully, the division retreated again, this time falling through the line of battle formed by General Couch, and going to the rear. They were not, as a body, engaged afterward. This retreat yielded up their camp to the enemy. In this second contest Colonel Bailey and Major Van Valkenburg, both excellent officers, fell whilst directing the movements of the First New York Artillery.

Between the points of General Casey's first and last resistance is about a third of a mile, and General Couch was a half-mile farther to the rear. It was not until half-past three o'clock in the afternoon that General Casey's troops fell back exhausted to General Couch's line, and thus, for three and a half hours, they resisted, and gave General Heintzelman's corps a chance to come up. The official report of General Kearney, one of the commanders of division in that corps, thus speaks of General Casey's conduct:—

"As it was, Casey's division held its line of battle for more than three hours, and the execution done upon the enemy was shown by the number of Rebel dead left upon the field after the enemy had held possession of it for upward of twenty-four hours."

When it is considered that six thousand men for three hours resisted the advance of more than five times their number, doing it with an immense loss and under a murderous fire of cannon and small arms, the conduct of Casey's division deserves praise instead of blame. The unavoidable rout of the One-hundred-and-third Pennsylvania caused all the storm of censure which has been undeservedly heaped upon a brave body of troops who nobly fought their first battle.

The commander-in-chief, in his telegraphic report of the battle sent from the field to the Secretary of War, censured General Casey's division. Subsequently, however, when time had given him a correct knowledge of the devotion of that division to its country's cause, he retracted that censure, except as to one brigade.

It is proper that General Casey's defence of himself should be given to the world. He and General Naglee both have repelled the accusations made against the division. General Casey says,—

"I think it my duty to add a few remarks with regard to my division. On leaving Washington, eight of the regiments were composed of raw troops. It has been the misfortune of the division, marching through the Peninsula, to be subjected to an ordeal which would have severely tried veteran troops. Furnished with scanty transportation, occupying sickly positions, exposed to the inclemency of the weather, at times without tents or blankets, illy supplied with rations and medical stores, the loss from sickness has been great, especially with the officers. Yet a party from my division took possession of the railroad-bridge across the Chickahominy, driving the enemy from it, and my division took the advance on the 23d day of May, and by an energetic reconnoissance drove the enemy beyond the Seven Pines. Notwithstanding all these drawbacks, and the fact that there were not five thousand men in line of battle, they withstood for three hours the attack of an overwhelming force of the enemy, without the reinforcement of a single man at my first line. The Fifty-fifth Regiment New York Volunteers reached my second line just before it was evacuated. If a portion of my division did not behave as well as could have been wished, it must be remembered to what a terrible ordeal they were subjected: still, those that behaved discreditably were exceptional cases. It is true that the division, after being nearly surrounded by the enemy and losing one-third of the number actually engaged, retreated to the second line: they would all have been prisoners of war had they delayed their retreat a few minutes longer.

"In my opinion, from what I witnessed on the 31st, I am convinced that the stubborn and desperate resistance of my division saved the army on the right bank of the Chickahominy from a severe repulse, which might have resulted in a disastrous defeat.

"The blood of the gallant dead would cry to me from the ground on which they fell fighting for their country, had I not said what I have to vindicate them from the unmerited aspersions which have been cast upon them."

General Naglee says,—

"The list of casualties shows that of the First Brigade there were taken into the action 84 officers and 1669 men; and that 35 officers and 603 men were killed, wounded, and taken prisoners,—being 42 per cent. of the former and 37 per cent. of the latter. Of the 93 of the Eleventh Maine that were led into the fight by Colonel Plaisted, 52 were killed and wounded.

"The brigade was among the last enlisted: it had been reduced more than one-half by sickness. That it fought well none can deny, for it lost 638 of its number: bodies were found over every part of the field, and where these bodies lay were found double the number of the enemy.

"The enemy, more generous than our friends, admit 'that we fought most desperately, and against three entire divisions of his army, with two in reserve, that later in the day were brought in.'

"For three and a half hours we contested every inch of ground with the enemy, and did not yield in that time the half of a mile. We fought from twelve M. until three and a half P.M., with but little assistance, and until dark, with our comrades of other regiments and of other divisions, wherever we could be of service; and when, at dark, the enemy swept all before him, we were the last to leave the ground.

"I am most happy to refer to the kind treatment extended by the enemy to many of the wounded of the brigade that were taken prisoners.

"None of the brigade, regimental, or company baggage was lost. Some of the shelter-tents, knapsacks, and blankets fell into the hands of the enemy, which was the natural consequence of being encamped in close proximity with the outposts.

"Conduct such as this, if it be not worthy of commendation, should not call forth censure; for censure undeserved chills the ardor and daring of the soldier, and dishonors both the living and the dead."

The enemy halted a short time at General Casey's deserted camp, and it was four o'clock before they again took up the line of march against General Couch's line of battle. At that hour the Rebel commander-in-chief ordered General Smith, with his division, which had hitherto taken no part in the contest, to march forward to the Old Tavern and down the Nine-Mile Road to attack the Federal forces on their right flank. General Couch had eight thousand men, with artillery, and he was in a short time reinforced by General Heintzelman's corps, numbering sixteen thousand. Against these forces were advancing the column of thirty-two thousand in front, and another of sixteen thousand on the flank. General Couch had some slight intrenchments, and the nature of the ground was somewhat in his favor. His position was a short distance north of the Williamsburg road, and his right flank was near the railroad.

General Couch's line of battle was not parallel to the enemy's front: it was obliqued in such a manner that the right became first engaged. It was half-past four when the renewed advance of the enemy brought them to General Couch's line, and the woods once more resounded with volleys of musketry. The Twenty-third Pennsylvania regiment, Colonel Neille, was the first engaged. Its gallant colonel went from one end to the other of the line, encouraging his men. He reserved his fire until the enemy came very near to him, and before his troops were able to discharge more than six volleys they and the enemy were face to face. Then the order was given to charge; and all along the line the glittering bayonets were thrust forward, and the regiment rushed upon the enemy with a shout. They gave way and scattered before it; but, as it came out beyond General Couch's line of battle, the enemy upon both flanks poured volley after volley into it. Having suffered most severely, the colonel ordered it back to its place. During this charge, which was over rough and uneven ground, many men stumbled and fell, besides those who were killed and wounded, and upon rising could not find their regiment. So seriously weakened by these losses as to be unable to muster a fourth of its number, the regiment re-formed upon the next one in the line, the First Long Island.

The battle which was thus commenced upon the extreme right soon became general along that wing. There it seemed to form a nucleus, and supports were poured in to the aid of the Federal troops. From the left, the Ninety-third and One-hundred-and-second Pennsylvania and Sixty-second New York were hurried across; and to the right, General Kearney, leading General Birney's brigade,—the first reinforcement from General Heintzelman's corps,—marched forward along the railroad and joined in the contest. He brought some twenty-seven hundred men to the aid of General Couch. Brigade after brigade of General Heintzelman's corps, with Generals Hooker, Sickels, Patterson, Berry, Jameson, and others, and cannon after cannon, came swiftly upon the field, and the regiments formed by their commanders in line of battle were soon engaging the enemy. Part of General Casey's division, too, bravely attacked a second time the foes who had previously forced them to retire.

General Birney has been blamed for his tardiness in reinforcing General Couch; but explanations since have certainly exonerated him. He commands one of the three brigades forming General Kearney's division, and that division is one of three forming General Heintzelman's corps. Early on Saturday, General Birney was ordered by his corps commander to advance along the railroad. He proceeded promptly to do so, and whilst on the march General Kearney sent him orders to perform another duty. He performed it, and then proceeded to execute his first orders, his brigade arriving at General Couch's post at about five o'clock in the afternoon. In the confusion incident to a battle, General Heintzelman, hearing of General Birney's delay, and knowing no cause for it, thought it deserved reprehension, and ordered the general under arrest. General Kearney, so soon as this was made known to him, explained the whole circumstance to his superior, who, seeing the injustice which had been done, sent General Birney his sword and replaced him in command of his brigade. Time has exonerated all parties from blame, and mutual explanations have settled a difficulty which might have resulted in driving a brave officer from the service.

Just as General Birney's brigade arrived upon the field, the Rebel General Smith, with his division, advanced through the woods and fields in line of battle and joined his forces with those of Generals Hill and Longstreet. Their commander-in-chief came with him. Forty-eight thousand of the enemy were thus attacking some twenty-six thousand Federal troops. The movements of the Rebels were personally directed by their highest officer. About this time, General McClellan arrived, and took command of the Union troops. Miller's and Brady's batteries were the principal artillery supporting General Couch's line, and they poured shot and shell into the enemy with fearful effect. Soon, however, some Rebel guns discovered the range of Miller's battery, and it was compelled to change its position. Three other Federal batteries also played upon the advancing foe. The scene at this moment was awfully magnificent. The faint smoke of the musketry arose lightly all along the lines, just so that the heads of the men could be seen through it; sudden gusts of intense white smoke burst up from the mouths of the cannon all around; bullets filled the air and whistled swiftly by, or struck into trees, fences, boxes, wagons, or, with their peculiar "thug," into men; and, far up in the air, shells burst with sudden flame, like scattered stars, and passed away in little clouds of white vapor, while others filled the air with a hissing, rushing noise, and hurried on to burst far in the rear. Above, the sight was grand; below, it was horrible. Every inch of space was packed with dead and wounded, the latter groaning, and clutching at the troops as they advanced or receded by them.

But no efforts could retard the advance of the enemy's overwhelming force. They rushed on, and General Couch's division had to retreat to General Heintzelman's line, unfortunately getting divided in executing the movement. General Heintzelman, seeing that the enemy were outflanking him, ordered the whole force to retreat, it being the only way to save it. Every one thought the day was lost, and all eyes were strained to secure a sight of the expected reinforcements. General Sumner was known to be advancing upon the right, and every man prayed that, like Blucher of Waterloo renown, it might be to turn the fortune of the day. The defeated and almost desponding soldiers, however, could see or hear nothing of him.

The greater part of the Federal troops upon their retreat fell back toward and along the Williamsburg road, the enemy following them. General Couch, however, knowing the strong force the Rebels were precipitating upon his right flank, and not thinking that his left and centre were falling back, went at the moment of the retreat to the right wing with three regiments to aid Brady's battery, which, with one regiment, the Thirty-first Pennsylvania, was bearing the brunt of the contest with the Rebel General Smith's advance. He had scarcely reached there, however, before he discovered his mistake, but too late to remedy it. The balance of his division had fallen back, and the advancing enemy had cut off his road of communication with it. His first thought was to send a regiment, upon a charge, down the road through the column of Rebels, and thus open a path to the rest of his command; and orders were at once given to the Sixty-second New York to prepare for the charge. It was too late even for that, however, for the regiment when half-way down the road found it blocked up by imposing masses of the enemy preparing for a charge toward it. Upon seeing the Sixty-Second coming at them with a run and with the deadly bayonet fixed, the enemy changed their tactics, and, breaking to the right and left, took positions in the bordering woods to give the Federal troops a deadly fire on both flanks as they passed through along the hastily-opened road. This caused all idea of a charge to be given up, and, recalling the regiment, General Couch retreated with his troops across the railroad, which was close at hand, and Brady's battery was at once placed in position to cover the road.

Had the Rebel General Smith known of the critical position of General Couch, he could easily have captured him and all his command. He was fortunately not aware of it, and, General Heintzelman's retreat allowing his comrades—Generals Hill and Longstreet—to advance, he passed to the south of General Couch, and, although cutting him off from part of his division, left him, for the moment, safe. Of course, in that handful of brave soldiers all thoughts were upon General Sumner, and all wondered at the delay of his expected arrival. Night was approaching, and a drizzling rain had commenced from the low, heavy clouds which hung lowering over the battle-field. All seemed disheartening,—the rain, the constant series of defeats, and the failure of reinforcements,—but still there were stout hearts with General Couch who never desponded.

After a consultation with his officers, the general concluded to remain where he was, and proceeded amid the rain to form a line of battle in the shape of an L, one side facing the westward—the direction of the enemy's approach—and the other the south,—the direction of the column which had passed to his rear. Having completed this, he proceeded calmly to await the course of events. He did not do it idly, however, for Captain Brady, of the battery, was sent out to examine the neighboring roads, and soon returned with the news that one leading to the rear would enable him to form a connection with General Birney, whose brigade was but a half-mile distant. Elated with this good news, General Couch resolved to maintain his position, and rode along the lines encouraging his men.

General Heintzelman retreated in front of the advancing enemy, along the Williamsburg road, fiercely contesting every inch of ground. Strongly-defended positions were behind him, and he knew that when he reached them he could check the victorious march of the Rebels. Delay was what was now wanted,—delay until the arrival of reinforcements,—and, whilst he anxiously awaited General Sumner's coming, he still repelled the attacks of the enemy. Step by step, however, they forced back his soldiers, and, although the general never despaired, the men began to despond and their repulses of the enemy became weaker and weaker. It seemed as if the dreary night of May 31 would come upon a discomfited Union army, and be its only salvation, when an unexpected misfortune and almost simultaneous attack upon the left of the enemy's victorious column turned the tide of fortune.

It is time now to describe General Sumner's movements, and explain the reason of his delay in reinforcing his almost defeated comrades. Upon the morning of the battle, General Sumner's corps was quietly encamped near New Bridge, across the Chickahominy,—General Sedgwick's division being a short distance above General Richardson's. Opposite the camp of the former there was an excellent bridge across the stream, built by the division, and known as Grapevine Bridge. A crazy affair, weak and shaky, was opposite General Richardson's camp. It was called Sunderland Bridge. General McClellan crossed the latter with his staff early in the afternoon, all on the full gallop to the battle-field, and just afterward the rushing torrent, caused by the heavy rains of the previous afternoon and evening, came along, roaring and surging, and seriously endangering the two bridges. The Grapevine bridge withstood the flood, but Sunderland tottered and shook, and finally sank beneath the surface of the water. In a short time it was rendered impassable.

At about three o'clock General Sumner received orders to cross immediately and march as speedily as possible to the aid of Generals Heintzelman and Keyes. Both of his divisions were at once placed under arms and started at a double quick march for their bridges. General Sedgwick found his—the Grapevine bridge—safe; but, fearing it might be endangered by fast marching when such a flood pressed upon it, he took his troops very carefully over. General Richardson, not so fortunate, found his bridge impassable, and was compelled to retrace his steps to his camp, and then march up to the other bridge and cross it. This caused him a long delay, and prevented his troops being engaged in the battle of Saturday.

General Sumner crossed with General Sedgwick, but the roads were so horribly cut up that, with all their exertions, the troops made but slow progress. Upon getting out of the swamps near the river, however, and reaching the higher ground, the roads were found to be in better condition. It was four miles and a half from General Sedgwick's camp to the Seven Pines. But two or three pieces of artillery kept up with the infantry of the division. Eight thousand troops marched with Generals Sumner and Sedgwick.

Just as Captain Brady was reporting to General Couch the good news of his being able to communicate with General Birney, the sharp eyes of the soldiers espied dimly through the drizzling rain a column of troops away to the right, upon the full run toward them. "Is it General Sumner?" was the question upon every one's lips, and all eyes were strained and every breath hushed during the first moments of uncertainty. At last all doubts were removed. The proper signals informed them that it was General Sumner, with the long-expected reinforcements. The news spread like wild-fire among General Couch's small but brave party, and never was a sight so gladly welcomed. The overjoyed soldiers could scarcely contain themselves; they would have shouted to express the intensity of their feelings, but all noisy demonstrations, as they would give warning to the enemy, were carefully suppressed.

Whilst General Sumner was thus marching to the relief of the wearied troops who had fought so bravely for hours, the enemy still kept up their victorious march after General Heintzelman's retreating forces. But in the midst of their success their commander-in-chief, General Johnston, who was pressing forward as briskly as he could, was hurled from his horse, severely wounded by the fragment of a shell. He was badly hurt, and had to be carried from the field. The Rebel troops in the vicinity, who saw the misfortune, were in consternation, and the most stringent means had to be resorted to to prevent the others learning the sad news. For a moment, all was confusion near the spot where the general fell, and, until General Smith, the second in command, could be sent for, the victorious army was without a head. The intelligence at that instant brought, that a large Federal force was preparing to attack the left wing, increased the disorder. General Smith was soon told of the disaster, and having learned the state of affairs at all points, after a brief consultation with the officers around him, determined to turn all his attention to the new enemies who had appeared on his left, those in front, as he supposed, being entirely defeated and cut to pieces. To carry out this plan, orders were at once despatched, checking the further advance of the column on the Williamsburg road, and the division which he had so lately commanded was formed in line of battle facing the North, and every thing was prepared for an attack upon the force which menaced their left flank.

As General Sumner's regiments one by one came up, the veteran general himself placed them in line. Brady's battery, of General Couch's division, was in position commanding the road by crossing which the enemy had cut off communication between the two portions of the Federal army. As regiment after regiment came quickly up, they were formed in line of battle to the right and left of this battery. The three guns of Kirby's battery, which had succeeded in forcing their way over the heavy roads, were also placed in position. All this was quickly done, and, not knowing exactly where the enemy would show themselves, the line stood facing the south, ready to give them a reception. That proved to be the right direction, for in a few minutes the Rebels were seen through the thick woods and along the road, advancing in line of battle. They came to the edge of the woods, and, when just outside of it, the whole force fell upon their knees and delivered their first fire. The Federal troops at once lay down upon the ground, and over, through, and past them there was a perfect rush of musket-balls. It sounded like the fierce crashing of the wind through the rigging of a storm-tossed ship. It passed over, and up rose the Federal soldiers, firing a volley, simultaneously with the opening of work by Brady's and Kirby's batteries. Each man, both infantry and artillery, worked as hard as he could. The officers rushed up and down the lines cheering and stimulating the men, and in every part of the field General Sumner seemed to be, his gray hair streaming in the wind as he shouted the words of command or praised the good practice of the gunners. It was a critical moment, for the enemy were forming for a charge. The hands of the soldiers flew as they loaded and fired their muskets, and such was the rapidity of the cannon-shots that it took five extra men to each gun to keep the ammunition supplied.

Captain Brady, of the battery, gives a graphic account of the scene at his guns at this moment. He says,—

"'Canister! canister!' was all I could repeat. Men fell and horses were cut down around my guns, but still there was no cessation in the cry for 'canister;' and the hurrying to and fro for more, with the mad gesticulating of the sweating rammers, as they sent home the charges, made a wild scene. 'Canister is out!' caught my ear, and in an instant, unthinking, I sung out, 'Shell without fuse!' The next moment our guns belched bursting shell and spherical case right in the face of the enemy. Just at this critical juncture they charged, advancing half-way in the field, right on our guns, scarce twenty yards from the muzzles,—but no farther: the 'rotten shot,' as one of the poor wounded Rebels graphically termed it the next morning, was too much for them. 'No one,' he said, 'could stand, for it flew every way.' Those that charged were buried there next day."

Not only in front of the battery was that charge resisted, but along the whole Federal line. In front of the handful of troops who had so bravely supported General Couch there was a fence, and behind it the men, upon their knees, were loading and firing, each soldier picking out his man. The enemy in their charge swiftly advanced toward that fence, but the fire was too murderous to be withstood. They wavered, but still came forward, and, when some ten yards from the fence, broke and retreated in confusion. Twice again the enemy charged, but neither time with such force or confidence as at first. Both charges were successfully resisted, and cannon after cannon of General Sedgwick's artillery—having forced their way over the roads—were being brought upon the field every moment, and added to the ability to repulse these attacks. Each instant of time the Federal troops seemed to grow stronger and the enemy weaker, and a few moments after the third charge the Rebels retreated through the woods, leaving all their dead and wounded behind them, and yielding General Sumner the victory. It was almost dark, after eight o'clock, upon a lowering, rainy evening, when the fierce contest of that memorable Saturday ceased.

Upon learning the disastrous result of the battle with General Sumner, the enemy's column, whose pursuit along the Williamsburg road had been stopped, was ordered back, and, retreating about a half-mile, rested for the night. The Rebel General Smith's division, commanded by Generals Whiting and Pryor, each having three brigades, was rallied after its repulse by General Sumner, and, having retreated but a short distance, there bivouacked. The enemy's front stretched from the Williamsburg road to the railroad, presenting two faces,—an eastern one toward General Heintzelman, and a northeastern toward General Sumner. Upon their retreat, Generals Kearney and Hooker at once moved their divisions forward, possessing themselves of the ground which had been fought upon during the last three hours of the battle. At dark

General Richardson's division of General Sumner's corps, which had been delayed in crossing the Chickahominy, reached the battle-field, and, passing in front of General Sedgwick's fatigued troops, halted in line of battle within hail of the enemy. General Kearney's division, with some remnants of General Casey's, was upon the left of the bivouacking Federal line. It contained the brigades of Generals Berry, Birney, and Jameson. General Hooker's division joined it upon the right, with General Sickles's Excelsior Brigade, —which held the Williamsburg road—and part of General Patterson's New Jersey brigade. Then came General Richardson's division, almost at right angles with General Hooker, and containing the brigades of Generals French and Howard and General Meagher's Irish brigade. General Sedgwick's division and the remnants of General Couch's were moved from the rear to the right of General Richardson. The divisions of General Sumner's corps faced the railroad. Thus lay the Federal troops during the stormy night of May 31, waiting for the Sabbath to renew the strife.

Whilst the fierce battle was raging at Fair Oaks, General McClellan sent orders to Mechanicsville—six miles distant and upon the right wing of the Federal army—to have a feint made as if the troops were intending to attack the enemy in strong force. Accordingly, a brigade from General Franklin's corps, with a battery, were placed in position for the supposed attack. The battery opened a fierce cannonading upon the Rebel works opposite the village, and the infantry marched in column down the roads and fields toward the Chickahominy. The feint had its desired effect. All the enemy's cannon in the vicinity commenced shelling, and their troops disposed themselves to resist an attack. A strong body which was passing down the roads toward Fair Oaks—apparently to the assistance of the troops engaged there—was halted, and turned back. This Mechanicsville battle lasted for three hours, and hundreds of shells were fired at the enemy, finally silencing all their guns. This diversion produced its effect upon the contest at Fair Oaks. It prevented the enemy's sending reinforcements to attack General Sumner.

It was after the contest had closed upon Saturday evening, that General McClellan—who from four o'clock in the afternoon had personally directed the Federal movements—turned, fatigued and wearied, toward his camp. Followed by his staff, he took the road toward Sunderland Bridge, which he had crossed early in the afternoon, and proceeded to the river. The bridge, as the reader knows, was almost destroyed by the flood: sunken and broken, the current surged over it, passing on in its headlong course, and every moment making the weak structure tremble to its very foundations. Expecting to find it still standing as when he had first crossed it, the commander galloped up to its former place—to see the bridge almost destroyed. The staff stood aghast at the appalling fact. But, nothing daunted, General McClellan dashed into the current, through which his horse safely carried him to the opposite shore. Admiring his courage and presence of mind, some of his followers crossed after him; but the majority passed the stream at Grapevine Bridge above. This was a daring act, but one which shows the perfect coolness of the general, after leaving one of the bloodiest battle-fields of modern times.

The night after a battle is worse than the contest; and the field of Fair Oaks was enough to try the nerves of the strongest. The cries of the wounded for water, and the sight of the dead—with the varied expressions of countenance, some biting a cartridge, others in the act of ramming their muskets, and in countless positions—covering every foot of ground, and in some places lying in heaps:—it is a horrid scene, of which one sight in a lifetime is too much. Yet, upon that dark, rainy Saturday night, amid such sounds and scenes, forty-eight thousand Rebels and thirty-two thousand Federal soldiers were waiting to renew the conflict upon the next morning,—the Sabbath.

During the night General Richardson sent out scouts and pickets across the railroad, which ran parallel to his line and in front of it, and prepared every thing for a sudden attack. He personally superintended the posting of the advanced guards. It seems that his division was the only one at all disturbed. About midnight his scouts across the railroad reported that the enemy in great numbers had come into the woods in front of them. The words of command could be distinctly heard as their regiments were brought up and placed in line of battle. This body of the enemy proceeded to fell the trees in front of them, so as to impede any advance the Federal troops might make the next day. Whilst this work was going on, and hundreds of axes could be heard hacking and chopping, lights were observed in the wood some distance to the right, and a company sent forward to reconnoitre came back and reported it to be a detachment of the enemy, numbering some two hundred and fifty men. Another small party, sent forward to confirm this report, came back with the news that it was correct, bringing some prisoners with them.

Just at daybreak upon Sunday morning, a mounted orderly rode out of the woods into the Federal lines and asked a colonel, who was standing by, where General Anderson was. "Here he is," said the colonel: "what do you want with him?" "I have a despatch for him from General Pryor," said the orderly,—when, to his utter astonishment, he was told that he was a prisoner. The despatch was taken from him and at once sent to the corps commander, General Sumner. It was written in pencil, and stated in substance where General Pryor was posted, and gave directions to General Anderson for the movements of Sunday. An officer who had had his horse shot under him confiscated the orderly's steed, and that gentleman was sent to the rear, to ruminate upon the fortunes of war.

At six o'clock upon Sunday morning, General Heintzelman, who commanded the Federal left, ordered reconnoissances to be made diagonally to the right and left of his position. The detachments sent out soon came in, reporting the enemy in strong force opposite both his flanks. The general then ordered General Hooker to prepare to attack the enemy in his front, where they lay in a wood. At about half-past six the division advanced to the attack: General Sickles's Excelsior Brigade was to charge the enemy, whilst General Patterson's poured volley after volley into them. Before commencing the attack, General Sickles encouraged his men with an appropriate speech, which was received with shouts. He then marched his troops along the Williamsburg road, filing into the fields upon the right. General Patterson's New Jersey Brigade formed upon the left of the road. The word was given to move forward, and, whilst General Sickles charged, the other brigade advanced, briskly firing at the enemy. They were received most warmly, and scores of Federal soldiers dropped out of the advancing lines. Steadily to the woods the charge advanced, however, firing a volley as it came to the edge, and, rushing in, driving the enemy before it, who broke and retreated in confusion. They were pursued for nearly a mile, each step increasing the enemy's disorder. Once they attempted to stand, but there was not enough time to form their lines. The charge came upon them too soon, and they broke again. This was the enemy's retreat upon the Federal left. Farther to the left, General Kearney advanced his division as the charge proceeded, driving the Rebels before him. General McClellan arrived early upon the ground and took command.

To the right the battle commenced raging as early as it did to the left. General Meagher, after giving the enemy several volleys, quickly advanced, starting upon the railroad, but pressing forward, driving the enemy before him diagonally toward the Williamsburg road, and moving in a line with the Excelsior Brigade, which advanced along that road. After a mile's march, the two brigades met, the Rebels, a demoralized mass, fleeing before them.

Farther to the right were the brigades of Generals French and Howard, of General Richardson's division, and General Sedgwick's division, and early in the morning the battle was commenced by General French's brigade advancing diagonally toward the Williamsburg road, at the same time the charges were made upon the left. The battle spread to the right of General French, and soon the whole of the troops were marching forward, cheering and firing, the enemy retreating before them. The Rebels resisted, but the force of Federal troops was too strong. Like their fellow-soldiers farther to the left, they could not withstand the attack: their lines became broken and confused, and the retreat was almost a disorderly rout. Rough ground, swamps, fences, woods, and trees contributed materially to the Federal success. The retreating enemy stumbled into and over them, breaking the ranks and adding to the demoralization. The Federal troops suffered somewhat from these obstacles, but the order of their lines was in most cases well preserved.

This simultaneous advance of the whole Federal line gained them the day. The enemy were driven on, through the plundered camps of Generals Couch and Casey, along the roads and through the woods for a mile beyond the Seven Pines, when the pursuit reached Fair Oaks. There, the enemy ceasing to offer resistance, it was stopped, and the position was at once strongly occupied, General Heintzelman being upon the Williamsburg road and General Sumner upon the railroad. Upon the evening of June 1, the two generals advanced a short distance farther, slightly beyond the Fair Oaks, and intrenched themselves.

The battle of Fair Oaks was over; and now came those solemn duties which, after a battle, are always the first thought of the soldier, the collection of the wounded and the burial of the dead. Stretchers and ambulances were brought upon the ground, and small parties detailed for the purpose began collecting the wounded. Upon a field scarcely a mile square, there were lying between seven and eight thousand dead and wounded men, many having lain there, trampled upon and mutilated by the marching troops, for twenty-four hours. Hundreds of those wounded early in the battle had perished for want of attention, and the others were lying where exhaustion had overcome them as they endeavored to crawl away from the terrible battle,—some hidden, some seen, amid the swamps and trees and bushes of that awful place. Their groans attracted the fatigue-parties, who speedily collected them, and they were sent back two miles to the rear to a hospital hastily established at Savage Station. But many were not carried from the field. Some were in inaccessible places; some were hidden; some overlooked; and, even whilst the collection was going on, others died, their poor bodies failing longer to perform their functions. Federal and Rebel were treated alike: —all found were sent to hospital.

The gathering of the wounded occupied Sunday and part of the evening, and, when all who could be found had been sent away, the burial of the dead commenced. The sorrows of the former labor of love were deepened. Parties from each regiment passed over the ground, finding their slain brethren; and as each comrade who had fallen in the terrible strife was seen lying dead upon the field, the searchers could be heard weeping over his fate. As they bore his body to the spot selected for its last resting-place, their sorrows would increase. Many a stout soldier engaged in that last act of earthly kindness has given way to emotions which since childhood never before overcame him; and as he gazed upon the grave which had been dug, or the mound the earth formed over it, his tears came thick and fast. A few green leaves or flowers tastefully decorating the grave, and a modest head-board which, in plain handwriting, tells who lies beneath, ornament almost all the graves of Federal troops upon that dismal field.

Day and night the burial proceeded, each hour increasing its horrors. Decay had begun in many cases; and the almost universal swamp forbade the digging of graves more than two or three feet deep. Scores of wounded men had rushed into the miry places, and, sticking fast, had died there, and their heads could be seen thrust out from the mud and water, the countenances telling too well the terrible death they suffered. In places to which the burial-parties could not go, to this day they remain where they died, grim beacons amid the awful desolation which surrounds them. For a week parties explored all parts of that battle-field to collect and bury the bodies, and when, two weeks later, the author visited the place, the stench was too horrid to be borne. Yet, amid all this, regiments were encamped, the necessities of a desperately defended siege keeping them there.

General Casey's camp was the saddest of all places upon Sunday afternoon. The scene there baffles all description. Caissons, with horses shot dead in their traces, ambulances, wagons, boxes, old tents, clothing, arms, and ruins of every thing used in war, filled the once clean and orderly camp. Some two hundred wounded men were lying there, who had fallen on Saturday and been in the enemy's hands all that night. They spoke kindly of the Rebels, and said they had been treated very well. The enemy's dead, mixed with Federal, were lying all through the camp. At one place, upon a small open space, not forty feet square, fifty-seven dead Rebels, besides others from the Union army, were counted. The wounded begged piteously to have the dead removed. The sight and stench were intolerable.

The Savage Station Hospital—to which the wounded were sent—was another sad place. It was, in some cases, forty-eight hours before wounded men could be attended to, and many lay for a whole day where the enemy's bullets struck them down. We owe to a correspondent of the New York "Tribune" a most pathetic description of the sorrows seen at Savage Station:—

"The poor, helpless, wounded soldiers,—how they suffer! Those away from water have inexpressible agony. Those in the wet,—how they contract new disease, and how they undergo torments from the chilly nights! And after they are bought to the hospital, the groaning everywhere over the three acres of lawn upon which they are laid, the cries for help, for food, for drink, for shade, the delirium of the dying, the blood, discoloration, disfigurement, and dirt and wretchedness, spread all over those three acres,—an uninterrupted stream of unfortunates pouring in from the battle-field, and another going out toward the great hospital-tent, as one by one they are taken to be cared for by the surgeons,—it is terrible. In that tent the scene is, if possible, more horrid. The ceaseless work upon the operating-table, the use of knife and probe by lantern-light, the dressing of ghastly wounds all night and all day, and the screaming of stout men under the surgeons' knives,—all this will render Savage Station a ghastly remembrance for years."

The battle of Fair Oaks has been claimed by both sides as a victory: by the enemy, because they captured Federal cannon, and drove their troops back upon May 31, and also after the end of the battle occupied a half-mile of ground formerly held by them; by the United States, because its army upon June 1 drove the enemy to Fair Oaks, and at the end of the conflict held possession of the principal part of the field. The Rebels made an attack upon the Federal troops, for the purpose of cutting off their left wing. That purpose was defeated: the left wing was not cut off, but, on the contrary, those who attacked it were compelled to retire. The capture of a few cannon—though their loss, to be sure, is one to be deplored—has nothing to do with gaining or losing a victory: ground lost or won, and advantages secured or yielded up, are the criterions by which to estimate success or defeat. The defeat of the enemy's purpose is a great Federal advantage, but still a half-mile was surrendered to the enemy. One success will counterbalance the other, and Fair Oaks may properly be considered a drawn battle.

In the Rebel commander-in-chief's official report, he sums up the results of the contest as follows:—

"We took ten pieces of artillery, six thousand muskets, one garrison-flag, and four regimental colors, besides a large quantity of tents and camp-equipages.

"Major-General Longstreet reports the loss under his command as being about 3000

"Major-General G. W. Smith reports his loss at... 1233

"Total...... 4233

"That of the enemy is stated in their own newspapers to have exceeded ten thousand,—an estimate which is, no doubt, short of the truth.

"Several hundred prisoners were taken, but I have received no report of the number."

General Hill's division was under General Longstreet's command.

The Federal commander-in-chief's official statement of killed, wounded, and missing is the following:—

	Killed.	Wounded.	Missing.	Total.
General Sumner's 2d corps......	183	894	146	1223
General Heintzelman's 3d corps.	259	980	155	1394
General Keyes's 6th corps.......	448	1753	921	3122
	890	3627	1222	
Grand total, killed, wounded, and missing.............				5739

About one thousand Rebel prisoners—among them General Pettigrew—were captured.

Upon June 5, General Kearney, proud of the bravery shown in the battle by his troops, issued the following order to his division:—

"HEAD-QUARTERS, THIRD DIVISION, THIRD CORPS, June 5, 1862.

"General Order No. 15.—1. Brave regiments of the division, you have won for us a high reputation. The country is satisfied; your friends at home are proud of you.

"After two battles, and victories purchased with much blood, you may be counted as veterans.

"I appeal, then, to your experience, to your personal observation, to your high intelligence, to put in practice on the battle-field the discipline you have acquired in camp. It will enable you to conquer with more certainty and less loss.

"2. 'Shoulder-straps and chevrons,' you are marked men: you must ever be in the front.

"Colonels and field-officers, when it comes to the bayonet, lead the charge; at other times circulate among your men, and supervise and keep officers and men to their constituted commands, stimulate the laggard, brand the coward, direct the brave, prevent companies from 'huddling up,' or mixing.

"3. Marksmen, never in the fight cheapen your rifles: when you fire, make sure and hit. In woods and abatis, one man in three is to fire, the others reserve their loads to repel an onset, or to head a rush. It is with short rushes, and this extra fire, from time to time, that so much ground is gained. Each man up in first line, none delaying, share danger alike. Then the peril and loss will be small.

"4. Men! you brave individuals in the ranks, whose worth and daring, unknown perhaps to your superiors, but known to your comrades, influences more than others; I know that you exist. I have watched you in the fire: your merit is sure to have its recompense. Your comrades at the bivouac will report your deeds, and it will gladden your families; in the end you will be brought before your country.

"5. Color-bearers of regiments, bear them proudly in the fight, erect, and defiantly in the first line. It will cast terror into the opponents to see it sustained and carried forward. Let it be the beacon-light of each regiment. The noblest inscriptions on your banner are the traces of the balls.

"6. Again, noble division, I wish you success and new victories, until, the cause of our sacred Union being triumphant, you return honored to your homes.

"By order of BRIGADIER-GENERAL KEARNEY."

And upon June 3 General McClellan caused the following order to be read at the head of every regiment:—

"HEAD-QUARTERS, ARMY OF THE POTOMAC, June 3, 1862.

"Soldiers of the army of the Potomac, I have fulfilled at least a part of my promise to you. You are now face to face with the Rebels, who are held at bay in front of the capital.

"The final and decisive battle is at hand. Unless you belie your past history, the result cannot be for a moment doubtful. If the troops who labored so faithfully and fought so gallantly at Yorktown, and who so bravely won the hard fights of Williamsburg, West Point, Hanover Court-House, and Fair Oaks, now prove worthy of their antecedents, the victory is surely ours.

"The events of every day prove your superiority. Wherever you have met the enemy, you have beaten him. Wherever you have used the bayonet, he has given way in panic and disorder.

"I ask of you now one last crowning effort. The enemy has staked his all on the issue of the coming battle. Let us meet him, and crush him here in the centre of the rebellion.

"Soldiers! I shall be with you in this battle, and share its dangers with you.

"Our confidence in each other is now founded upon the past. Let us strike the blow which is to restore peace and union to this distracted land.

"Upon your valor, discipline, and mutual confidence the result depends.

"GEORGE B. McCLELLAN,

"*Major-General Commanding.*"

CHAPTER VIII.

THE COMMENCEMENT OF THE SIEGE.

When General McClellan had fought the battle of Fair Oaks, and intrenched himself there, his army was placed in the position occupied by it, with but slight alterations, during the entire siege of Richmond. The Federal troops were upon both sides of the Chickahominy,—three corps upon the Richmond side, and two with General Stoneman's command upon the other. The enemy were confined exclusively to the right bank, scarcely a single scout crossing the stream. One corps of Federal troops afterward crossed toward Richmond, making four upon that side, and General McCall's division of Pennsylvania Reserves, which arrived on June 18, were added to the force which the subtraction of that corps weakened.

The Federal position on the Richmond side of the river was a strong one, fully intrenched, and supported by large masses of troops. The left wing, General Keyes's corps, rested upon the White Oak Swamp, a mile and a half south of the railroad, and six miles east-southeast of Richmond. In front of this corps, pickets were advanced a short distance beyond the intrenchments, which were a little over five miles from the capital. General Heintzelman was encamped to the right of General Keyes, his intrenchments being the same distance from the city. General Sumner, to the right of General Heintzelman, had the railroad passing directly through his encampment, and his front line was the same distance from Richmond as the others. These three generals were all encamped upon or near to the Fair Oaks battle-field, and their troops sickened by scores. The ground they occupied was in wet weather a swamp, and in dry, half of it was covered with stagnant pools. Timber originally covered three-fourths of the surface, but military operations had converted the whole into a most forbidding wilderness. Acres upon acres of forest were "slashed," that is, cut off about five feet from the ground, so that the butts will rest on the stumps, the tops falling over. This slashing is done to prevent the passage of the enemy's troops, or to clear the ground for the effectual use of artillery; and the cut timber is called an "abatis." This destruction gives the most shocking appearance imaginable to a wood,—that of an abandoned waste without any thing to redeem its barrenness. Slashing was done on an extensive scale in the neighborhood of Fair Oaks.

Trees on the battle-field, which were not cut down, all bore marks of the war. Shells were imbedded in their trunks, and musket-balls had marked them in dozens of places. The swamps were in little patches upon all sides, some bare and open, some concealed by the woods. Here were graves of Federal and Rebel, side by side, with huge trenches filled with dead, many of them but half covered with earth, while a stench almost too stifling to be borne filled the air. Upon this place, shocking to every sense, McClellan was obliged to keep a force under arms: it was changed, however, every third day.

General Smith's division of General Franklin's corps crossed to the right bank of the Chickahominy upon June 5, taking a position upon a high hill east from Richmond, and bordering upon the river, called Lewis's Hill. Here he at once intrenched himself, building a strong earth-work, known as Fort Davidson,—being so named in honor of one of the most talented of his brigadiers. This hill commanded the enemy's works both to the west and north, and was the counterpart of another high hill just below Dr. Gaines's mansion upon the opposite side of the river. The remainder of General Franklin's corps crossed upon June 18, and encamped between General Smith and General Sumner. This corps was thus the right wing of the army engaged in the siege; the troops across the river being an army of observation, watching the enemy to prevent his getting to the rear and cutting off their supplies.

The Federal army proper thus presented nearly four miles of front to the enemy, the left flank resting upon White Oak Swamp, and the right upon the Chickahominy. The former was upon an almost flat surface; the latter, upon hills. All had intrenchments, the first parallel of the siege-works, before them. Between the left wing and the James River, in a line running toward the southwest, was at least five miles of open space, uncontrolled by the United States army, through which guerrilla parties constantly passed to the lower parts of the Peninsula. As the siege progressed and the army advanced, this space slowly closed, but still it was wide enough open, up to the time of the movement to the James River, to allow the enemy an uninterrupted passage.

Across the Chickahominy, General Porter's camps

surrounded Dr. Gaines's house, and extended two or three miles northwest of it. His artillery commanded all the Rebel hills, from General Smith's position upon Lewis's Hill up to those opposite Meadow Bridge, a mile and a half northwest of Mechanicsville. The Federal pickets in front of that village were the nearest soldiers to Richmond, being but four miles distant, in a north-northwesterly direction. Meadow Bridge, General Porter's extreme right, was the Virginia Central Railroad crossing, and was slightly over four miles north of the capital. His corps was the main body of the army of observation, and presented a front of four miles to the enemy. The troops of General Stoneman, the remainder of that force, were most erratic in all their actions. To them was given in special charge the prevention of the passage of guerrilla parties around from the north of Richmond, who might cut off the Federal supply-trains. Such a duty required his cavalry forces to keep a watch through all that section of country. One day they would scour all along the Virginia Central Railroad, past Hanover Court-House, and to Ashland, twenty miles north of Richmond. The next they would pass across the Peninsula to White House, reconnoitring for miles north of the road connecting that point with Mechanicsville. At all times they were upon such expeditions, capturing the enemy's trains and numerous prisoners, and keeping the railroads to the north of Richmond constantly impassable.

This army of observation had a far finer country to encamp upon than their brethren who were conducting the siege. High hills, running streams, and pleasant woods all contributed to their comfort. The troops were generally healthy, being far removed from the swamps and battle-fields. The country they held is well worth a description. Southeast of Dr. Gaines's house, there was a long hill sloping down to the fields bordering the river. It was occasionally wooded and occasionally bare, bending around with the river, until lost in the distance. No gorges or gullies seemed to break its symmetry. Its top was smooth and level; its side descended abruptly to the fields. These fields, submerged in wet weather, furnished the richest pasture in dry. Hundreds of horses fed upon them, and beyond were the bridge-builders and pickets of the Federal army,—the one working, the other watching. Below Dr. Gaines's house, this long and beautiful hill had ceased to be of any military value, the Federal positions upon the opposite side of the Chickahominy being so far advanced as to deprive it of any importance. If warlike things were not upon it, however, there were others which will bear description. A house half-way down the slope was a bleak monitor of the desolation which had swept past it. Every board had been torn from it and carried off, leaving only the frame standing. The wind moaned through it and the rain beat in, no obstacle opposing their progress. Not a living thing approached it. On the top of the hill, and (such was its abrupt rise) almost above this deserted house, was a small burial-ground, enclosed with one of the most tasty fences ever seen in Virginia. This little spot was the centre of a vast field. Myrtle covered the ground within it, and an oak and cherry threw a grateful shade around. It had once been carefully attended, the myrtle trimmed and the trees pruned, but their rank luxuriance was now its greatest beauty. This was the cemetery of the Govan family, who seem to have once been the owners of all that neighborhood. A dozen graves of them and their relatives reared their white tombstones, all of Northern make, from the midst of the omnipresent myrtle.

Above the Gaines mansion the country was wooded, though the land was still as high. The front sloped down to the river, and was covered with enormous trees. This was the condition of the surface for a third of a mile, when open ground again appeared. On this open ground were part of General Porter's camps, and encamped in a vast field were the reserve artillery of the army of the Potomac. The entire Federal position, all the way to Meadow Bridge, was this elevated ground. gently rising and falling, with its front sloping off at various angles to the fields and swamps on the river's edge. For a fourth of a mile from the woods to the right of Dr. Gaines's house, the country was open. Beyond that, thin fringes of woods ran along, at first on the hill-top, and then on the slope.

It was behind these fringes that the greater part of the Federal army of observation was encamped, they affording a complete mask from the enemy across the river. General McCall's division was the farthest northwest of the army. Beyond his camp the hills became high again, and the woods thick, very few open spots being on the front. A large portion of General McCall's troops were always at Mechanicsville, as a picket in force. Here the hills were very high, and mostly covered with woods. Mechanicsville was a small village of a half-dozen houses and beer-shops, a half-mile from the river. Several days' shelling from both armies had almost battered it down. A road ran to the river here, and crossed it on a bridge which the enemy had broken. This was the Mechanicsville turnpike, one of the direct roads to Richmond. To the right of this road was a woods cleared of undergrowth, which had been used as a beer-garden. During Federal occupation it served for a camp. The beer-saloon was back of this woods, and had been completely ransacked. A house upon the opposite side of the road had been the prettiest one of the village, and, being the least injured of all, was used as a hospital. Flower-beds were tastefully planted in the front yard, honeysuckles and woodbines being trained up the trellis-work porch. A large vegetable-garden, which had been well cared for, extended along the roadside, some distance toward the river.

Beyond the beer-garden, all the way to Meadow Bridge, the country was open, being a high hill sloping down toward the river and the railroad. The fields in front of all these hills were strongly picketed, their tops being crowned by numerous pieces of artillery. Picketing in the Chickahominy swamps was always a wet, disagreeable duty, besides being highly dangerous, from the constant watch kept up by the enemy's sharp-shooters. Picket-shooting became general upon both sides, in the latter days of the siege.

The different portions of the army drew their supplies from different stations on the railroad. The army of observation sent to Despatch Station for food, and to Forage Station for forage. These were two supply-posts, a half-mile distant from each other, and some ten miles from White House. They were five miles distant from General Porter's camps. His troops frequently sent their wagon-trains all the way to White House for supplies, principally of forage. The supply of food at the issuing-stations was always ample.

The besieging army had two posts at which to get supplies. General Keyes and General Heintzelman sent to Savage Station. This, in addition to being an issuing-station, was also an immense hospital, some thirty tents and huts and houses being required to accommodate the sick and wounded. There will be occasion to speak of it again, in describing the march to the James River. Generals Sumner and Franklin drew their stores from Orchard Station, on the railroad at the seven-mile post. This was the nearest one to Richmond, and was within three hundred yards of the line of intrenchments. In a direct line it was scarcely five miles from the capital, and the enemy's shells, on many occasions, fell quite near it. Marks of the Fair Oaks fight were seen on all sides, and graves reared their humble head-boards from the midst of piles of provisions. This issuing-depot, though at first but a small one, finally eclipsed all the others. Generals Keyes and Heintzelman left Savage Station and drew from Orchard, and for the last two weeks of the siege it fed three-fourths of the army. A small hospital was located there, and at it the first processes of embalming were gone through with, the bodies being sent to White House for the work to be completed. An immense commissary business was daily transacted at Orchard Station. Captain Henry N. Swift, of Dutchess county, New York, was chief officer of the post, and performed his duties with the greatest urbanity.

In front of the line of Federal camps and intrenchments, and between it and the enemy, there was always a belt of country about a mile wide, upon which there were no visible signs of either army. Creeping and hiding, on the one side of this belt, Federal scouts and pickets lurked, and on the other, near enough almost to talk, were those of the enemy. This was the great neutral ground of the siege. Cannon-balls and shell sped over it, and skirmishes and battles were sometimes fought upon it, but usually it seemed silent and deserted, not having upon it a single sign of a living being. In front of the besieging army this belt was a series of grain and grass fields, interspersed with a great deal of forest. The Chickahominy valley was the neutral ground in front of the army of observation.

Of course, the only real knowledge had of the enemy's positions by the soldiers and subordinates of the army was that gained by careful observation from the numerous hills held by the Federal troops. The reports of scouts and spies and deserters, and knowledge gained from balloon-ascensions, were carefully reserved for the higher generals. Every one, however, could see a great deal,—enough to show that the enemy had line after line of earth-works, redoubts terracing up the hills, and intrenchments upon the tops of them, strong forts to command all the important passes, and rifle-pits wherever attacks were expected from the Union troops. Ever since Richmond was first threatened, the enemy have been building fortifications around it. During all the time our army lay in front of Washington, before the Bull Run disaster, they were digging and building. Whilst Manassas was threatened, it was notorious that the enemy, fearful of the consequences of abandoning that place, were working night and day to prepare Richmond for an assault and siege. They held Manassas until the capital was ready, and when General McClellan brought his army in front of it, he found a series of earth-works constructed in the most perfect manner by scientific officers. The enemy scarcely struck a spade into the ground during all the siege. All such work had been done, and well done, long before.

Vague rumors have reached readers in the North as to the number, position, and strength of these fortifications, but very little that is reliable. The Richmond "Dispatch" of July 21 professes to give a list of fortifications surrounding Richmond, which is perhaps correct, although it is impossible to judge by any knowledge possessed in the North. This list gives them in regular order, with their condition at that date, and it deserves reproduction here. They are as follow:—

"Beginning on the north side of James River, west of Richmond, and coming around with the sun, from left to right:—

"No. 1. On the high part of the old fair-grounds; not yet completed; work in progress.

"No. 2. On the new fair-grounds, commanding the approaches by way of the Deep Run turnpike and the Bush Hill road; not completed; negroes at work on it; northeast of No. 1.

"No. 3. Three miles northwest of Richmond; a very strong work; completed.

"No. 4. Two and a half miles nearly north of the capital; commanding the approaches by the Brook turnpike; east of No. 3.

"No. 5. A little more than three miles north of the

city; commanding the approaches from Brook Run Bridge and Meadow Bridge; northeast of No. 4.

"No. 6. A mile and a half nearly north of the city, rather near the latter, but admirably situated on a slope, that can be swept for two miles by its guns. This fort was built a year ago; south of No. 5.

"No. 7. Two and a half miles northeast of the capital, between the Virginia Central Railroad and the Mechanicsville road; built last fall; northeast of No. 6.

"No. 8. Three miles northeast of the city; commanding the approaches from the Mechanicsville bridge. This fort was built while General McClellan's headquarters were on Dr. Curtis's plantation, only three miles east of it, the Chickahominy being between; northeast of No. 7.

"No. 9. Two and a half miles northeast of the city, east of the Mechanicsville road and west of Dr. French's plantation. A beautifully finished work, with outworks, abatis, &c.; commenced last winter, and finished early in the spring; south of No. 8.

"No. 10. Nearly four miles northeast of the capital; commanding the approaches from several fords on the Chickahominy. There is a large magazine in this fort. General Johnston passed much of his time here while the Union army was encamped on the left bank of the Chickahominy. There were some guns in this fort then, which used to throw shells at random toward the Chickahominy. The fort was hidden by dense woods before it, but these have been cut down during the last six weeks. It is east of No. 9.

"No. 11. Two miles nearly east of the city; built nearly nine months ago. It commands the approaches by the New Bridge road; southwest of No. 10.

"No. 12. Three miles east of the city, commanding the approaches from Woodbury Bridge. Immense gangs of negroes were employed on this work, and it was built very rapidly, the negroes working day and night, at the same time that the engineer brigade were building the Federal bridges. It is believed to be very imperfect in its construction, and is east of No. 11.

"No. 13. Three miles nearly east of the capital; a work of great strength and admirably situated. There are some heavy guns in this fort, and also some rifled guns, which it is said carry a ball four miles with accuracy; all of which have been here since early in the spring. There is also a large magazine. It is southwest of No. 12.

"No. 14. Two miles southeast from the city, commanding the turnpike from Williamsburg, a small, but strong work of admirable construction; south of No. 13.

"No. 15. Two miles south of the city, on the left bank of the James River; unfinished, and the work on it not progressing rapidly. It is west of No. 14.

"No. 16. Three miles southeast of the city, and two miles west of the Seven Pines; built since the battle there, and men are still at work on it. It is designed to command the approaches from the Williamsburg stage-road, and is east of No. 15.

"No. 17. More than three miles southeast of the city, and nearly south of the latter work. It commands the approaches by the Charles City road and the Central road. The work on it is still progressing.

"No. 18. Four miles south of the city, on the left bank of James River; unfinished.

"No. 19. Four miles nearly south of the city, and east of No. 18. It commands the Newmarket road and the Osborne turnpike. The work on it is still progressing.

"No. 20. More than four miles southeast of the city, and east of No. 19. It commands the Central and Newmarket roads.

"No. 21. Six miles south of the city, commanding the Mill road. This is not a work of any great strength.

"Crossing the river now, we come to—

"No. 22. Fort Darling, which has often been described. It was commenced as long ago as April, 1861. Its position is such that all vessels sailing to Richmond have to pass it; that its guns can be fired down upon all vessels coming up the river, while no vessel can get its guns sufficiently elevated to fire at the fort. Since the attack upon the fort by the Monitor and Galena on the 17th of May, the fort has been greatly strengthened and the armament has been greatly increased.

"No. 23. Six miles south of Richmond, on the right bank of James River. Built since the attack on Fort Darling. Casemated, and has a powerful armament, with guns trained to bear on river-craft.

"No. 24. Immediately south of the city, on the right bank of James River. Not finished, but work progressing.

"No. 25. Three miles south of the city. Commenced in April last.

"No. 26. Three miles nearly south of the city, and west of No. 25; well situated.

"No. 27. Three miles southwest of the city. Work in progress.

"No. 28. Three miles west of the city, on the right bank of James River."

Of these fortifications, a refugee from the South thus speaks:—

"He reports Richmond to be encircled with fortifications of the most extensive character. Those north of the city are fully armed, and manned by experienced artillerists. Those on the south side are comparatively neglected, for the reason that they anticipate no danger in that direction.

"Fort Darling, at Drury's Bluff, is now completed, and mounts twenty-two guns of the heaviest calibre, principally rifles, and the face of the work is constructed in such a manner as to resist the passage of any projectile. It is constructed first of eighteen-inch square timber, over which is a plating of four-inch iron, the whole placed at such an angle that any shot striking it must glance and fly off, without the possibility of doing damage.

"Obstructions of the most substantial character have been placed in the river opposite and above Fort Darling; and the most rabid of the Rebels of Richmond advocate the entire filling up of the river between Drury's Bluff and Rocketts, and the construction of a railroad for army purposes, leaving the river to find a new channel.

"He estimates the force of Rebels in Richmond at the commencement of the seven days' fighting to have been between two hundred thousand and two hundred and fifty thousand men."

The observations of those not in the great secrets of the army, of course, were confined to mere sight-seeing, with the aid of telescope and field-glass. These gave a perfect view of the appearance of the enemy's position from the Federal works, which, to all who cared nothing for the hidden sights beyond, was in the highest degree satisfactory. The entire front presented by the enemy being some eight miles in length, its description would be much like the views of a panorama; and perhaps a series of views from different Federal hill-tops would be the best way of conveying to the reader an adequate idea of the appearance of the outposts of Secession.

On the Federal left there was no good point of observation. The country being low and flat, or at best very gently rolling, and almost covered with woods, forbade the idea of finding any commanding spot from which to view the front. From the swamp protecting the left wing all the way to and across the railroad, the enemy's front presented a succession of woods and fields with occasional earth-works and batteries. The frequent woods hid the principal part of the defensive works, and their locality was only known from the shells they threw at the Union camps. It was a poor spot for sight-seeing or sketching, and it was rarely that an artist ventured to use his pencil there. In front of the Federal works, at the point where the railroad passed out, the enemy were effectually covered by woods, on the edge of which their pickets watched, and behind which they had all their batteries. The country was swampy and very nearly level.

The first good view to be had of Rebeldom was in front of General Franklin's corps, at his left, where he joined General Sumner. At that place there was a wheat-field rising to a hill on the Federal side. It was here that negro pickets were first discovered on the enemy's outposts. The wheat-field ran down the side of the hill, and at the bottom it stopped, a grass-field gently ascending for nearly a half-mile on the other side to a woods filled with the enemy. Rebel pickets came to the low ground. In front, just on the edge of the woods, was a strong earth-work, with guns pointed at the spot where the spectator is standing. A short distance to the right another redoubt bristled with cannon, and a battery farther beyond kept up a constant duel with General Porter's guns across the Chickahominy. An old house in ruins was also upon that side, and a tall chimney standing alone, without a house to own it, was a hundred yards to the left. Two houses, one with a beautiful garden, were just within the enemy's picket-lines, and no doubt were head-quarters for their picket-reserves. This was the plainest view to be had of Rebel earth-works, batteries, and pickets, in full operation. Seeing it, however, was a dangerous operation. Anywhere else but in standing wheat, with an opportunity to "duck" whenever a hostile rifle was aimed, it would have been too perilous a venture.

The ramparts of Fort Davidson, General Smith's post, and the extreme right of the besieging army, was the next point from which a good view could be had. The enemy's works in sight were the same as those seen from the wheat-field, with the addition of a few more seen endwise upon the hills on the upper part of the Chickahominy. The view of Rebel manœuvring was not very good, even though Fort Davidson was almost always occupied in resisting their artillery attacks. Too much woods intervened to allow of extensive sight-seeing. The great attraction here, however, was the view of the valley of the river. Every thing done by the enemy upon the hill-sides and lowlands on their side of the stream could be distinctly seen, and, of course, accurately reported. This view extended for several miles, a bend in the stream closing it away in the distance. General Porter's and General McCall's positions, on the high hills across the Chickahominy, were easily discerned from Fort Davidson.

Here the river must be crossed, and the reader taken to the other side. There the Chickahominy valley ran along between the two armies, both being posted on high hills, which presented, on the one hand, fine points of observation, and, upon the other, grand views, glorying in all the hues of summer and all the romance of a mountain-range.

Dr. Gaines's house, or rather the ground just to the left of it, is a spot from which could be had one of the best views of the field of operation. The view from it on the Federal side to the left and right has been given on a previous page; and now the description is to be of that in front. From this hill, across the stream, two miles distant, is to be seen Fort Davidson, appearing as a huge square earth-work. Its importance, wedged in between the river and the enemy, can be discerned at a glance. The Stars and Stripes wave upon the ramparts. Beyond, wagons are parked, and to the rear there is an extensive camp. A half-mile to the right of the fort, and equidistant from the point of observation, just on the crest of a hill, are a Rebel battery and earth-work, two of those seen from the wheat-field, and the neighboring woods cover other masked ones. Passing the eye down the hill from the battery, a breastwork, almost concealed by bushes, can be discovered, though it is half hidden by the intervening trees which grow beside the river. Coming nearer, but still on the opposite side of the stream, Rebel scouts prowl about and sharp-shooters lie in the tall grass, each one ready to shoot some unwary Federal picket. But the most attractive view presented from this hill was the admirable one of the Federal and Rebel positions upon the opposite side. One moment's glance from this commanding eminence would suffice to explain the salient points of both armies. Federal officers availed themselves of this; and the never-changed signal station to the left of Gaines's house was an evidence of the value of the secrets there disclosed.

To the front and left of Hogan's house—the one with the beautiful oak-tree—there is a second hill, giving a tolerable view of the opposite ridge. Here an angle of woods across the stream hides Fort Davidson; but the view farther to the left, down the valley of the river, is magnificent. For miles and miles there is a succession of dark swamp, yellow field, and brown hill-side, until all blends in the blue sky at the horizon. That view is most charming. The appearance of the Rebel front is almost the same as when seen from Dr. Gaines's house, the view, however, being more extended to the right. Batteries on the ridges, with woods on their sides, is the rule with all the hills opposite this one. This spot, like the other, was also a valued signal station.

A third eminence, a half-mile farther to the right, is the next point of observation. This gave a view of the opposite hill, somewhat confined, yet of great interest. There were batteries and woods, as upon the ground viewed from Gaines's and Hogan's houses, but opposite this hill a road ran much used by the enemy's troops, and of course closely watched by Federal artillerists. It had one or two exposed gaps, and the guns were always in range for them. As the road was constantly travelled, the Federal gunners were continually at work. Fearful execution must have been done by the hundreds of shells poured into those gaps. Many a Rebel regiment when exposed upon that road to Federal fire has ignominiously run. This hill was frequented by all lovers of exciting artillery practice.

Five hundred yards to the right of this, upon the low ground,—for there the fringe of woods protecting the camps was upon the hill-side,—was one of the best places for viewing the disposition of Federal and Rebel pickets. The enemy's hills, across the river, were bare of woods, and for miles their whole surface was a series of cultivated fields,—one or two small patches of trees alone breaking the continuity. Being upon low ground, of course the view from this spot was greatly restricted. The gaps in the wood, the prominent points seen from the last hill, are to the left, and farther on that side—almost hidden by trees—the waving of Fort Davidson's flag could be detected. The flag must have been four miles distant; and from the moving of the leaves, so momentary were the glimpses had of it, the sight almost seemed an optical illusion. In the swamp in front, and upon both sides, Federal pickets were watching the enemy,—an occasional rifle-crack giving evidence of their faithfulness. Across the stream, upon the gradually-ascending hill, Rebel picketing could be viewed in all its perfection. Companies deployed, skirmishers moved out and in, reserves were posted, and vedettes patiently sat in their saddles, on the wide-stretched fields of grain. Every movement of the enemy could be plainly discerned. Upon the crest, behind all these pickets, the enemy had what kept the Federal troops from attacking them,—a series of the strongest earth-works, with plenty of cannon upon them. Only one or two of these numerous guns were ever used, and they were brought to bear occasionally upon an exposed road on the Federal side, along which troops sometimes marched.

Standing upon the turnpike at Mechanicsville, another interesting scene was presented. There, for a mile to the right and left, the enemy's hills could be examined. Upon their tops were forts and earth-works of the strongest character, and their sides—except where roads broke through it—were one universal forest. Three or four houses peeped out from among the trees there, one of which, the prettiest, was the Rebel general's head-quarters described in a preceding chapter. Heavy guns were mounted upon the enemy's works opposite Mechanicsville, and their light ones occasionally gave evidence of their presence by shelling Federal pickets. By ascending trees beside the turnpike, smokes and other indications of Richmond could be seen.

Just above Mechanicsville, half-way between it and Meadow Bridge, is the last hill from which a view could be had,—as the ground beyond slopes down toward the Virginia Central Railroad, the extreme right of the Federal position. Here the face of the opposite country changes, the ranges of hills upon the two banks of the river coming together and almost obliterating the valley. The thick woods still prevail upon the enemy's hill-sides, and their crests are as well provided with earth-works and batteries. There was always a fear that the Rebels, under cover of the woods and swamps, would attempt a crossing at Mechanicsville, and, to resist it, that village—though really only a picket ground—was always well provided with artillery and infantry. Across the river, two most striking objects were seen from this hill-top. The road to Richmond—a city only four miles distant—can be seen, in every part, as it ascends the opposite slope. It runs directly from the point of view, and every rut and clod is visible until it crosses the highest point, to descend upon the other side. The other object, in a different situation, would seem insignificant; but there, giving rise to so many thoughts and feelings, it was the greatest sight of all. Just to the right of the road a spire, rising above the tree-tops, stood out in bold relief against the sky. Thousands went to study that spire. It was the only part of Richmond which could be seen from the Federal lines. From General McClellan down to the lowest private, all earnestly viewed it.

The positions of the enemy in front of the Union army were very strong, and, in some cases, impregnable. They had used their time and talents well in the fortifications surrounding Richmond; and this poor description of how they appeared to the Federal soldiers may help to satisfy those anxious to understand the history of a war as yet wrapped up in almost unintelligible newspaper-accounts of battles, skirmishes, and raids.

To garrison their works and defend their city, the enemy had an immense army. At the commencement of the siege it was divided into eight grand divisions,—

each one corresponding to a Federal army corps, and commanded by Major-Generals Huger, D. B. Hill, Longstreet, Smith, Magruder, A. P. Hill, Rains, and Ewell. General Huger was opposite the Federal left wing, and the others were in regular succession around to the right. General Jackson, with his force, was also, for the principal part of the time, opposite the right wing of the Federal army. Hê and his forces were absent in the Shenandoah valley, however, from the 20th of May to the first week in June. In addition to these forces there was a large body of cavalry under the command of General Stewart, aided by Colonel Fitz-Hugh Lee.

The shell which wounded the enemy's commander-in-chief, General Johnston, at the battle of Fair Oaks, although it confused the Rebels, was the saddest shot for Federal success that has been fired during the war. It changed the entire Rebel tactics. It took away incompetency, indecision, and dissatisfaction, and gave skilful generalship, excellent plans, and good discipline. It removed the first commander, General Johnston, and replaced him by a most eminent leader, General Robert E. Lee. Before the battle of Fair Oaks, Rebel troops were sickly, half fed and clothed, and had no hearts for their work. On the 1st of June, General Lee commenced his efforts to reorganize the dissatisfied and mutinous army. He removed their camps from the swamps, and placed them in healthy situations. He procured supplies of wholesome provisions, particularly fresh beef and bread. He redressed many wrongs the men had suffered, attentively listening to their just complaints. He soon found his efforts crowned with success: mutiny and dissatisfaction almost universally disappeared; there were no more cries for food, no more outcries against oppression. The troops improved in appearance. Cadaverous looks became rare among prisoners. The discipline became better; they went to battle with shouts, and without being urged, and, when in it, fought like tigers. The wounding of General Johnston was one of the best things for the enemy which had ever happened.

A more marked change for the better never was made in any body of men than that wrought in his army by the sensible actions of General Lee. What effect it had upon Federal success can scarcely be estimated. Harder fighting, greater loss of life, and infinitely more work at picketing and intrenching, were undoubtedly some results. Whether subsequent disasters to the Union arms were caused by General Lee's humane regard for his army, time alone can decide.

CHAPTER IX.

THE INCIDENTS OF A SIEGE.

IN the siege of a city which is well defended, there are many incidents which are parts of the daily routine, and which, to be understood, need an explanation. In a narrative of events these are constantly referred to, but never described, and the un-military reader generally loses half the enjoyment which the perusal of a perfectly understood narrative would give. For instance, picketing is constantly spoken of or referred to, yet few civilians have more than an indistinct idea of what picketing is. So of an intrenchment: they know it is earth piled up, and have seen pictures of forts, but how piled, and how it becomes such an excellent means of defence, they are at a loss to comprehend. It is a great fault in description to take it for granted that the meaning of military terms is a part of every man's knowledge. Many a befogged reader has to his sorrow discovered the contrary. It is the intention to devote a few pages to a description and explanation of what will be constantly referred to in the subsequent history of the siege.

Sieges very often give rise to BATTLES. Small skirmishes, or artillery duels, or sorties, may rapidly increase in proportion, until the number engaged, and the ferocity of the contest, well deserve the name of a battle. It is at such times that war rises to its highest sublimity, and those fortunate ones who happen to be in a safe place where the progress of the fight, or some parts of it, can be seen, are vouchsafed a boon that any one might envy. Very few men have ever seen the whole of a battle. A thousand obstacles intervene to prevent it. Hills obstruct the view of what is passing upon their opposite sides, and hide the more distant valleys. Woods—always a favorite place for combatants, into which one or the other of the opposing forces will always go—prevent a view of what is passing within them. Houses, usually garrisoned, are often fiercely fought around, yet the shrubbery and shade-trees surrounding them allow but an occasional glimmering of the military operations. And then the great distance at which an observer must be to be safe from the death-dealing shells so freely distributed on a battle-field, is quite an obstacle to his discerning individuals or obscure movements. All these things intervene to prevent a view of an entire battle-field; but usually parts of it can be seen, which, for military strategy and bloody carnage, are a fair index of the whole.

Soldiers in battle see very little of the great work which is in progress around them. Each man is too earnestly engaged in performing his own duties, to waste any time in idle gazing. Usually lying flat upon the ground, with a fence or a tree before him, he loads his musket, picks out his man, and fires at him,—doing all as quickly as possible. Men so busily engaged scarcely heed the whistling bullets which fly past their ears or strike against the tree or fence in front of them. Shells, however, they always notice. Those deadly missiles rush through the air with a noise like a rocket, and, until fighting battles becomes a confirmed habit, the soldier is, as it were, compelled to follow them in their course, dreading the instant at which they burst and scatter their deadly fragments around him.

In battle there is one moment when every man's heart is in his mouth, and during which the cowards, if there are any, will always show themselves. The enemy's volleys of musketry come too fast to be resisted by like musket-shooting; or they are assembling for a charge; or some of their batteries have too deadly a range to be allowed any longer to work unmolested. In all of these cases the remedy is to be administered at the bayonet's point. A charge is ordered, sometimes of a regiment, sometimes a brigade, sometimes a whole division. The men are ordered to form in line of battle. In such a case there is always a moment or two of delay. Then, exposed to the deadly fire of the enemy, with nothing to occupy his mind but thoughts of the thousands of bullets flying past him, each instant some of them striking his brethren, whose groans are heard even above the din of battle, the bravest will falter. Those moments of delay are the ones to test true courage. On some occasions the mental agony has been too awful to bear; whole regiments have broken, and run to cover, all the reproaches of their officers failing to have any effect. Experienced commanders dread those idle moments, for no man is proof against the effects of that terrible agony which the suspense gives him. But the delay is over. "Trail arms! Double quick! March!" is shouted by a dozen prancing horsemen. Off starts the line, and, before ten feet of ground is passed over, every man has forgotten the torturing trial of the previous moment. An earnest, all-absorbing attention to the work before him has supplanted it. The charge proceeds; the enemy's fire becomes more deadly; the artillerists work faster; the infantry fire with greater precision. Dozens of soldiers drop, killed or wounded, from the rapidly-advancing ranks. Still they approach the enemy, each man looking intently before him, avoiding snares and pitfalls, and endeavoring to single out an opponent from the thick-clustering groups of the foe. The charge proceeds; it is within fifty feet of the enemy's cannon. "Charge bayonets!" shouts the commander. "Charge bayonets!" is echoed by every officer, and, with a yell which can be heard for miles,—a yell never heard off the battle-field, so demoniac and horrid that men in peaceful times cannot imitate it,—every musket is raised to the breast, and a long row of glittering bayonets appals the foe. Among the cannon the troops rush, still yelling and shouting, and the artillerists who are not bayoneted, or do not escape, are shot by the officers' revolvers. Past the cannon the line goes with headlong speed, the file-closers spiking or breaking them. The troops rush on at the enemy's infantry. All firing of musketry from it has ceased: other things are thought of; offence is forgotten in the anxiety for defence. The officers endeavor to rally it for a charge, but the avalanche of glittering bayonets and terrific shouts swiftly coming upon it is too much; the soldiers cannot stand quietly and meet the attack: they break, and flee; and, whilst they are ignominiously running away, the word "Halt!" stops the progress of the victorious charge. It has done its share of the work; the enemy has been put to flight, and it remains for the artillery to complete the victory. "About face!" and "Double quick! March!" soon clear the ground, and Federal shells, rapidly sent after the retreating foe, decide the contest.

An observer may see all this, if obstacles do not intervene; and many have done so. But, if distant gazers do not see all, they have a correct idea of the general scope of a battle, and are always better able to give a description than those who take part in it. From their point of view, they may see the whole Federal line of battle with all its movements, or the entire Rebel line; or they may observe the progress of affairs on portions of both. To them the sight is far more impressive than to the soldier, whose duties so engross his attention that he scarcely has time for a moment's thought. They see the lines advance or recede, and know all the strategy of the contest. How often have they witnessed a well-contested fight, where neither party seems to have the advantage, or where one is gradually defeating and driving the other, when a stealthy column is discovered cautiously marching along some hidden road to take one or the other on the flank and thus decide the battle! Rebel flanking-parties seldom caught Federal soldiers: their lynx-eyed signal-men were perched about on too many hill-tops. They gave the generals warning. At other times, perhaps, these gazers would see the secret planting, by one or the other army, of masked batteries, commanding places to which their opponents would be drawn by well-arranged flights or retreats, when a deadly fire would for a moment stagger and break the lines. Many strategic movements could be observed by distant sight-seers, whose circle of vision commanded a great extent of country.

The progress of the battle, however, usually engrossed every one's attention. Bursting shells could all be traced, and their effects in many cases plainly seen. A continuous roar of musketry filled the ears, and the frequent discharges of cannon, as grape and canister, solid shot or shell, were launched at the opposing parties, constantly varied the sound. Shell after shell would rise above the carnage, swiftly pass in its curve, and burst, leaving its mark in smoke floating in the air, and scattering its fragments upon all below it. The moving of the sound of the musketry, and the cheers of the victorious armies, indicated the advances and retreats. The spots from which cannon were fired were changed also. They would advance or recede, or, if spiked, become silent. Thus would the view be during the whole time of the battle. Gradually increasing smoke, curling up from all parts of the field, usually obscured it, but cannon-shot and musketry could always be heard, and bursting shells seen. Approaching night ended all battles. It stopped the pursuit by victorious armies, and closed all doubtful contests.

A SKIRMISH was the name given to a small contest, where the victory being decided either way had no effect upon the general result. Small numbers, very little fighting, and a great amount of cheering were the usual incidents of all skirmishes. They occurred at all times and in all places. A picket shooting one of the opposite side would provoke retaliation, which in its turn would bring on an attack, which always resulted in a skirmish. A regiment stationed upon a picket tour might be attacked, and a skirmish was the consequence. The essence of a skirmish was, that its result, no matter how decided a victory it might be for either party, had no bearing upon the progress of the siege. The troops were all taught a skirmish drill, to be used upon such occasions, which consisted in spreading themselves at wide distances,—each man, whilst he observed the general course pursued by his company, using his weapons in such manner as seemed to him best. Skirmishers in battle or upon a march are small parties sent out to reconnoitre or scour the woods, or beat up ambuscades and masked batteries. By them the skirmish drill was also used.

During the progress of the siege, Federal artillery commanded every spot from which the enemy could make attacks, and a dozen shells from them would quickly scatter an attacking party, and end a skirmish in a very short space of time. The commander-in-chief was very careful of his pickets, and always had artillery placed to defend them, and attacks by sharpshooters or stronger parties resulted badly for the enemy. A genuine skirmish, in which artillery took no part, very rarely occurred, but, when it did, would usually be most ludicrous. Two regiments, a Federal and a Rebel, are standing opposite to each other. The Rebels make a charge, and rush upon their opponents with a yell. Away go the Union troops, running for cover, firing half a dozen shots at the advancing enemy. The charge being balked, the Rebel regiment retreats, perhaps previously discharging a volley, when out start the others from behind the trees and bushes, yelling and screaming upon a full charge after the first. Away goes the first on a run to its cover, which it usually reaches, and, receiving a volley, races the swift-running Federals back. If artillery, from one side or the other, does not interfere, the two regiments will run each other back and forward for hours, until sheer exhaustion compels them to stop. Then they report one man killed and two wounded, in each regiment, and brag of their exploits for a week.

A column sent out to advance to and capture some point always presents the most interesting skirmishes. The taking of Mechanicsville was almost enchanting,—the manœuvring of the troops and out-generalling of the enemy were so brilliant, and yet so easily understood. Its capture was entirely accomplished by skirmishes. Though well defended, a battery of artillery and brigade of infantry, aided by a detachment of cavalry, advanced four miles into what had previously been an unknown country, held by the enemy, drove in their pickets, dislodged them from rifle-pits and woods, and finally compelled them to evacuate the town and rush pell-mell across the Chickahominy. This was all done by manœuvring and strategy. The enemy, outflanked several times, believed the Federal troops to be in much stronger force than they really were. Scarcely any regular volleys were fired; a musket-shot was rarely heard, and, when it did come, it was from a skirmisher. Two or three shells beat up a wood, through which skirmishers cautiously advanced. When Mechanicsville was approached it received a thorough shelling, which made the enemy quickly leave it, and in their retreat along the turnpikes and roads, and across the Mechanicsville and Meadow bridges, shells burst all about them. Accuracy in artillery practice, and proficiency in skirmish drills, secured for the United States the possession of Mechanicsville.

Skirmishes were sometimes as exciting, to those viewing them, as battles. A correspondent of a leading newspaper thus describes the first skirmish he saw:—

"We are all in camp together, sitting about doing nothing,—the officers in their marquees, the men in their tents. A cavalry-man rides swiftly along the road leading from the outposts to head-quarters. In an instant he is dismounted, enters the general's tent, is out again, vaults into the saddle, and away he gallops along the road he came. An aid runs from the tent to the different regimental head-quarters:—'Be ready to march in five minutes, light marching-order.' A few seconds more, and the whole camp is aroused; the greatest listlessness is changed to the greatest activity. Cheering and yelling at the prospect of a brush with the enemy, each man seizes his gun, hastily examines it to find if it is in perfect order, puts on his cartridge-box, canteen, and haversack, places himself in line, and is ready for marching. Then the regiment is drawn into line, and all stand with true military stoicism awaiting the order which will send them to confront the enemy.

"But foot-soldiers are too slow for newspaper-men, and, hastily picking up some friends, away we go across field and fence, through mud and swamp, bound for the scene of action. A threatening storm, whose distant thunder had been muttering for an hour, warns us of its approach by a few large drops scattered over the ground. We stop an instant, put on our water-proofs, start again, and, urging our horses to their utmost speed, plunge through the rain. We rush past sentry, vedette, and signal-man, unheeding any challenges they might give. Shoulder-straps and head-quarter passes are our passports through what would otherwise be great difficulties. An hour's ride brings us to the outposts, and when we rein in our panting horses, we find the storm passed over, its clouds hanging like a black pall behind us. A regiment of troops stands in a road in marching-order. On the right, three black dangerous-looking Parrott guns, ready loaded, each with gunner holding lock-string, are pointed at a pass some five hundred yards in advance, where the road enters a wood. On the left, some thirty yards from the road, is an old Virginia manor-house, recently deserted by its owners, and having some curly-headed negroes, half frightened, half pleased, poking their heads out of the doors and windows. In the front yard, two brass twelve-pounders stand, pointed at the same pass as their three black-looking brethren on the right, each one ready to belch forth fire and smoke at an enemy. Cavalry are drawn up in order behind the cannon. Officers stand about, and, though all seems prepared for a most fearful fight, laughter and conversation proceed the same as if no danger were near.

"Directly an aid comes galloping along the road from the advance beyond the wood, whispers a word in the ear of the commanding officer, and then, receiving an order, swiftly returns to the place whence he came. A moment more, and the cannon are limbered up, and, the infantry and cavalry preceding them, they all march off to take a position in the advance. We follow, finally passing through the troops, and getting to the front. The infantry take a new position in the road beyond the wood, sending out skirmishers in force to the right. The cannon are rapidly wheeled into a road to the left, turned into a field, unlimbered, and accurately aimed at a hill and wood where the enemy had made their appearance. We take our stand with the battery, and from there could see a wide expanse of country. The wood commanded by the artillery seemed a mile distant. A cavalry vedette of four horsemen were a few feet to the left of us. Each man was mounted, and all eyes were bent on the wood. Directly a detachment of infantry march up the hill, stop at the entrance of the wood, fire some volleys into it, and then enter and disappear among the trees. We wait minute after minute in breathless suspense, but they do not appear, nor do we hear answering shots from the enemy. Save an occasional remark from our own men, all is still as death. The birds are singing and insects chirping; two or three cows are quietly grazing in front of us; away in the distance, over the ridges, we can see a fringe of woods, bearing away to the left, but not a human being is in sight.

"No one can truly describe his feelings upon such an occasion. The enemy he knows to be near him, but he cannot see them. His own friends in the Union army may be killed and wounded beyond the wood, yet he knows it not. Not more than fifty men and a few field-pieces are around him. On the road to the right, the regiment is resting on its arms. His bosom heaves and swells at what he imagines to be passing. He wishes to be in the thickest of the fight, yet knows not how to get there. Weapons he may bear upon his shoulder or by his side, yet, burning as he is with zeal to use them, no object is presented on which to wreak his vengeance or show his courage."

A RECONNOISSANCE is a body of men, usually cavalry, sent out to explore an unknown section of country, discover the enemy's positions, and ascertain his force. It may be of two kinds,—a "reconnoissance" simply, in which the detachment sent out, if opposed, is not to fight, but return; and a "reconnoissance in force," or an "armed reconnoissance," which is directed to give the enemy battle if resistance be offered, and, in all events, to carry out its instructions to the utmost extent, exploring the entire country over which it is directed to go. These latter were usually made by strong bodies of men, an army corps, with all its artillery, being sometimes sent out. Reconnoisssances were the great means of collecting information of the enemy's position, strength, and apparent intentions. Armed ones were usually successful.

A SORTIE was an attack made by the besieged party upon the besiegers. When closely pressed, or when desirous of annoying the Federal troops and preventing their working in the trenches, a column of the enemy would suddenly rush out from behind some mask, and, protected by a furious fire of artillery, attack the men at their labor. These sorties were always feared, and the strongest bodies of troops were posted at points where they were anticipated. They were seldom successful, the spiking of one or two cannon, and an hour's delay in the work, being usually their worst results. Furious battles sometimes marked the repulse of a sortie, and artillery were always brought extensively into play. Being generally prompted by desperation, they were rarely well planned.

The practice of Union artillerists during all the siege of Richmond was excellent. With splendid cannon and the best ammunition, accurate aim and deadly execution were always sure to result. Many of the artillerists in the army of the Potomac were Germans, whose natural taste for war always seems developed to its greatest perfection when they are given the management of cannon. No men ever watched more closely for opportunities to exercise their guns. When placed to protect pickets or bridge-builders, or to command a pass, seldom did harm come to the former or an enemy march through the latter, whilst a cartridge remained in the ammunition-boxes. These Germans were brave, too. On the battle-field no Federal cannon ever was captured until its last shell had sped, its horses lay dead, or itself lay broken and useless. And even then the gunners rarely deserted their favorite. Killed, or wounded, each one could be seen upon the ground around it. Like the Irish as infantry soldiers, the Germans as artillerists were among the most admired of the troops,—the pride of the officers, the envied of the men.

Several admirable specimens of artillery practice occurred during the siege, a description of two or three of which would amply repay perusal. Artillery was always in batteries, each battery having from four to six guns, and these were distributed in pairs over any space necessary to be guarded. If bridge-building was in progress in the swamp, the battery to protect it would be posted in the most eligible situations upon the neighboring hills. A pair of guns usually took a position from which they could command all the approaches to the bridge upon the enemy's side, thus insuring against infantry attacks and sharp-shooters. Another pair were generally posted away to the right at a point where they were able to silence all the enemy's guns which could annoy the party in the swamp. A third pair, placed upon the left, performed equally good service with the batteries upon that side. Now, if the bridge-builders were attacked in any manner, Federal shells would always successfully resist it, driving back infantry, scattering sharp-shooters, or silencing cannon. The builders did not have to fire a musket.

On the 1st of June, an artillery duel took place at Mechanicsville. It was an excellent specimen of practice, and well worth describing. In the front of the Federal lines there were several batteries, all commanding the hills and woods across the Chickahominy. About three o'clock one afternoon, two brigades of Rebel troops and a long train of wagons were espied wending their way along the crest of the hills. They were two miles distant, and horsemen were prancing about upon the hill-sides nearer the river. Soon a Rebel battery came along, unlimbered its guns, and by the aid of a glass the gunners could be seen training their pieces. Fun being anticipated, the Federal soldiers clustered in groups behind their guns and in the edge of the woods, though none of them were sufficiently exposed to be visible to the enemy. The Rebels had six guns visible, and placed them in pairs at three different positions, each about one hundred yards distant from the other and just in front of their lines. The brigade halted a moment, and then retired to the woods in the rear, and the baggage-train whipped up and drove swiftly across the open space in front of the guns. In five minutes the last wagon had disappeared behind the trees to the left; and, at that instant, two companies of infantry left the Federal camp, marching at quick time down the road toward the bridge. One turned into the field on the left not twenty yards from the bridge, and, presenting full front to the enemy, halted there. The other continued on down the road and stopped near the bridge, three or four men crossing and boldly invading the enemy's country, thousands of soldiers of both armies observing them with intense interest. Directly, off goes the Rebel gun farthest to the right of the six, and a cloud of white smoke flirts up into the air, followed by another, nearer, from the bursting shell, whose fragments flash into the water just above the bridge. The lazy report comes long after, such is the distance and the time taken for the sound to travel. The gun has undershot its mark, and the company still stands in the road, patiently awaiting the pleasure of their Rebel majesties on the distant hill. Off goes the middle gun of the six, and the first one a second time, both almost at the same instant, the shells curvetting through the air, one plunging into the woods, the other into the water in front of the brave soldiers, but still flying wide of their mark and doing no harm, unless it be the ploughing up of a square yard or two of Virginia soil, or the barking of a few Virginia trees. A fourth gun blazes out at the extreme left of the battery; and then the middle one again; and then the extreme left a second time. All three shells, falling into the water and bursting there, give the old bridge a shower-bath. No one is hurt, and a cheer from our troops announces their safety.

Thus far the work has all been upon one side, and the Federal artillerists have stood idly beside their guns, watching the bad shooting of their opponents. The word is given; and to the right and left the Federal bull-dogs commence growling. Shell after shell goes whirring through the air, all bursting in and over the wood into which the Rebel brigade retired. Not one misses its mark, and two come into rather close proximity to the battery. The gunners stand a moment, giving a parting salute by a ball, which, for all the good it did to them, might as well have never been shot; for it burst about a mile from any Federal troops. Then they stopped, and never fired a shot afterward, every one beating a swift retreat to the woods. Not a Rebel was to be seen where, an hour before, they were swarming, and for twenty minutes afterward the Federal guns sent shell after shell, some crashing among the trees, some falling in the field, and some going away over the wood and bursting, perhaps, at the very feet of the astonished people of Richmond. Not a single reply came from the Rebel guns; they were mysteriously withdrawn from sight, and the Secessionists—horse, foot, and dragoon—retreated from the Union cannon, when a small party of hardly fifty men braved every shot which treason could aim at them. When the contest was over, and the last shell had burst, the two companies retreated from their positions, and were warmly welcomed back to camp by their delighted comrades.

When the distinguished Spaniard, General Prim, visited the army, being a noted military character, reviews of all arms of the service were given him, and, among others, a review of artillery practice from the hill to the left of Hogan's house, from which there is so grand a view down the Chickahominy valley. Being watched by so distinguished a visitor, of course the gunners did their best, even excelling their usual good practice. The general took great interest in what was passing before him, several times aiming the guns. Very few artillery skirmishes were ever witnessed to better advantage than the one reviewed by General Prim. The battery was upon a high hill at a point where the river made a slight turn. Immediately in front was a rich field of grass, upon which cavalry-horses were pasturing. Then came the swamp and stream, and beyond them fields and hills,—the ones to the right being held by the Rebels, and those to the left by the Federal troops. There was not a half-mile between the earth-works of the two armies. Both were equidistant from the battery whose practice was to be reviewed. The contest was opened by the enemy, who shelled the Federal batteries across the river. A signal officer with his flags and attendants was slightly to the left of General Prim, and another was in the swamp beside the river. After a short delay, the command was given to open fire. There were two twenty-pounder Parrott guns, and they kept at it for an hour as fast as the gunners could load and aim them. Two more were afterward brought on the field, but they threw no shell.

Standing behind the gun, the course of the rapidly receding shell could be distinctly traced as a gradually lessening black spot in the air. It could be followed until it struck the earth, and the explosion marked the place long before the report was heard. The guns kicked but little upon being fired. The strangest part of the whole grand performance, however, was the noise made by the rapidly revolving shell as it flew through the air. It was like a puffing locomotive starting a train of cars,—at first slow, then faster and faster, till it culminated in an unchanging whiz and a dull boom from the explosion.

It was a most picturesque scene,—the hills and woods away in the distance with the smoke wreathing up from the conflicting batteries there,—the narrow stream beneath, with the thousands of soldiers scouting, picketing, and bridge-building; the vast plain, with horses and cattle quietly grazing, scarcely noticing the shells which flew over their heads; and, nearer still, in the group clustering about the distinguished Spaniard, the staff officers in their glittering uniforms, following each shell with their eyes, and the attendants and escorts behind them, all looking as if they might as well be colonels and generals too. All this, illuminated by the slanting rays of a setting sun, was a view worthy the pencil. But nightfall broke it up. The glittering foreigners with their American friends rode swiftly off to head-quarters, and the artillerymen disposed themselves for their nightly vigil.

With all their admirable skill, however, the German gunners had one fault: they would keep up an incessant talking. The harder they worked, the more and louder they talked. When, pressed by necessity, they fired their guns with a rapidity which almost seemed unattainable, each man's tongue would run with the speed of a steam-engine. This continuous chattering was their only fault.

In the enemy's artillery there was much room for improvement. It was weak in calibre, and generally very poorly managed. Their aim was inaccurate, and the missiles seemed to go anywhere but to the spot upon which they were intended to fall. The enemy was largely supplied with guns of the best quality, some domestic, but also large numbers imported. He had vast quantities of expensive shells of English manufacture, with which he was very lavish. The powder was good, and the ammunition for artillery was in part from abroad: the bags for cannon-cartridges came apparently from England, being packed in large boxes as imported, and made of a fabric (moreen) not manufactured in the United States. Occasionally their field artillery threw grape and canister, but it was very rarely done. There was a long distance between the artillery outfits of the two armies. With the Union troops the artillery was the greatest boast.

INTRENCHING was also an incident of the siege. In fighting an enemy with so strong natural and artificial defences as those surrounding Richmond, the only way in which success could at all be achieved was by counter trenching and digging. This was evident to every soldier in the army, and the commander secured all his posts by intrenchments. At night thousands of soldiers would labor with the spade and dig a work which when seen the next morning would astonish both armies. These trenches, in many cases, were made in such a way as to compel the enemy to abandon some of his works. Every one made was of use, and all compelled the enemy to gradually fall back, and draw in their outposts, yielding up to their grasping opponents commanding hills and redoubts from which they had often been annoyed.

Negroes and prisoners were not used for throwing up earth-works,—the latter for the very obvious reason that they would bring the enemy upon the Federal troops or run off to the Rebel picket lines every time they were put to work. Negroes were not suited to the labor. They worked too slow and made entirely too much noise. Besides, they took but little interest in the war which was going on around them, many failing to comprehend its meaning. However slow and noisy may be the workmen upon defensive lines when no enemy is near, the greatest secrecy and celerity are required in digging the intrenchments for a besieging army: a moment's delay, or the slightest noise, is often fatal to all engaged.

A party of trench-diggers generally went upon a dangerous excursion. Detachments from regiments were usually designated as the working parties, and each one was informed of the hours between which it would labor. These detachments were always of sufficient numbers to be spread over the whole work at once. An earth-work four hundred yards long required three hundred laborers, who, if the soil was hard, worked in pairs, one with the pick and the other with the spade. The relieving detachments generally lay on the ground a short distance back of the trench, and a brigade of infantry and a battery of artillery—the supporting parties in case of an attack—were still farther to the rear. All these would keep behind the crest of a hill, or under cover of woods, so as to be out of the enemy's observation. Dark nights were always selected for trench-digging; and, under the stimulus of danger and the injunctions of officers, the work proceeded with unusual rapidity and quietness. The first effort of each man was to cover himself, a narrow ditch being dug, and the earth being thrown up on the side toward the enemy, an allowance for a narrow ledge being made between the ditch and the pile. Two hours sufficed to place all in safety, when the work proceeded more leisurely, and the sides and bottom were smoothed off. Four feet deep and three feet wide was the general rule in the commencement of a trench. When daylight came, of course all labor was ended, and every one was disposed so as to resist an attack. The first work being completed, it could be altered and enlarged at leisure. If intended for a fort or siege parallel, the ditch was widened to fifteen feet or more, and deepened, the earth being thrown and embanked upon the Federal side. For rifle-pits, or a mere protection to pickets, the trench was left as originally made. It is surprising with what secrecy intrenching parties labored. Earth-works have been dug within fifty yards of the enemy's pickets, and have never been discovered until daylight revealed them. The art of intrenching needed all its skill in the siege of Richmond, and that skill was generally at hand.

PICKETING is not an incident of sieges only: it is employed whenever two armies are extended in front of each other, and its use is to watch the enemy's movements and give timely notice of all indications of offensive operations. At least one-eighth of the infantry force of the army before Richmond was constantly upon picket duty. Regiments took picket tours twenty-four hours at a time, upon the expiration of which they were relieved by others. A regiment going upon picket marched to the extreme front of the Federal position, with loaded muskets and unfixed bayonets. It would proceed to the edge of the nearest wood to the enemy, when such disposition of forces was made as was best suited to the nature of the ground. All relieving of pickets was done in the morning, except in dangerous places, where the change was made just after dark.

If a field, with the enemy upon the other side of it, was beyond the wood, a spot to the rear of the wood, or in it, would be selected where all the roads and paths met, and each captain was instructed that in case of an attack it was to be the rallying-point of the regiment. Then, upon each road or path, near the edge of the wood, but in such manner as to be hid from the enemy's observation, one or two companies were posted, and each post thus garrisoned was named a "picket reserve." The companies not detailed as reserves were always attached to one or the other of them, and from these men would advance out into the field as far as was necessary to observe the enemy's movements, and dispose themselves in a line across it, from a point opposite the extreme left reserve to one opposite the extreme right. The men stood fifteen or twenty feet apart, and the line they picketed was the "picket tour." Rows of men stationed at the same distances connected this front line with each of the reserves. The duty of the picketers was to continually watch the enemy before them, and send along the lines connecting them with the reserves a report of every thing which took place, no matter how slight. The reserves were always ready to reinforce the men in front of them, and two or three cavalry soldiers, detailed as orderlies to the commander of the picketers, stood ready to carry to the nearest brigadier whatever news it was thought necessary to send him.

Picketing along the Chickahominy was somewhat different. The picket at the Mechanicsville bridge was always well arranged, and guarded an important pass. It was a type of all that was done in the swamp. The disposal of reserves in the woods was similar to field-picketing, but the front line scarcely ever could advance directly forward. Tortuous paths through the swamp, generally centring at a point away on one side, took each man to his post, and over these he would have to go, managing to keep out of the water by all sorts of gyrations, until he reached his place in the picket tour. Observations of Rebel movements were telegraphed to the right or left along the line, according as on the one side or the other it led to a picket reserve. Men upon such posts usually kept themselves hidden. To watch the bridge a separate line, with its own reserves, was always sent out. Two companies stood at the edge of the woods, three hundred yards distant from the bridge, and a third picketed in front of them. The fence by the roadside was thickly grown with weeds and bushes, and along this fence, hid in the foliage, a line was posted, each man within low-talking distance of the other. This line ran from the reserves to the bridge, and at the middle of it there was a sort of reinforcing guard of a dozen men. Just at the water's edge, lying flat on the grass, perfectly hidden from view on all sides, were six or seven men, who watched the bridge and the road beyond, and sent word of the slightest movement back along the line to the reserves, where the commander was always stationed. Thus was watched the most dangerous pass across the Chickahominy.

Men from the two armies being constantly upon picket opposite to each other, a sort of tacit agreement in many places sprang up, that neither should fire at the other. This was all well enough, as it saved valuable lives, and enabled the pickets to attend better to their duty as watchmen. But from this an excrescence arose which the commanders of both armies endeavored to repress: the men would get to talking to one another, and finally to exchanging food for newspapers. Before Richmond it was very common to find pickets engaged in conversation, each one telling the other the news, and frequent exchanges were made of Northern for Southern newspapers, and of Southern whiskey for Northern salt. Upon one occasion, whilst a New Jersey regiment was upon picket, the Federal scouts were served out their allowance of coffee, and one of them, observing a Rebel wistfully gazing at his steaming cup, invited him over to partake. He came, drank the coffee, went slowly back, looked around, and asked how many times a month the Federal troops had such good coffee served out to them.

"Oh, three times a day," replied the Jerseyman.

"Three times a day! Why, if that's true, I'll not stay a moment longer in the Confederate army. Here; I give myself up!"

And the man actually yielded himself up a prisoner.

Several good stories are told of picketing-incidents. Both of the following will amuse the reader:—

"Yankees are proverbial for shrewdness, cunning, and jokes; and when Yankee and Rebel play together to see who is the smartest, the Rebel usually comes off second best. The Fifth Maine infantry, containing some of the 'cutest Yankees in the land, was on picket duty one afternoon. About three o'clock some of them discovered a pair of wheels, and put their heads together to find out what to do with them. While deliberating, a squad of Rebel officers, elegantly dressed and mounted on splendidly-caparisoned horses, made their appearance on a hill about a mile distant, and commenced spying all about with their field-glasses. This made up the minds of the Yankees. The wheels were hidden, and a party sent off which came back with a round, black-looking log and a slow-match. The log was lashed to the axle, and then all waited to see what the Rebel squad would be at. Directly every field-glass in the whole party was bent on the Yankee pickets, when out came the extemporized cannon, which, with great formality, was pointed in range for the hill on which the curiosity-hunters stood. It was loaded and primed,—when, lo! away go the brave Rebels, each one trying to get ahead of the other, the horses galloping, the riders urging them faster, and over the intervening space went a shout of derision from the Yankee group, which no doubt was like a thorn in the side of each of the easily-frightened foe."

"A picket invited a Rebel scout to partake of his cup of coffee, and, after drinking it, the Secessionist, to testify his gratitude, instructed his benefactor after the following fashion:—

"'Now, you see, our posts are opposite each other. Well, the man that comes on after me I'll tell not to shoot, and he won't; and I want you to do the same with your relief. But the fellow what comes next but one after me, look out for him: he's a d—d Louisianian.'"

VEDETTES are closely allied to pickets. They are cavalry soldiers sent out in parties of three or four, to observe the movements of the enemy. They have positive commands to keep as much as possible out of sight of the foe, and unceasingly on the alert for the slightest movement in any direction. They are usually placed so that they can be seen from the Federal outposts, in order that any signal they may make will be noticed by the pickets. Their system of signalling is quite limited, being but a few motions made with the sword, indicating some prearranged messages, such as, "a large force approaching in front;" "enemy's pickets have fallen back;" "enemy advancing on the right," &c. These motions are arranged and given so as to attract as little attention as possible. Vedettes are very useful, and a sharp-eyed cavalryman, who makes a good one, will always command the high opinion of his officers.

The extensive swamps in the neighborhood of Richmond made THE BUILDING OF ROADS AND BRIDGES a frequent incident of the siege. These were always constructed by detachments of troops under the superintendence of the engineer corps. General McClellan dispensed orders for roads and bridges with no miserly hand. Four or five crossed the Chickahominy within as many miles. Corduroy roads ran in all directions through the swamps, and every general had his roads leading wherever he wished. The construction of them was very rapid. A detachment of men cut the timber and cleared it of branches. Wagons hauled it to the spot where it was needed, and another detachment constructed the work. One description of a road and bridge will give an idea of all.

Woodbury Bridge, and its approaches, was the greatest structure of the kind built by the army. It was commenced and completed in six days, and crosses the Chickahominy River and Swamp. It is over a mile in length, two hundred yards being a pile-bridge. Its course is zigzag across the swamp, and diagonally across the river. On either side, until it reaches the piles it is a corduroy road, and throughout it is fifteen feet in width. The road is composed of cross-layers of timber, and the foundation is upon solid ground. On each side, a ditch of four feet wide and two deep is dug, and the earth is banked on the upper side to act as a barrier against freshets. The superstructure is gravel, several inches thick, laid both on the road and the bridge, and making a perfectly level pavement. The bridge itself—across one of the quietest streams in a dry season and one of the most raging in a wet one—is firm and solid as a rock. Piles, beams, and braces, all of rough hewn timber, support a corduroy roadway which is capable of bearing the heaviest burdens. Artillery-trains galloping across did not disturb it, and marching columns of soldiers scarcely caused a tremor. Woodbury Bridge was named after the lamented commander of the regiment which constructed it,—Colonel Woodbury, of the Fourth Michigan. It was the admiration of every passenger.

A small board nailed to a tree at the centre of the structure showed its paternity. The modest words upon it were:—

"WOODBURY BRIDGE,
"ON THE WAY TO RICHMOND.
"BUILT BY THE VOLUNTEER ENGINEER CORPS,
"FROM JUNE 8 TO JUNE 14, 1862."

The completion of such a structure in the short

space of six days, half the time rain pouring in torrents, is in the highest degree creditable, and reflects great honor upon the citizen soldiers who performed the labor.

All these incidents of the siege, building intrenchments, roads, and bridges, added to the bad weather and the enemy's admirable defences, delayed the forward progress of the Union forces. General McClellan advanced as rapidly as was possible: no army nor no general could have moved faster. Obstacles were opposed to them that unmilitary men would scout at, but which, when foolishly attacked, rendered certain a mortifying repulse. There was delay in the siege,—great delay; but it was of a character that no human being could avoid. It was delay caused by natural reasons, and the necessarily slow progress of a war of intrenchments. The siege advanced as speedily as any other ever did, and was marked by many events honorable to the Union arms. If the next siege of Richmond progresses as rapidly and as well, all should be satisfied.

CHAPTER X.

THE SIEGE.

WHEN the human body has ceased from a labor which required great exertions, its energy and spirit are weakened and depressed in proportion as they were previously strengthened. The stimulus of danger or excitement no longer holds sway upon the brain and gives the muscles additional vigor. It has gone, and has left behind it a prostration proportionate to the greatness of the exertion. As with individuals, so it is with bodies of men, and so General McClellan found it after the battle of Fair Oaks. That severe contest commanded all the energy and ability of his army, and when it was over the troops needed relaxation and rest. For several days, therefore, the active operations of the siege seemed to be almost suspended, and neither army was disposed to renew the bloody battle which had killed and wounded over seven thousand men. The generals upon the Federal left wing promptly strengthened their positions, and the commander-in-chief began the construction of his siege-works, but, excepting slight skirmishes, scarcely a battle was fought for many days after the contest at Fair Oaks.

The siege of Richmond was commenced upon the 2d of June. Previously, the Federal troops were being placed in position, but upon that day the real work began. It ended upon the 25th of the same month, and upon the following day was the first engagement of the famous seven days of retreat. Richmond was invested for twenty-four days, and during that time the besieging army, almost solely by means of intrenchments, advanced their line, in some places a mile, in others a half-mile, capturing earth-works, prisoners, and arms, and slowly nearing the city. Had the statements of the superior force opposed to the Federal troops, which filled both Northern and Southern newspapers, and which were endorsed by spies, scouts, signal-men, and balloonists, and even by the commander-in-chief himself, been then believed, and had the almost daily requests of General McClellan for reinforcements been favorably considered, subsequent disaster would perhaps have been avoided, and the enemy, instead of threatening the Federal capital, have been compelled to surrender their own. Misfortune, that harsh and cruel teacher, has now, alas! too late, convinced the Government and people of the truth of the accounts of Rebel strength, and of the need the army of the Potomac had of additional aid.

The first military movement after the battle of Fair Oaks was made upon June 3, by General Hooker. His division was sent out upon an armed reconnoissance along the Williamsburg road. They advanced a mile, to a point within four miles of Richmond, without meeting the enemy in any force. Rebel pickets kept in sight, but retreated before the Federal troops. The division returned without loss, in the evening.

Upon the 5th of June, every thing being prepared, General Smith's division of General Franklin's corps successfully crossed the Chickahominy. They struck their tents at four o'clock in the morning, and shortly after left their camp near Hogan's house, passing over Grapevine Bridge. The entire division did not arrive at its station upon Lewis's Hill, about a mile from the bridge, until eight in the evening. General Burns's brigade of General Sumner's corps had previously garrisoned the hill, and yielded it up to General Smith, the brigade marching southward to rejoin its corps, which held the railroad.

On the previous two or three days, and also upon this one, strange phenomena were visible from Mechanicsville. Huge smokes, covering the entire surrounding country, rose from the woods beyond the river. They began each day about noon, and continued until dusk, but after nightfall no fires could be seen which would aid in explaining the cause. Contrabands who came into the lines previously had reported that immense amounts of tobacco had been carried out of Richmond and piled some two miles from the city, where it was saturated with turpentine. If the stories told by these men were true, it may have been the burning of the tobacco which caused the smokes. No solution of the mystery, however, has yet been given, and, like many other things which have occurred in the Confederate States, it may be that the cause of these strange smokes never will be explained. At this time, artillery duels commenced to become quite an important part of the siege. Where they had previously occurred at long intervals, or not at all, they now became incessant, and of course, owing to the superiority of Federal cannon, usually resulted in the discomfiture of the Rebels.

For two or three days, balloonists and signal-men upon the right wing had observed bodies of troops passing down the roads from Northern and Northwestern Virginia, and disappearing in the woods, as if intending to encamp. They were accompanied by artillery, wagons, and all the paraphernalia of an army. There seemed to be from fifteen to twenty thousand of them, and, from certain peculiarities observed by the signal-men, and also from information given by spies and deserters, they were supposed to be the division commanded by General Jackson, who had been in the valley of Virginia, making General Banks retreat before him, and in turn retreating before Generals Sigel and Fremont. He had now come to rejoin the Rebel army, which he had left about the time General McClellan was at White House, and brought with him a large reinforcement. General Jackson remained near Richmond until the retreat, in which he figured conspicuously.

Until June 8, save the continued artillery practice, no military movement was made by either army. The enemy were constructing a formidable earth-work about two miles from Woodbury Bridge, upon which they employed large numbers of negroes, and the Federal troops were actively engaged in building roads and bridges. Indeed, such was the swampy nature of the ground upon which they were encamped, that engineering labor was kept up incessantly until the middle of June. Woodbury Bridge was completed upon the 14th. Several skirmishes happening upon the 8th and 9th varied the monotony of these proceedings.

The principal one was an engagement between the enemy and General Burns's brigade of General Sumner's corps. This brigade contains four Pennsylvania regiments, commanded by Colonels Baxter, Owen, Morehead, and Wistar. Colonel Baxter's regiment was the first attacked. It was upon picket duty, and in front of the picket tour a space about twenty yards wide had been cleared from the woods, to prevent the enemy from surprising the Union pickets. Behind the pickets were some rifle-pits. The enemy suddenly appeared in front of the regiment and furiously attacked it, first with infantry and then with artillery. The other three regiments were brought up, and Colonel Baxter's retreated to join them, yielding up the rifle-pits. In a few moments, however, the colonel ordered a charge, and the enemy were driven out of the pits; but, being reinforced, they were recaptured. Again the regiment charged, driving the Rebels out a second time, and afterward successfully held them against all attacks. The enemy's loss is not known, as they carried all their dead and wounded away. The Federal loss was nine killed and twenty-nine wounded.

Upon the same day, detachments of the Ninety-fifth Pennsylvania regiment and of the Eighteenth and Thirty-first New York, whilst engaged in bridge-building, were attacked by the enemy's sharp-shooters, who were, however, soon scattered by Federal artillery. But one man, a private of the Eighteenth New York, was wounded. General Sumner the next day advanced his pickets a short distance along the railroad,—a movement which provoked a furious artillery fire from the rebels. General Sumner's cannon, of course, replied, and, after an hour's work, the enemy's firing ceased. None of the Federal troops were injured, and the new picket tour was successfully maintained.

Upon the 12th of June, General Burnside was at General McClellan's head-quarters, and in close conference with him. A Fortress Monroe correspondent of a

Northern newspaper says that when he returned there from the army before Richmond, he announced that he "was and always had been part and parcel of the army of the Potomac." These two generals always labored together, and had the utmost confidence in each other, and at their conferences formed plans which in many cases have proved successful. General Banks, too, was an officer who had a high opinion of the commander of the army before Richmond,—an opinion which was reciprocated. The three are now (September, 1862) together, and, it is to be hoped, will vindicate their country's cause in this hour of her greatest danger.

The enemy, although they had been very quiet for some time, had matured the plan of an expedition which, for rash daring and complete success, has scarcely an equal in history's annals. This expedition was "Stewart's raid," and under that name posterity will hear of it when others far more important will have been forgotten. Upon the 12th of June, General J. E. B. Stewart, of the Rebel cavalry service, with two regiments of infantry, twelve hundred horse, and two guns, and accompanied by the son and nephew of the Rebel commander-in-chief, left the enemy's camp, upon a mission originally intended merely as a reconnoissance to the country northwest of Mechanicsville, for the purpose of ascertaining the Federal force in that direction. Being an expedition of much danger, it was composed of picked detachments, and was conducted with the utmost secrecy,—General Stewart alone of all his command having any knowledge of its object. He went from the extreme left of the Rebel lines, and, as he says in his official report, "purposely directed his march toward Louisa," encamping on the night of the 12th near Hanover Court-House.

Early the next morning, his camp was broken up, and, without flag or bugle-sound, the stealthy march was resumed. Four companies of the United States cavalry were at that time picketing some six miles back of Mechanicsville, near the road to White House. At about one o'clock in the afternoon General Stewart's force came suddenly upon them, bringing their artillery to the front and opening fire. The Federal cavalry, under command of Captain Royall, formed in line preparatory to making a dash, when the Rebel infantry came forward and fired a destructive volley at them, which was instantly followed by a charge from their cavalry. This caused the Federal troops to fall back to the White House road, the enemy pursuing them, destroying their camp and capturing several prisoners. The Federal troops, upon reaching the road, retreated to the Chickahominy.

Having thus defeated the out-picket and ascertained the Union force there, it became a question with General Stewart whether he should return to Richmond, or, although not so ordered, make a bold attempt to cut off the supplies of the Federal army by destroying the railroad. How he resolved to do the latter, he tells in his report:—

"In a brief and frank interview with some of my officers I disclosed my views; but, while none accorded a full assent, all assured me a hearty support in whatever I did. With an abiding trust in God, and with such guarantees of success as the two Lees, and Martin, and their devoted followers, this enterprise I regarded as most promising.

"Taking care, therefore, more particularly after this resolve, to inquire of the citizens the distance and the route to Hanover Court-House, I kept my horse's head steadily toward Tunstall's Station. There was something sublime in the implicit confidence and unquestioning trust of the rank and file in a leader guiding them straight, apparently, into the very jaws of the enemy, every step appearing to them to diminish the faintest hope of extrication. Reports of the enemy's strength at Garlick's and Tunstall's were conflicting, but generally indicated a small number. Prisoners were captured at every step, and included officers, soldiers, and negroes."

Having fully made up his mind, General Stewart, sending his infantry back to Hanover Court-House, proceeded toward Tunstall's Station, and upon arriving opposite Garlick's Landing, upon the Pamunky, sent part of his force to destroy whatever could be found there, the main body continuing on to the railroad. The detachment sent to the river burned two schooners and a large number of wagons, and captured several prisoners and many horses and mules. All reports agree that the conduct of the enemy whilst at the Landing was most barbarous. Teamsters, who were unarmed, were shot down in cold blood, and one account states that even women and children were murdered. The party, having done all the damage they could, rode briskly off with their spoil to rejoin their comrades.

Nearly all of the enemy had been residents of the part of Virginia in which they were rioting, and, of course, possessed an accurate knowledge of the roads. This aided them greatly in their undertaking, and, indeed, without it the expedition could never have succeeded. The main body, after the force sent to the Pamunky was detached, rode briskly to the railroad, and, being rejoined by them, stood prepared to wreak vengeance upon the first train which appeared. Part were upon a hill through which the road had been cut, lining it upon both sides, and others hid behind trees and fences. Soon a distant whistle announced the approach of a locomotive from the Chickahominy. It was running rather fast, and to it was attached a long train of cars. When it reached the place where the Rebels were stationed, some of them appeared and hailed the engineer to stop. Suspecting the character of the intruders, however, instead of checking he increased the speed, and, jumping upon the tank with the fireman, crouched among the fuel. Scarcely had he done so, when a deadly fire was poured into the train from all directions,—many bullets being aimed at the locomotive in the hope of striking the engineer.

There were numerous passengers on the cars, mostly laborers, civilians, and sick and wounded soldiers, and a general effort was made to jump off, and, if possible, elude the enemy's fire. Several succeeded, and hid themselves in the wood; but the quickly increasing speed of the train prevented the majority from following their example. The cars, however, were soon out of reach of the Rebels, and the engineer, fearful of pursuit or of meeting more enemies, increased the pressure of steam so that the train almost flew over the distance between Tunstall's Station and White House.

There the news of what had occurred spread like lightning, and there was the utmost consternation among the sutlers, civilians, clerks, laborers, and negroes who inhabited the canvas town which had sprung up on the Pamunky. Lieutenant-Colonel Ingalls, of the quartermaster's department, was the officer in command, and, under the fear of impending danger, he mustered the few soldiers who were at the place, and armed the civilians and laborers. He also placed all the money, records, mails, and other valuable property of the United States upon a steamboat in the river. The panic among the sutlers was beyond all description: each one expected utter ruin, and awaited, with an anxious heart, the approach of the enemy. They did not come, however, and White House, though it was so soon to be destroyed, had a short respite.

The Rebels, having been foiled in their designs upon the railroad-train by the presence of mind of its engineer, set to work to burn a small bridge near Tunstall's Station and to take up some of the rails from the road-bed. Before the work was finished, however, some apprehension frightened them away, and, a body of troops sent from White House opportunely arriving at the station, the flames upon the burning bridge were extinguished. The enemy marched southwest from the railroad, and encamped for the night of the 13th about two miles from it. The next morning, laden with booty, they crossed the Chickahominy some distance below Bottom's Bridge, proceeded west until they struck the "River turnpike," and returned on it to Richmond.

The Federal loss from this raid was severe. There were four men killed, some thirty wounded, and twenty captured at Tunstall's Station and its vicinity. Several of the Fifth cavalry were captured, and Captain Royall, of that regiment, was wounded. In the skirmish with the cavalry near the White House road the Rebels acknowledge to have had a captain killed. Over three hundred thousand dollars' worth of Federal property was taken or destroyed, and numerous casualties occurring among the laborers and others at Garlick's Landing have never been reported. The enemy were particularly harsh toward the negroes. Every one found was compelled to go along with them. Numerous prisoners whom they captured subsequently escaped. The great result of the expedition, however, was its proving the vulnerability of the long railroad-line over which all the Federal supplies were carried.

One of the novel circumstances connected with this Rebel raid was the arrest of a newsboy who came into the Federal lines a day or two after. About ten o'clock in the morning he suddenly appeared among the pickets, crying out in true newsboy style, and endeavoring to sell his papers, a bundle of which was under his arm. They had been issued that morning, and the most prominent article upon the editorial page was a long, minute, and exaggerated account of General Stewart's expedition. The boy, who was not more than twelve years of age, was taken to General Slocum, and there gave an account of himself. He said that the feat of the cavalry, in passing completely around the besieging army, had given the people of Richmond ecstasies of delight, and it was proposed to him that, for a slight reward, he should take across the Chickahominy a number of newspapers containing an account of it, and dispose of them in the Federal army. Nothing loath, the boy consented, and, taking as many as he could carry, he was passed through the enemy's lines, and across the river upon a slight log bridge hidden in the grass and weeds. Of this bridge an account will be given upon a subsequent page. Having successfully passed the swamp, he appeared among the Federal pickets and began selling his papers, and had nearly finished when he was taken into custody and sent to General Slocum. His newspapers were disseminated through the camps, and the falsehoods and boasts they contained gave the soldiers infinite amusement.

Other guerrillas besides those of General Stewart's command were hovering upon the rear and flanks of the Federal army. Upon the 14th of June a party was discovered prowling about the country upon the opposite side of the Pamunky, near White House, and their object was supposed to be the destruction of the shipping at that place if an opportunity offered. Another squad was reported to be at Charles City Court-House, and a third near Williamsburg. General McClellan at once took measures to break up these roving bands, and, upon the 16th, two cavalry expeditions were sent out. One, commanded by Colonel Averell, went northward across the Pamunky to the Mattapony, but the guerrillas he was in search of had fled before he reached that river. He destroyed a bridge, however, and captured a large number of wagons and carts laden with supplies for Richmond. Several prisoners were taken, and some grain destroyed. The other reconnoissance, commanded by Colonel Gregg, marched to Charles City Court-House, and succeeded in recapturing a number of mules which had been driven off by General Stewart.

Both expeditions were quite successful, and not a soldier in either was hurt.

Whilst the raid was being made, little else of interest took place before Richmond. The enemy evacuated the hills opposite Mechanicsville upon the 15th of June, no doubt intending to entice the Federal forces over and subject them to a destructive fire from the batteries. The movement was unsuccessful, however, and the Rebels soon returned to their old stations. The day before, a sharp artillery-fire was opened upon General Sumner's camps. It lasted some three hours, and one man was killed and one wounded. General Heintzelman's pickets were also attacked; but the enemy were repulsed. Numerous arrests of disloyal inhabitants were made subsequently to Stewart's raid, and they were sent North as prisoners of war. The work of the siege steadily proceeded, and the enemy were daily compelled to yield up ground to their advancing opponents.

General Slocum's officers had long suspected that there was some means of crossing the Chickahominy in front of the lines picketed by their troops, and the appearance of the Rebel newsboy confirmed the suspicion. The division was at that time upon the extreme right, not having been moved across the river until June 18. In order to discover what means the enemy had of passing the stream and swamp, General Slocum ordered Colonel Henry L. Cake, of the Ninety-sixth Pennsylvania regiment, to make an expedition to the borders of the river and thoroughly explore it. Upon the evening of the 17th of June, the colonel prepared for his dangerous journey, and at nine o'clock, accompanied by three officers and fifty picked men, left his camp for the swamp. He first directed his course to a house near the river, which was the station of a picket reserve and belonged to a man named Sydnor, and made it the base of operations. Having ordered his men to load their muskets and unfix bayonets, the whole party cautiously proceeded outside the Federal picket line and entered the swamp. After penetrating some distance, they reached a cleared place near the borders of the stream, where they halted. Here Colonel Cake left the greater part of his force, and, with Major Martin, Captain Anthony, and a few soldiers, directed his steps along what seemed to be a path through the tall grass. A short and silent march brought them to a rise in the ground, running parallel with the river; and, leaving his body-guard, the colonel went forward with Major Martin to reconnoitre. Pistol in hand, they stealthily crept up the little hill and peeped over its top. At first all appeared dark and dreary; but soon a moving body could be discerned a short distance in front, and an application of the night-glass disclosed a half-dozen Rebels sitting amid the grass.

This was quite a discovery, and as quietly as they had ascended it they retreated down the hillock and returned to the body-guard. The party then moved forward, and, continuing along the path a short distance, were halted again, and their commander went forward to make another reconnoissance. Here the path turned shortly and seemed to pass across the little ridge, and as stealthily as before he crept up and again looked over. The first sight which met his gaze was that of a tall Rebel, standing, musket in hand, upon the river-bank. He was evidently mounting guard; and to find what he was watching became the next object. The night-glass was again brought into requisition, and every thing near was carefully scanned, until down amid the bushes the end of a log was seen. The colonel was on the hunt for a bridge, and that was circumstantial evidence that one might be there. Moving slightly to one side to obtain a better view, he applied the glass again, when, lo! dimly through the darkness a log bridge was seen, scarcely wide enough for a man to walk upon it, running across the swamp, from one little spot of solid ground to another, until it was lost amid the foliage which grew in such profusion all around. Noting its precise situation, he cautiously returned to his companions, and, taking another look over the ridge at the point where he had discovered the party of Rebels, they were found to have fled. Something had evidently frightened them. Marching on, the main party was soon reached, and, completely wet through from their contact with the grass and weeds, the whole of them returned to Sydnor's house. It was nearly two o'clock when Colonel Cake and his party reached their camp.

The next morning, a report was made of the result, and the bridge was doubtless broken down by the shells thrown there by the artillery. The discovery of this place broke up one means of communication with the enemy. Spies no doubt crossed there. Negroes would be seen near Sydnor's house and suddenly disappear, and others would as suddenly appear. Sydnor was strongly suspected of aiding these men in their dangerous business; and Colonel Cake was highly commended for the successful manner in which he executed his difficult commission.

Upon June 18, General McCall, with his fine division

of Pennsylvania troops, arrived at General Porter's head-quarters. He had come from Fredericksburg as a reinforcement to General McClellan's army, and his force was added to General Porter's corps as an additional division. General McCall had eight thousand troops, including some cavalry and artillery. At noon on the 18th, General Slocum's division, whose watch upon the right wing had thus been relieved, broke up camp and joined the besieging army. They crossed the Chickahominy upon Woodbury Bridge, and arrived at their allotted place between Generals Sumner and Smith at about seven o'clock in the evening.

Upon the same day, General McClellan, accompanied by his staff, made a grand review of the army. He commenced at General Keyes's camps, upon the left wing, and passed along to the right, being everywhere received with the greatest enthusiasm. In all possible ways the soldiers expressed their admiration of a general whose modesty and military genius have won for him a place in the hearts of the thousands of men composing the Union armies.

This review was not barren of results in other ways than display. The cheering, as it had been the first heard for weeks, and such loud and universal shouts, extending from one end to the other of the Federal line, seeming to portend some great disaster to the enemy, they were all anxious to ascertain its cause. A general, who was said by some captured Rebels to have been intoxicated, accordingly ordered forward a brigade to seize some Union soldiers, in order that they might be questioned about it. These troops attacked the position held by General Burns's brigade, but were met by a perfect storm of shell, grape, and canister, and after a short contest were driven back. Several prisoners were captured,—among them an orderly-sergeant, who said that the Federal fire was too tremendous for any troops to withstand. But one man was killed, and one wounded, in General Burns's brigade.

Upon the 19th and 20th of June, several attacks were made upon Federal pickets, particularly in front of General Heintzelman's corps. They were all successfully resisted, however. The principal skirmish lasted for more than an hour, and was between the Twentieth Indiana regiment of General Kearney's division, and a large force of the enemy. The regiment bravely stood its ground, and the Rebels, finding they could make no impression, retreated. A Federal lieutenant and three privates were wounded. The attacks upon the next day were principally by artillery, intended to annoy the troops working in the trenches. No harm was done, however. The prisoners captured at this time all reported that Beauregard's army was coming into Richmond, and that large reinforcements were daily arriving. A member of Governor Letcher's guard, captured at Ashland by General Stoneman's cavalry, also told the same story.

Upon the evening of the 21st, the Federal left wing was very much disturbed. At about six P.M. the Rebels made a bold but injudicious dash at a redoubt on the left of the Williamsburg road. Three regiments pushed up toward it in fine style, firing upon the picket-guards with great impetuosity. They were received with grape and canister from two field-pieces, and by very sharp musketry from a long rifle-pit whose existence they had not suspected, and speedily turned about, retreating with some loss. They kept up alarms all night, and at three o'clock in the morning a brigade was sent against another redoubt still farther to the left. This also had no result. These alarms were imagined to be preliminary to an attack in force the next morning; but not a single gun was fired all day. It was a hot, silent, and serene Sabbath.

The 23d of June was also a remarkably quiet day, almost devoid of skirmishes, and, from their movements, the enemy were supposed to be contemplating an attack. Their pickets in some places were drawn in for a half-mile, the ground vacated being promptly occupied by Union troops, who secured themselves with intrenchments. During the night a terrific storm, lasting some three hours, passed over the camps. The wind blew a hurricane, and levelled tents and trees in all directions. The Federal troops were under arms at daylight the next morning, to resist the anticipated attacks; but the enemy, after a few slight demonstrations, finding themselves effectually resisted at all points, retired. Upon the same day General Casey was assigned to duty at White House, General Peck taking command of his division.

Upon the 24th a reconnoissance was made to James River by Captain Keenan, with two companies of cavalry. Understanding from citizens residing on that river that a gunboat had of late been signalling the shore, he obtained permission to undertake the opening of communication with her, and left the camp of General Peck's division the preceding afternoon. He found that General Wise held a position opposite Fort Darling, with his command of five thousand troops, being the extreme right of the Rebel army. Their pickets also extended along the river-bank below the fort for several miles, and, as they were closely posted, the captain determined to hazard the probability of capture, and go aboard alone. Before daylight he penetrated the enemy's picket-line, and forced a negro, whom he found in a house near by, to row him to the Galena—for such was the gunboat. He remained on board until the approach of daylight warned him to be away, when he returned to his camp, having fully accomplished his mission.

June 25 was a most eventful day. It closed the siege of Richmond; for upon the 26th General McClellan changed his policy from offence to defence. From morning till night the woods and hills resounded with the constant reports of cannon and musketry. At Mechanicsville, the Federal troops were going through manœuvres which will be detailed in the following chapter, and which were intended to entice the enemy across the Chickahominy. General Porter's cannon, at Dr. Gaines's house, in conjunction with signal-men upon Lewis's Hill, were engaged in driving the enemy from some earth-works. And upon the left of the besieging line the lamented Kearney and gallant Hooker were fighting one of the most brilliant actions of the war. Everywhere there was success for the Federal arms, and the day was a fit one to close a siege which could be no longer continued, from the lack of reinforcements to counterbalance the great additions made to the Rebel army.

The contest between General Porter's artillery and the Rebel earth-works proved the great usefulness of the signal corps. Dr. Gaines's house was distant a mile and a half from General Smith's position upon Lewis's Hill. Two strong intrenchments, and a battery, very annoying to the Federal troops, were about a mile in front of the hill, but hidden from General Porter by intervening woods. Guns were planted upon the hills near the house, and a signal-man stationed upon Fort Davidson, where he could be seen by another who was with the battery. The enemy, since early morning, had been throwing shell at the Federal pickets, compelling them to retreat. When all was in readiness, the ball was opened, and the batteries, directed solely by the signal-officers,—for their mark was concealed from them,—began firing. The Rebels, of course, continued their shelling, and, finding themselves likely to be disturbed, redoubled their exertions. Spectators near the signal-station could see the entire operation,—the Rebels loading and firing their cannon, and the Federal shells at first flying wide of their mark, but coming closer as they were directed by the swings of the flag. The shells gradually fell nearer and nearer. After each one had fallen, the signal-officer, accurately noting where it burst, would send word over the river, and the next one would be sure to drop closer to the Rebels.

The two earth-works and the battery were in a line, the battery being nearest the Federal cannon, and the farthest earth-work a third of a mile more distant. The battery was silenced first; then the earth-work in the centre of the three received a bombardment so terrific as to compel every Rebel to slink away; then the farthest one caught the storm, and all were compelled to flee, carrying away dead and wounded by scores. The whole Rebel force were perfectly at the mercy of a Union battery, whose gunners never saw the spot they were hitting, but who gazed only upon a small flag waving and swinging away off upon the ramparts of Fort Davidson.

The ground in front of General Heintzelman's corps, upon the left wing, had been for almost a month a bloody duelling-place for the pickets of General Hooker's division upon the one side, and those of Generals Longstreet and D. B. Hill upon the other. It was a swamp. The little processions of dead and wounded which at eventide daily came in from its leafy shades were nothing to the deadly influence of the malaria, which sent hundreds of brave soldiers to hospital. Every military and sanitary consideration required that the Federal picket line should be removed from the eastern half of this swamp to its breezy open edge upon the west, where it would be in view and within pistol-shot distance of the enemy's camp, placed beyond a wheat-field, and stretching a mile or more in length, being defended by rifle-pits and three bastioned forts filled with men and bristling with cannon.

General Heintzelman accordingly received orders to advance the picket line; and, to do so, his entire corps was placed under arms, and at eight o'clock on the morning of the 25th, General Sickles's Excelsior Brigade and General Grover's brigade, both of General Hooker's division, were advanced to the attack. They entered the wood, driving the enemy's picket line before them to its reserve, some distance to the rear. These pickets made a stout resistance, which enabled General Hill's division, to which they belonged, to come up and meet the Federal troops. The battle now commenced, and the firing became hotter and hotter. General Kearney sent forward Generals Berry and

Robinson with their brigades as a reinforcement to General Grover, who held the left. Part of General Patterson's brigade, and the Second New York regiment, together with the Nineteenth Massachusetts, a regiment of General Sumner's corps, were also pushed forward to the assistance of General Sickles.

The Federal line, thus reinforced, slowly advanced, driving the enemy before it, until half-past nine, when it was brought to a stand-still. It was evident that the Rebels were in great strength in front, and the contest was kept up for an hour with intense fury. Finally, their line began giving way, showing the first symptoms of defeat, in front of General Grover's position. His brigade was immediately pushed forward, and the Rebels, once fairly started, retreated quite rapidly. Soon the advancing Federal troops broke out into the open field upon the western side of the swamp, when the enemy, being reinforced, rallied, and again attacked them. A hard contest ensued, ending with the enemy's repulse.

At this moment an order was received from the Federal head-quarters that the pursuit should be stopped and the troops withdrawn to the original line.* This caused great astonishment, and could not be understood; but, of course, it was complied with. With heavy hearts the soldiers turned to retreat, halting, at about half-past eleven, at their old line upon the eastern edge of the swamp. There they remained until

---

*** This order was misconceived,—not being a positive order: it was intended to take effect under certain contingencies, and its spirit was not fully represented in its delivery.**

one o'clock, when General McClellan rode upon the field. All were in amazement at the unaccountable command to retreat; and, seeing the position of affairs, the general-in-chief at once ordered a second attack. This was greeted enthusiastically, and once more the troops advanced, in the same order in which they had already done so well.

Generals Kearney and Grover, upon the left, found but slight resistance; but in front of General Sickles the fighting was very severe. There the enemy had gathered a strong force, and seemed determined to defend the point at every hazard. The battle raged until two o'clock, when General Palmer's brigade, from General Keyes's corps, was ordered up in support of General Sickles. It at once advanced and engaged in the contest. Osborn's battery of four guns was also sent into the Williamsburg road, to throw shell over the woods into the enemy's camp. To do this, the missiles would have to pass over the heads of the Federal troops in advance. Such practice is always very perilous: shells either fall falsely, or the distance is miscalculated, and misfortune ensues. So it was in this case. An officer and several privates of the Seventh Massachusetts regiment, deployed in the woods as skirmishers, were hurt,—some fatally. The firing was at once stopped.

A section of Derussy's battery was then sent along the Williamsburg road, and took its position in the midst of General Palmer's brigade, at once opening fire. This was kept up for some minutes, during which the volleys of musketry almost ceased. At the same time, the artillery of General Sumner's corps, farther to the right, began shelling the woods in front of them, and soon the gunners had it all to themselves. The enemy also brought their cannon forward, and had the range of Derussy's battery so accurately that he was compelled to withdraw. The Federal line pushed forward, however, and, aided by General Sumner's artillery, it again drove the enemy completely through the woods, halting upon the outer edge of it. The battle then almost ceased, occasional contests between skirmishers alone occurring, until six in the afternoon, when General Kearney, upon the left, led General Birney's brigade, which had not been previously engaged, against the enemy. Aided by Generals Grover and Robinson, he pushed forward, driving the Rebels completely out of the woods. For some minutes the firing was very fierce, but it soon subsided.

The attack having been successful, dispositions were then made to hold the advanced line during the night; and the Excelsior Brigade, having fought gallantly all day, and being very much fatigued, was relieved by General Palmer. Soon after dark, large bodies of Rebels were brought up in front of his position, and a battery was also pushed forward. At ten o'clock the enemy suddenly advanced and poured a volley into the Second Rhode Island and the Tenth Massachusetts, who held the front. Some confusion ensued; but the men were soon rallied, repulsing this threatened advance and driving the enemy back with considerable loss. The contest was not again renewed by either army.

The loss of the Federal troops in this engagement amounted to six hundred killed, wounded, and missing. It has been named the "Battle of the Five Oaks," and was the last contest of importance before the retreat.

Upon the 26th, 27th, and 28th of June there were constant fighting between the two armies, and upon the 28th General McClellan abandoned his siege-works before Richmond, to make the celebrated march to the James River.

CHAPTER XI.

THE RETREAT.

THE difficulties thrown into the way of the historian who attempts the compilation of an intelligible account of the battle of Fair Oaks are increased tenfold when he essays to give a description of General McClellan's march to the James River. Seven days of retreat and conflict, a march of twenty miles, the transportation of the baggage of a great army, and the confusion caused by thousands of horses, wagons, cattle, and troops retreating by poor roads first across the enemy's front and afterward with their forces constantly attacking the rear,—all cause the utmost trouble to the narrator who endeavors to reconcile the statements of those who have written of it. The same misgivings, therefore, which were had when a description of the battle of Fair Oaks was attempted, are felt whilst writing this chapter, and the same indulgence, it is trusted, will be extended the author should he be unable to tell all, or to tell without errors, the sad yet thrilling story of the famous retreat of the army of the Potomac.

It was about the 20th day of June when General McClellan first became aware of the daily arrival of reinforcements at Richmond. They entered the city upon the railroads from Petersburg, Danville, and other places in Southern and Southwestern Virginia, and their number was constantly reported by trusty scouts.

Without these additions the Rebel army was considerably more than one-third larger than that of their opponents. With them it was more than double the Federal army. The precise time at which these reinforcements first arrived at the capital is not known, but it could scarcely have been earlier than the 15th of June,—nor can it be stated whence they came. They may have been part of the army which evacuated Corinth at the end of May, or they may have been new levies under the conscription act, or else they had been employed for coast-defence and were withdrawn when the capital was found to be in such imminent danger. Such is the control had in the South over the press and the people that scarcely a glimmering can be obtained of the route by which these troops came, or the places where they had previously been in service.

Their number is variously estimated. Some have placed it at one hundred thousand, whilst others have not gone so high. The opinions of officers of the besieging army varied, whilst the statements of contrabands and refugees—although the marvellous accounts given by so many of them have caused all to be regarded with suspicion—have made the entire force of the Rebels, at the time of the retreat, to number from two hundred and twenty-five thousand to two hundred and fifty thousand men. From all the reliable information which can be procured, the troops who came into the city during the few days between the 15th and 26th of June numbered fifty thousand; and this force, added to the army already there, increased its strength to about one hundred and seventy-five thousand. To meet this vast multitude General McClellan could not muster more than eighty-six thousand troops.

The Rebel commander-in-chief seems to have changed his policy to an offensive one about the 23d of June, for on that day and the next his troops made numerous attacks all along the Federal lines, evidently for the purpose of feeling their strength. General McClellan appears to have decided upon his course at the same time, as upon the 24th he commenced to act in accordance with it. His intention at that time was to entice the enemy in as great numbers as possible across the Chickahominy, and then, taking advantage of their absence, to make a sudden dash with his entire force along the railroad and the Williamsburg road and enter the capital in triumph. He changed it subsequently, however. Seeing the stubborn resistance with which his left and centre were greeted at the battle of the Five Oaks, and correctly judging that before very long General Lee would attempt to turn his flanks or overwhelm his centre, he abandoned the idea of attacking Richmond, and, weighing all the chances, finally decided upon making a march to the James River, where his siege-operations could be aided by the gunboats.

It is curious what little things will sometimes cause great events. Upon the 24th of June General McClellan, in accordance with his first plan, sent orders to Mechanicsville that every effort should be made to entice the enemy across the river. During the previous night the Rebels were heard at Meadow Bridge making noises such as the throwing down of lumber from wagons and its preparation for bridge-building. This being reported to the commander-in-chief upon the 24th, he rightly judged from it, and the resistance made to Generals Hooker and Kearney upon the next day, that the Rebel General Lee had commenced his offensive movements,—how they were to be made being indicated by the noises heard at Meadow Bridge. All fears of his turning the Federal left, or precipitating his forces upon the centre to break the army in two and cut it to pieces, were set at rest: General Lee intended to cross the Chickahominy and to turn the right flank, annihilate General Fitz-John Porter's isolated corps, disperse General Stoneman's cavalry, cut off the supplies, and then, recrossing, to drive the rest of the Union troops into the swamps and mud-holes of the Peninsula. Having ascertained the enemy's designs, General McClellan at once ceased the siege-operations, excepting so far as they were necessary to conceal his intention, and began his arrangements for the retreat.

The history of the retreat naturally commences with the movements at Mechanicsville. During the afternoon of the 23d of June, the Rebels, in strong force, commenced preparations for throwing two bridges across the stream, and were met by a determined resistance on the part of the Federal troops. When darkness came, the artillery were still throwing shell and the pickets firing at each other, but the bridge-builders had been driven off. After dark, the enemy renewed their exertions; but the terrific thunder-storm of that night, precipitating a perfect deluge upon them, compelled them to leave the work. Upon the 24th, General McClellan's orders to retreat from the outposts and endeavor to entice the enemy were received. Accordingly, General Fitz-John Porter withdrew the troops from Mechanicsville and from Meadow Bridge, and concentrated them upon the left bank of a small stream known as Beaver-Dam Creek. Near Ellison's

Mill, about a mile southwest of Mechanicsville, he built intrenchments, and also dug a rifle-pit, northeast of the village, near Oakland. General McCall's division were the troops near Mechanicsville.

Upon that day, save an occasional cannon-shot, nothing was done by the Rebels, and upon the 25th they continued equally inactive. During the night, however, they renewed their efforts upon the bridges, building two above Meadow Bridge, one at that point, and mending the one opposite Mechanicsville. These were not finished until the morning of the 26th. About noon, the enemy made an attack upon a portion of General Stoneman's division, near Hanover Court-House, evidently for the purpose of accomplishing an outflanking movement upon the right and engaging the attention of Federal officers in that direction. Immediately after, they commenced a vigorous cannonade from their works opposite Mechanicsville, and from batteries above and below. Two Federal batteries were sent out, and replied to them,—one from the Mechanicsville road, and the other from the hill to the right, from which the Richmond spire is visible. About this time, the wagon-trains of General Porter's corps were ordered to cross the Chickahominy at Woodbury Bridge, and during all the day and evening the heavy teams were lumbering across the river and parking upon the other side.

The Federal troops, at noon upon the 26th, were posted along Beaver-Dam Creek. General Reynolds's brigade of General Porter's corps was the right of the line, being near Oakland, and holding the rifle-pit there. General Seymour's brigade joined it upon the left, the line extending to the river. General

Meade's brigade was held as a reserve. These troops were all from Pennsylvania, and composed General McCall's division. The remainder of General Porter's corps was near Dr. Gaines's house.

At about two o'clock, General A. P. Hill's division of the Rebel army began crossing the stream above Meadow Bridge, and an immense force was, before three o'clock, upon the left bank of the river. The troops of Generals Longstreet, G. W. Smith, and Jackson also crossed subsequently; and, indeed, during all the 26th, 27th, and the morning of the 28th, columns of troops could, by the aid of a glass, be seen from Fort Davidson, marching toward the various bridges which had been hastily built. It was supposed that over forty thousand crossed during the day and night of the 26th, twenty thousand more upon the next day, and that by noon upon the 28th full seventy thousand Rebels were upon the left bank of the Chickahominy.

The first attack was made upon the Federal right, General Reynolds's brigade. They were posted in a hilly piece of woodland, with a ravine in front. The Bucktail regiment, commanded by Colonel Simmons, one of the most talented of the Federal officers, was upon picket duty. Almost before they knew it, the enemy had surrounded several companies of the regiment who were near Meadow Bridge. The men were brave, however, and not to be captured without a struggle. They attacked the Rebels, and cut their way out of the toils. With much loss, and leaving numbers as prisoners, they joined their comrades who were in the rifle-pit near Oakland.

The Rebels, in overwhelming force, then advanced upon the entire Federal line. Fiercely they fought over the rifle-pit, and with equal earnestness endeavored to drive General Seymour from his works near Ellison's Mill. At six o'clock the battle raged with its greatest fury. Advancing to the rear of Mechanicsville upon a low, swampy piece of ground, the constant attacks of the Rebels, and the desperate defence of General McCall's handful, made the conflict indescribably terrific. A cavalry charge of the enemy was so well opposed that it was broken up, and the troopers, dismounting, fled for their lives. Hundreds upon hundreds of Rebels were mowed down, as they endeavored to wallow through the mire.

General McCall had early sent information of the posture of affairs to his corps commander, and about half-past six, accompanied by General McClellan, General Morell's division came upon the field. One brigade, General Griffin's, was at once placed in battle-array, relieving two of General McCall's fatigued regiments. The Fourth Michigan and Fourteenth New York formed in front, and the Sixty-second Pennsylvania and Ninth Massachusetts to the rear of them. A battalion of Colonel Berdan's Sharp-shooters also drew up in line with the others. About seven o'clock, the enemy attempted to break the front formed by General Morell. To accomplish this, numerous efforts were made, but they were all boldly and successfully met. The enemy then transferred his attention to the troops farther to the left, but was also resisted there. The battle ceased at half-past nine, and the tired soldiers of both armies rested upon their arms. The Richmond newspapers acknowledge that their forces were repulsed upon the 26th.

All night long, parties were engaged upon both sides

in collecting the wounded and burying the dead, and, for fear a night-attack might be made, a strong picket force was stationed along the lines. General McCall and his staff bivouacked in the open air, and must necessarily have passed a sleepless night. The silence was occasionally broken by a picket gun, but no demonstrations were made by the enemy. At three o'clock upon the morning of the 27th, the sleepers were aroused, and the whisper passed from ear to ear that the Rebels were upon the move. The picket firing became more frequent, and it was evident that they intended to renew the attack. At daybreak, finding the enemy were rapidly closing upon the right flank, General Porter—in accordance with the plan of General McClellan to give the enemy battle, but to slowly retreat before them—ordered the whole force to fall gradually back to his camps near Dr. Gaines's house. The movement was conducted in a most satisfactory and orderly manner, there being scarcely a single mishap. The rear of the column, as it marched toward the camps, was admirably protected by the Ninth Pennsylvania Reserves, assisted by Robertson's and Easton's batteries. The enemy followed very cautiously, as if they feared they were being ensnared. But few Federal soldiers were hurt in the retreat. Having reached Dr. Gaines's house, the troops were at once disposed in line of battle to meet the Rebels.

The line formed extended from the river to Coal Harbor, presenting a front of nearly two and a half miles. Commencing upon the left, the extreme flank was held by General Meade's brigade. He was joined upon the right by General Butterfield. Then followed, successively, the brigades of Generals Martindale and Griffin, and the division of General Sykes. The extreme right of the line, at Coal Harbor, was held by General Reynolds, of the Reserves. General Philip St. George Cooke, of the cavalry, had his brigade slightly to the rear, and General Seymour was in position to support the centre of the line. There were twenty thousand infantry and about one thousand cavalry; and some sixty pieces of cannon were distributed upon the eminences held by the Federal troops. All belonged to the corps of General Porter.

The enemy had moved down the Chickahominy as fast as the Federal troops retreated. They advanced in three columns; one along the river, one upon Gaines's Mill,—a mile inland,—and another upon Coal Harbor. They were in much stronger force than the troops opposing them, and, when the battle of the 27th began, General McClellan's plan of enticing a large number of Rebels across the Chickahominy had been successful, and he now began sending his wagons and camp-equipage toward the James River.

About noon the enemy, from their position near Dr. Gaines's house, opened fire upon Fort Davidson across the river. General Smith's batteries at once replied to it, and almost instantly every Rebel gun along the whole line in front of the besieging army commenced a furious fire at the Federal earth-works. Expecting an attack, the troops were placed under arms, and, in order to balk any attempt the enemy in front of General Porter's corps might make to cross Grapevine Bridge, General Slocum's division of General Franklin's corps was marched to the west end of it and bivouacked. The bridge was at three in the afternoon broken down by detachments of the Ninety-sixth Pennsylvania and Third Vermont.

The Rebel Generals Lee and Longstreet made their head-quarters at Hogan's house, and at one o'clock they directed an advance upon the Federal line. A heavy fire of artillery was opened, and the skirmishers in the centre commenced the contest. The Union cannon at once replied, and the skirmishing extended along the entire front.. Soon the pickets were called in to the lines, and the real battle began. At a few minutes past two the infantry became engaged, and at that time there could not have been less than sixty guns in action in the Federal ranks, and there were as many on the opposite side, and a dense cloud of smoke rolling up from all quarters almost obscured the field.

At half-past three an attack was made upon the Federal centre, held by General Martindale, but it was repulsed with fearful loss. After this there was a short lull in the conflict. It being evident that the enemy were so much stronger than the Union forces, General Slocum's division and Generals French and Meagher, of General Sumner's corps, were ordered to cross the river to the aid of General Porter. They crossed at Woodbury Bridge, General Slocum going to the right of the line and the others reinforcing the left. Nearly fourteen thousand men were thus added to the Union army. At five o'clock the enemy concentrated a large force around Dr. Gaines's house, to make a charge upon the left of the Federal line. They descended the hills in immense masses, and gave an excellent opportunity for artillery practice. An incredible amount of spherical case shot, grape, and canister was thrown among them, and at the proper time the infantry opened fire.

Although a great number were killed and wounded, it did not seem to have the slightest effect upon the advancing columns. They marched steadily forward, and poured a terrible volley into the Federal lines, which thinned them greatly. Though desperately resisted, the vast force soon began to tell, and it became evident that General Porter's line would be compelled to give way. The troops of General McCall's division were nearly exhausted, having been in the battle of the preceding day and having passed the night without sleep. The onset of the enemy had its effect. By force of superior numbers they broke the Federal line, and the left wing began falling back.

At the same time it was discovered that the enemy was turning the right flank, and they had already opened an artillery fire upon it. The two attacks, one upon each wing, gave the victory to the Rebels. The centre and right began to give way, and soon the entire line was retreating toward the river. The enemy seized upon the auspicious moment, and, with furious yells, rushed forward upon the broken ranks. The horses attached to the Union batteries upon the left were nearly all killed or wounded, and as the cannon could not be drawn from the field they fell into the hands of the Rebels. Twenty-six guns were thus captured.

To contend any longer was useless. The Federal position was lost, and for the time all attempts to rally the men were in vain. The command was given for the troops to retire in order across the Chickahominy, and the regiments commenced moving in that direction. It was nearly dark. The fight had been desperate, and, after some few demonstrations, the enemy did not seem inclined to press upon the Federal rear. Generals Slocum, French, and Meagher formed a second line of battle about a half-mile back of the first, the object being more to protect the retreat than to renew the contest with the enemy. The battle was ended, and at nine o'clock the covering regiments retreated, and by daylight the next morning all were upon the right bank of the river, with the bridges broken down behind them. The sick and wounded who could not walk had to be left upon the field: they were in a hospital which had been hastily established near Woodbury Bridge. The greatest praise is due General Fitz-John Porter for the admirable manner in which he conducted the retreat.

The enemy, of course, remained in possession of the field; and the Richmond "Dispatch" thus describes its appearance:—

"Money was found quite abundantly among the slain. Some men in interring the dead often searched the pockets, &c.,—one man finding not less than one hundred and fifty dollars in gold; another fished out of some old clothes not less than five hundred dollars, another one thousand dollars in Federal notes. Watches, both gold and silver, were found among the spoils; one lucky individual having not less than six chronometers ticking in his pocket at one time. As a general thing, more money was found upon the dead on the field than on any other of which we have heard.

"Clothing in abundance was scattered about, and immense piles of new uniforms were found untouched. Our men seemed to take great delight in assuming Federal officers' uniforms, and strutted about serio-comically, much to the amusement of dusty, powder-begrimed youths who sat lolling and smoking in the shade. Every conceivable article of clothing was found in these divisional camps, and came quite *apropos* to our needy soldiery, scores of whom took a cool bath, and changed old for new under-clothing, many articles being of costly material and quite unique.

"The amount of ammunition found was considerable, and proved of very superior quality and manufacture. The exact amount captured we have not yet ascertained; but, from the immense piles of boxes scattered through the camps, we conjecture that the enemy had laid in quite an unusual supply, expecting to use it, doubtless, upon our devoted men; and so they would, doubtless, did our troops stand, as they do, at 'long taw,' and not come to 'close quarters.'

"The cannon and arms captured in this battle were numerous, and of very superior workmanship. The twenty-six pieces were the most beautiful we have ever seen, while immense piles of guns could be seen on every hand, many scarcely having the manufacturer's finish even tarnished. The enemy seemed quite willing to throw them away on the slightest pretext, dozens being found with loads still undischarged. The number of small arms captured, we understand, was not less than fifteen thousand, of every calibre and every make.

"The Federal wounded were collected together, and formed a very large field-hospital. The court-yard of a farm-house was selected, and scores could be seen reclining on the grass, and expert surgeons operating with much skill and zeal. By mutual agreement, surgeons are not considered prisoners of war: hence, at the close of the late battle many Federal surgeons remained behind, and their services seemed very much appreciated by the men. As many as could be were conveyed to town and attended to, good conveyance being furnished, and much care manifested for their welfare."

A separate movement, deserving notice, was made upon the 26th of June. The Seventeenth New York and the Eighteenth Massachusetts regiments, under the command of Colonel Lansing, were ordered to proceed to a place called Old Church, some six miles east of Mechanicsville, and intercept the Rebel General Jackson, who was on his way to cut off Federal communication with White House. Arriving upon the ground, pickets were posted, and scouts sent out to ascertain the location of the Rebels should they be in the vicinity. Falling in with their pickets, these scouts reported that a large force was marching down the road from Hanover Court-House. The enemy succeeded in cutting off Colonel Lansing's communication with the main body of the Federal army, at that time fighting upon the banks of Beaver-Dam Creek; and, keeping a good guard upon his rear, he proceeded to Tunstall's Station, upon the railroad.

By the advance of the Rebels upon June 27, General Stoneman's command was also cut off. Upon the 26th he had been scouting near Hanover Court-House, and, after doing all he could in the contest of that and the next day to harass the enemy's flank and rear, he retired to White House.

General Cooke, the commander of the cavalry attached to General Porter's corps, has been censured for not properly supporting the Federal troops during the engagement of the 27th. His official report seems to contradict any such charge. In justice to a gallant soldier, the following extract from it is given:—

"I have the honor to report the operations of the cavalry reserve in the battle of June 27.

"Its extraordinary duties and exposure for the day or two previous, in covering the right and rear of the army, had caused the detachment of about half of my forces under Brigadier-General Emory, and which that morning were ordered to retire on a different line.

"In obedience to orders, I left Coal Harbor, and arrived on the field of battle about the hour the enemy began his attack. I selected a position, and disposed my force in contiguous close columns. Of the First brigade there were present two and a half squadrons Fifth Cavalry and three squadrons Lancers, Colonel Rush; of the Second brigade, Colonel Blake, only two skeleton squadrons First Cavalry (and the provost-guard), under Lieutenant-Colonel Grier.

"About six o'clock P.M. I observed all the infantry of the left wing—in rear of which was my position—giving way, and three batteries, which in reserve positions had been silent the whole day, opened a violent fire upon the advancing lines of the enemy. Without orders, of course, I instantly conducted the Fifth and First Cavalry to the front, and deployed them in two lines, a little in rear of and just filling the interval of the two right batteries: this was under a warm fire of musketry and shell. I instructed Captain Whiting, commanding the Fifth, to charge when the support or safety of the batteries required it. I instructed Colonel Blake to support the Fifth, and charge when necessary. I then galloped to the left, and placed the Lancers on the right of the third battery, Second Artillery, Captain Robinson. I found it limbering, having been wholly unsupported. I ordered the fire reopened: the position was not very good for the matter in hand, but the renewed fire was continued until the rest of the army had retreated and the enemy was nearer the only line of retreat than we were. I then ordered the battery to retire, and, when it was all to the rear, I fell back about four hundred paces with the Lancers, and found the enemy checked at the brow of the hill by a most brave handful of infantry. I was told part of the Ninth Massachusetts and my First Cavalry were in line on the slope a little in rear of them. I then formed the Lancers, and ordered the First Cavalry to take post on the left of the infantry; but, by an unhappy misconception of the order, they advanced close upon their rear. While they were in motion, Colonel Childs, Fourth Pennsylvania Cavalry, reported to me with an only squadron of his regiment in hand, expressing a noble devotion. I sent him to join the left of the First; and this was done with a precision and bravery which would have honored veterans. Thus was withstood, under a hot fire of infantry, the advance of the enemy at the brow of the hill. Then a battery of ours which had been posted four or five hundred paces in our rear, in the obscurity of evening and of smoke and dust, opened a fire of shrapnel, which fell among us instead of the enemy. I then ordered the cavalry to retire, having been informed a second or third time that General Porter had ordered a retreat, and which he has informed me he had *not* done. The infantry were near the cover of a ravine leading to the rear, and retired at the same time. Having reached the hollow under and safe from the fire of our battery, I formed once more the First and the Lancers.

"The enemy made no further advance.

"It was a hard duty given this half of the Fifth Cavalry; emulation of the habitual devotion of our artillery was a strong motive. I was determined on this occasion that they should not be sacrificed nor lose their guns.

"The charge of the Fifth Cavalry failed to be carried home: the left squadron had but one officer present, the gallant Captain Chambliss, and when he fell it broke and threw the rest of the line into disorder. Its success, beyond enabling the batteries to get off, was impossible. It lost most severely, and did not rally. The First Cavalry then retired in line, covering the retreat of the batteries. Its subsequent action has been given.

"The Sixth Pennsylvania (Lancers), under its gallant Colonel Rush and his fine officers, performed its duties handsomely."

During the early morning of Saturday, June 28, Federal batteries were planted upon the hills west of Woodbury Bridge, where they commanded all the approaches and fords, and could for some time, at least, prevent the enemy from crossing. At ten in the morning it was discovered that the Rebels in strong force were still crossing to the left bank of the river, and it became evident that they intended to move down to the railroad and cut off communication with White House. That this had not been done on Friday night was certainly surprising; for the enemy had free access to that part of the Peninsula.

At five o'clock on Friday afternoon, a train of cars destined for White House left Savage Station. They were nine or ten in number, and filled with wounded soldiers. Though much apprehension was felt, the train passed safely over the road. It returned during the night, bringing the mails and Philadelphia and New York papers of June 26. These were the last received from White House. The last train left Savage Station on Saturday morning about eight o'clock, with some four hundred wounded, and got safely through; the telegraph worked till about eleven o'clock A.M., the last message being sent to Philadelphia by Captain Arthur McClellan to the general's family. Another train then at Savage Station was withheld. The railroad-bridge —a point of the utmost consequence, being directly in our rear and the key to our position—was held coolly and gallantly, to the last moment of usefulness, by General Naglee, and then effectually destroyed.

Excepting a furious artillery fire, and a contest in front of General Smith's intrenchments, no attack was made by the Rebels upon June 28. The battle in front of the earth-works is best told by a Richmond newspaper:—

"About eleven o'clock on Saturday, Captain Moody's battery opened fire upon the intrenchments of the enemy, located just beyond Garnett's Farm. The battery fired some ten or fifteen minutes, and meanwhile a body of infantry, consisting of the Seventh and Eighth Georgia regiments, moved up under cover of the fire from the field-pieces. The Eighth, in advance, charged across a ravine and up a hill, beyond which the Yankee intrenchments lay. They gained the first line of works and took possession of them; but, it is proper to state, this was unoccupied at the time by the Yankees. The fire of the enemy was murderous, and, as soon as our men reached the brow of the hill, rapid volleys of grape, canister, and musketry were poured into them. It was found almost impossible to proceed farther; but the attempt would have been made had not orders been received to fall back, which was done in good order, still under fire."

The Federal troops who met the enemy in this contest were four companies of the Thirty-third New York and three of the Forty-ninth Pennsylvania, numbering some five hundred men. Colonel Lamar of the Eighth Georgia was mortally wounded, and Lieutenant-Colonel Tower and a number of privates sent into camp as prisoners. The bravery of this handful of men, in repulsing vastly superior numbers, cannot be sufficiently praised. The enemy acknowledge a loss of one hundred and eighty-eight men.

The narrative of the retreat must now be suspended to allow of a description of affairs at White House. General McClellan, so soon as he had matured his plan, sent orders for the evacuation of the post. Upon June 25, the day after the order was received, matters progressed there as usual, with the exception that the landing of stores from the transport had ceased, whilst those already on shore were rapidly loaded upon wagons and sent across Bottom's Bridge to the Federal left wing. Several steamers, with vessels in tow, laden with forage and subsistence, had also sailed down the river, with orders to proceed to City Point on the James River.

This change in the course of transportation caused considerable comment and speculation. Some supposed the stores sent down the Pamunky to be intended for the supply of General Burnside's army, which, rumor said, had reached the James River and was co-operating with General McClellan. An order was also received from head-quarters upon Wednesday, the 25th, to prohibit any one from coming forward to the lines on any consideration whatever, unless he belonged to the army. This order was so peremptory that even those connected with the press, some of whom had come to White House to forward their letters by the mail-boats, were prevented from returning, and others who had smuggled themselves through were promptly sent back.

On the same day General Casey came from the army in front of Richmond and took command of the small land-force, not exceeding six hundred men, and in the evening was notified to prepare at any moment for the entire evacuation of the post, and the preservation, as far as practicable, of the public property. Similar orders were also given to Lieutenant-Colonel Ingalls. Communication was at once had with the fleet of gun-boats in the Pamunky near White House, and a division of men, armed with axes, proceeded during the night to cut down the trees surrounding the White House, and afterward all along the shore above and below the railroad-bridge, so as to give free play to the guns.

On that evening there was a report that a body of Rebels were approaching the Pamunky. The trains on the railroad were kept running as swiftly as possible, carrying forward nothing but ammunition and munitions of war, with siege and rocket trains and field-pieces.

On Thursday morning it was found that the gunboats had all taken position in front of the landing, with their ports open and their guns run out. This, and the equally astounding discovery that the trees had been cut down, gave great activity to all the camp-followers congregated at White House. The quartermaster's office was thronged by those anxious to procure transportation to Fortress Monroe, and the population was rapidly depleted. The morning train from the front reported all quiet, with the exception of certain mysterious movements not comprehensible to civilians. The immense stock of stores and forage at Despatch Station, eleven miles from the Pamunky, were being hastily carried away, and subsequently it was learned that an immense train of wagons had been running from that place all day. In the evening it was announced that not a box, bale, or barrel remained.

Throughout the day the greatest vigilance was observed in and around the head-quarters of General Casey, who had pitched his tents on the lawn in front of the White House, the building itself being occupied by the Sisters of Charity. The stocks of goods piled on the landings were rapidly diminishing, as the wagons carried them off. The railroad-trains moved steadily forward with ammunition. Cavalry scouts were sent out to different points, and preparations made for obstructing the roads. And at dusk a panic was occasioned by the discovery that bales of hay had been piled over and around the stores still remaining at the wharves—indicating the probability that during the night it might become necessary to apply the torch.

Whilst all this was doing on shore, the numerous steamers and tugs in the river, some fifty in number, had been busy towing to West Point long lines of laden transports. The vessels still scattered about the harbor were also collected and prepared for towing. Some seven hundred craft were at White House two days before. On Friday morning, the tow-boats were still moving down the river with their convoys, and vessels at the landings were being loaded with stores from the shore and moved out into the stream.

There was also great commotion among the crowds of contrabands employed as laborers. They soon understood that danger was apprehended, but, being assured by Lieutenant-Colonel Ingalls that they would not be left behind to meet the vengeance of their masters, they worked with renewed energy. Stores and munitions everywhere disappeared from the landings, and were being packed on the wharf-boats and the vessels contiguous. The wives and children of the contrabands also made their appearance, and, being sent on the canal-boats, were floated out into the stream.

The mail-steamer, which should have left early in the morning, was detained, and at eleven o'clock a despatch announced that General Porter had driven the enemy before him, repulsing them three times with terrific slaughter, and was then ordered by General McClellan to fall back. This despatch was the signal for renewed energy in the work of evacuation, and all the quartermasters' papers and valuables, and the chests of the paymasters, were taken on board the mail-boat. The household furniture and servants of some officials following, it increased the excitement among the sutlers and camp-followers. Some of the former became so panic-stricken as to sell out their stocks at half-price, and hastened on board the boat. Others, however, determined to keep their goods and to take the chances. That there was an intention on the part of General McClellan to evacuate White House as soon as his movement in front should be perfected, there was no doubt, but for what cause, no one there knew.

At three o'clock in the afternoon, the following despatch was received from head-quarters:—

"We have been driving the enemy before us on the left wing for the past half-hour. Cheers are heard all along the lines."

This increased the panic, and was the signal for a change in the programme. The valuable property was taken off the mail-boat and placed upon another steamer, and the former, taking vessels in tow, was at once sent down the river.

On Saturday morning, the work at White House was nearly completed, and, though numerous vessels still remained in the harbor, there were plenty of tow-boats to take them quickly out of danger. At nine o'clock a train of cars was sent toward the Chickahominy, but before an hour had elapsed it returned, reporting the enemy to be approaching Despatch Station, and at once the tugs and vessels sailed down the river, and every thing on shore was destroyed. At seven o'clock in the evening, the Rebels appeared upon the river-bank, and were greeted with a tremendous bombardment from the gunboats. Very little of value was left there, and, as at all other places vacated by the Federal troops during the retreat, nothing fell into the hands of the enemy but the camp-grounds and rubbish, which the Union officers did not think it worth while even to burn.

At ten o'clock on Sunday morning, the 29th, Lieutenant-Colonel Ingalls and Captain Sawtelle were before Yorktown with an immense fleet, on their way to the new base of operations upon the James River. Since a very early hour of the previous day, General McClellan had been deprived of his telegraphic communication with Washington. He abandoned its use several hours before the wires were cut, doubtless being fearful that the enemy might, by some means, become acquainted with the tenor of his despatches.

Such was the end of the far-famed supply-post at White House.

We will now return to the army beyond the Chickahominy. Upon Saturday afternoon, the retreat to the James River began. All the teams and cattle were sent in a southerly direction across the White Oak Swamp. At the same time General Morell's division left Woodbury Bridge, where they had been since the end of the previous day's battle, and marching past Savage Station, across the railroad and the Williamsburg road, they entered the swamp and crossed it, halting near Charles City, where they were the next day joined by other portions of the army.

During the night, orders were given Generals Franklin, Sumner, Heintzelman, and Keyes, whose troops still held their old positions before the Rebel capital, to destroy every article of commissary stores, ammunition, and hospital supplies for which transportation could not be furnished, and, abandoning their camps, to gradually withdraw their troops toward Savage Station. Orders were also sent the surgeons at the hospital there to instruct all the wounded who could walk to start immediately, and move toward Harrison's Point, on the James River. All the ambulances which could be found were loaded with the wounded who were in a condition to be moved; but many hundreds whose lives would have been destroyed by an attempt to remove them were left under the charge of surgeons detailed for the purpose, and turned over to the enemy, as had been done by them at Williamsburg. Two days before, four car-loads of ammunition had been sent up from White House for the use of a siege-train, and unloaded. It was replaced on the cars, and, a full head of steam being raised in the locomotive, they were started off down the railroad toward the burned bridge across the Chickahominy. Every moment the speed increased, and, whilst at the highest, the train reached the river, tumbling in with a terrible crash.

The last evening spent at Woodbury Bridge was one of solemn grandeur. On the Federal side, a solitary company of cavalry guarded the end of the destroyed bridge, and soldiers burned the few valuable articles which were lying about. Camp-fires were lighted as for a vast army. Stragglers, tired almost to death, lay upon the ground, sleeping, each marked feature sunk into perfect rest. A few wagons were still there. The vast plain, once filled with all the pageantry of war, was dotted all over with fires, but, save that one cavalry company, not a single human being was on all its surface. Across the river, brightly reflected upon the clouds, were the lights of a Rebel camp; and their forces no doubt lay upon the bloody field which bore so many of their dead.

On Saturday evening at ten o'clock, the last of the Federal army had left Woodbury Bridge and were in full retreat toward Savage Station. The night was dark and cloudy, threatening rain. Numbers of straggling soldiers were mixed up with the wagons as they proceeded. Midnight brought them to the station; and there was the first horror of the journey. The sheds and tents of the hospital were filled to overflowing with sick and wounded, whom exposure and battle had rendered helpless. That railroad-station will always be a sad spot in the recollections of all who saw it.

From Savage Station, all the way to the James River, the retreat had to be conducted by two roads, one of which crossed the stream bordering White Oak Swamp by a rude log bridge, so imbedded in mud that every wagon had to be assisted at the crossing. Over these roads a vast army, with all its baggage, passed. About two thousand wagons and twenty-five hundred head of cattle were part of the baggage of the Federal troops. The White Oak Swamp bridge was some six miles from the station, and, from one end of the road between them to the other, wagons, horses, soldiers, cannon, pontoon-boats, caissons, ambulances, and every thing conceivable which can be used by an army, were at times brought to a halt. At almost every step, an officer urged them on. Twenty rows of wagons stood side by side, teamsters swearing, horses balking, and officers shouting. Babel was a second time seen on earth. And over all could be heard General Fitz-John Porter, as he urged his horse up a hill, shouting to a wagoner not to block up the entire road. Many soldiers, straggling through the blockade, passed the swamp, and when they reached the beautiful country beyond, completely tired out, lay down on the ground and slept during the heat of the day. Thousands lay there, belonging to every regiment in the army. Thus passed Sunday morning; and toward night all aroused to continue their weary journey.

General McClellan, upon the 28th, had made his head-quarters near Savage Station, and at one o'clock on the morning of the 29th he ordered his tents to be struck, and, with his staff and escort, proceeded toward White Oak Swamp. General Smith had charge of the rear, and was ordered to hold his position near the Chickahominy until the wagons were at a safe distance, and then slowly to follow them. At about daylight he began to retire over the road the baggage-trains had taken, and, shortly after, Generals Sumner, Heintzelman, and Keyes gradually changed their front so as to make it face the north, thus protecting the retreat from all attacks either of forces sent from the direction of Richmond or from the Chickahominy. The enemy, having discovered the movement, began to press after, but made no attacks until late in the day. By noon on Sunday, all the artillery, except that required to protect the rear of the retiring column, and also all the wagons, were well on their way to Charles City. General McCall followed immediately after them. Then came Generals Porter, Franklin, and Keyes, with their corps, General Heintzelman protecting the rear. Several attempts were made to flank him, but they were all unsuccessful, and the retreat was conducted in perfect order.

It was about two o'clock on Sunday afternoon that the first real attack of the enemy was made upon the rear-guard. So rapidly did they approach that the officers had barely time to place the men in position to receive them, before fire had been opened and a furious assault made. Reinforcements were poured in to the aid of General Heintzelman, and the troops successfully resisted the attack. The Rebels advanced in solid masses to within a short distance of the Federal artillery; and the effect of the guns was fearful. The battle lasted until dark, both sides suffering severely, when the enemy withdrew. This battle was fought near Savage Station, and in the evening the main body of the army encamped near Charles City, six miles distant from the James River by one road, and fifteen by another.

During the day the Eighth Illinois Cavalry, commanded by Colonel Farnsworth, had been sent over the longest road, to ascertain if it was clear of the enemy. It ran through dense woods in a circuitous manner. The reconnoissance returned, reporting favorably, and at dusk a long train of wagons, preceded by the cavalry-regiment, commenced moving from Charles City toward the James River. General Keyes's corps was assigned to the rear of this column. At an early hour the next morning, the head of the column, without accident, and without meeting any resistance, reached the river at a point two miles west of Harrison's Landing.

The short road, which was nearer Richmond, was not so free from Rebels. On Sunday morning, a squadron of cavalry which had been sent out to reconnoitre returned with the information that the enemy were about a mile distant from the camp. Their strength was not known, but was supposed to be small. At seven o'clock in the morning, the pickets reported that some Rebel cavalry were marching along this road toward Charles City. Dispositions were at once made to receive them, and two pieces of artillery were planted in a concealed position, having the range of the road along which the enemy were approaching. A volley poured into them caused a most precipitate retreat, and General Martindale's brigade of General Porter's corps at once occupied the ground upon which the cavalry had appeared. In the afternoon, Generals Morell and McCall, with their divisions, and a large amount of artillery, were sent forward to open the way to the James River. They moved cautiously, and, after a few slight skirmishes, reached Turkey Bend. Late in the night a train of wagons, followed by infantry, began moving along the road, and upon Monday morning, the 30th, General McClellan broke up his camp and encamped that evening on the river-bank at Turkey Bend.

When an aid sent from Generals Morell and McCall rode back and reported to General McClellan that the road was open to the James River, a thrill of relief ran through the entire army; and, when the troops reached the stream, the sight of the green fields skirting its banks invigorated all. It was upon the top of Malvern Hill that the view first broke upon the weary soldiers' gaze, and it was there that the commander-in-chief, expressing the belief that, with a short time to prepare, the position could be held against any force the enemy were able to bring against it, disposed his forces to resist their anticipated attacks. This hill was but three miles from Turkey Bend.

About noon the Rebel columns came up, and the troops on Malvern Hill were ordered in line to meet them. General Keyes was upon the right flank, holding the longest road, and General Smith was at his rear to support him. On his left was General Sumner's corps; and then came Generals Hooker and Kearney, on the extreme left. Generals Slocum and McCall were held in reserve. The line was nearly three miles in length, and covered all the roads by which the Rebels advanced.

At two o'clock the contest was opened with artillery; but at first the firing was not very severe. An hour later, an advance was made upon General Sumner by an immense mass of the enemy, and the battle at once became hot and bloody. General Slocum's division was called upon at half-past three to reinforce General Sumner, and for more than two hours a furious fight was carried on, ending at six o'clock with the enemy's repulse.

Whilst this contest was raging in the centre, a demonstration was made against an earth-work which had been hastily thrown up on the extreme right; but a dashing charge of a brigade from General Smith's division drove the Rebels back.

But the severest part of the battle was upon the left. General Heintzelman was sorely pressed all the afternoon, and the engagement there continued with great severity until nearly dark. He fell back almost half a mile to obtain a better position, and the terrific attacks of the enemy often seemed too strong to be resisted. It was only the superior qualities of the soldiers, under the lead of veterans like Generals Hooker and Kearney, and the excellent management of General Heintzelman himself, that saved the day on that portion of the field.

Again and again the enemy resorted to those tactics which had been their main reliance in the previous battles. Their generals seemed to be utterly regardless of human life. If an advantage could only be achieved to repay the loss, they cared not how many of their army lay struggling with death after they had fought the Federal troops. Overwhelming numbers were precipitated on some point in the line, in the hope of breaking it, or against a battery, trusting to capture it; but, with the veterans Heintzelman, Kearney, and Hooker to resist them, it was done in vain.

At six o'clock the Rebels made a furious onset, which, almost by main force, bore back the Federal left. It was then that General McCall's wearied division, the last of the army in reserve, was brought forward to assist the defence. But what an awful reception they met! Cannon and musketry were poured into them with terrible havoc, and in a very few moments they were broken and pushed back, with hundreds lying dead and wounded on the field, General McCall captured by the enemy, Biddle mortally wounded, and Kuhn killed. The Reserves had tried to do too much, and were almost annihilated.

Seeing the desperate condition of affairs on the left, General Sedgwick's division was sent to aid it, from the centre, and Generals Hooker and Kearney rallied for a final and desperate charge. Four batteries of artillery were brought forward and advantageously posted. They opened with disastrous effect, and at the same time the Federal troops, led by their Generals, made an impetuous charge against the surging masses of the enemy, and, with the aid of the cannonade, soon broke the opposing columns and ended the contest. Nearly a thousand prisoners were captured by this charge.

At about four o'clock in the afternoon, the aid of the gunboats upon the James River had been called in to the assistance of the left wing. The Aroostook and Galena took position about a mile above Turkey Landing, and opened fire, shelling in the most effective manner the vast columns of the enemy advancing along the river-road to attack General Heintzelman. The gunners could not see the road, but a signal-officer, in an exposed position on the top of a house situated on a hill, directed the range of the guns, and their shells were thrown with such precision as to cause the enemy great loss and materially impede his operations, besides causing him to abandon a battery in the line of fire, which was secured by our advance.

A young Rebel officer, writing to the Charleston "Courier," gives a most graphic account of this terrible battle on Malvern Hill:—

"About five o'clock P.M. the enemy were reported occupying a very strong position just in our front, where they had fortified. Our artillery was ordered out to open on the enemy, and a brigade of Georgians and Alabamians to support it. No sooner had our guns opened than they were dismounted, the caissons torn to atoms, and the horses and men piled and mangled together. Other batteries were ordered out, with the same success, and the few horses and men who were left came dashing back, panic-stricken, and sought refuge in flight. Then we saw what was coming. Our brigade was sent to the front to support the one already sent out, and, forming in line, we marched to the skirt of woods which separated us from the open ground where the enemy had formed to receive us. His position could not have been better selected. Upon a hill about half a mile in our front were placed thirty siege-guns and twenty light batteries, manned by United States regulars, while in front the ground descended gradually to our position, midway between which and their batteries was a line of thirty thousand of their best troops, who were selected to cover their retreat to their gunboats, two miles distant. Upon this line and their batteries we advanced. For the first half-mile we marched, the shells burst round us incessantly. After that, just as we got in the woods, the gunboats opened on us with their broadsides of rifled guns, the shells from which came hurtling through the woods, crashing and bursting, and tearing down numbers of the largest trees in their course. Then came the grape and canister from the batteries in our front; and soon the musketry opened, actually sweeping down whole lines of men in our front and from our own ranks, and making our path one over dead and dying men. We passed over four lines of men, who, sent out before us, were unable to stand the fire, and lay close to the ground, from which no threats or persuasion could move them. Our men trampled them into the mud like logs, and moved on in an unwavering line, perfectly regardless of the numbers who were falling around them.

"But we pushed on until we found the line we were to support within six hundred yards of the battery; and there we halted under cover of a hedgerow, and lay down to rest. The line in front of us, unable to stand up in front of the fire, had lain down, while the troops in our rear poured several volleys into us, wounding and killing many men. Finding our place untenable, between friend and foe, General Kershaw proposed to the general in our front to charge the battery and let us support him. This he refused to do. Kershaw then offered to charge it with our brigade, if they would support him after he took it. This they also refused, and, as the Georgians and Louisianians on our right were moving up, we could not fire without injuring them, and we could do no good where we were. We were directed to fall back to our original position and reform line of battle. I held the position with our left wing until the right was out of range, and then directed the left to retire, I keeping some distance in the rear and falling back very slowly. No sooner had our men fallen back than there came a portion of the Confederate soldiers dashing past me, panic-stricken and huddled together like sheep, presenting elegant marks for the grape and cannon-balls, which cut paths through them and hurled them writhing and digging into the mud and water of the swamp. One man, in his haste to get out of danger, shoved me on one side, and just at the instant a canister-shot tore his head off and spattered my face with his blood and brains. As you may suppose, I was not much vexed at his impoliteness. On our way out we passed over the ground which we travelled in going in, and found men lying dead in every direction. Upon reaching the rear we were marched into a skirt of woods to rest for the night, the fight having now closed and the enemy ceased firing. When morning dawned, they were gone again, having reached James River and being safely under cover of their gunboats. Early in the morning I rode over the battle-ground, our brigade having been marched up to occupy it; and the sight which was there presented beggars description. Entering the field at the point where our artillery had been posted, I came upon numbers of dead and dying horses, who, with the drivers and gunners, lay in a pile together, the several dismantled guns, their caissons fired and blown up by the enemy's balls, all presenting an aspect of desolation and ruin. Then came the point at which our infantry lines advanced through the open field and engaged those of the enemy. For a mile the ground was thickly strewn with the dead and dying, showing with what energy our men had advanced, and with what energy they were repulsed. Men, mangled in every conceivable manner, to the number of ten thousand, were strewn out before me. The painful details of our own wounded I will spare you, but will pass to the enemy's side of the field, where one-half of the number lay. There were men with their arms and legs and hands shot off, bodies torn up, features distorted and blackened. All this I could see with indifference, but I could not but pity the wounded. There was one poor devil with his back broken, who was trying to pull himself along by his hands, dragging his legs after him, to get out of the corn-rows, which the last night's rain had filled with water. Another, with both legs shot off, was trying to steady the mangled trunk against a gun stuck in the ground. A fair-haired Yankee boy of sixteen was lying with both legs broken, half of his body submerged in water, with his teeth clenched, his finger-nails buried in the flesh, and his whole body quivering with agony and benumbed with cold. In this case my pity got the better of my resentment, and I dismounted, pulled him out of the water, and wrapped him in my blanket,—for which he seemed very grateful. One of the most touching things I saw was a couple of brothers, both wounded, who had crawled together, and one of them, in the act of arranging a pillow for the other with a blanket, had fallen, and they had died with their arms around one another and their cheeks together. But your heart will sicken at these details, as mine did at seeing them, and I will cease."

The battle of Malvern Hill was by far the most severe of the seven days' battles. The loss on both sides was terrible; and, as the enemy still maintained a threatening attitude, as a matter of precaution, the wagons at Turkey Landing were all sent off to Harrison's Point, farther down the river. The entire army rested on its arms during the night of the 30th.

Early the next morning the fight was renewed by the enemy, who evidently expected to crush the Federal army. After an engagement of three hours, with much loss on both sides, the Rebels retired, leaving their opponents the field. At three o'clock in the afternoon, a second advance was made, but it retired under a heavy fire from the gunboats and artillery, without having ventured near enough for the infantry to become engaged. This was the last contest between the two armies.

The most prolific imagination cannot realize a true view of this retreat, and pen-pictures avail very little in its description. On Sunday morning the enemy discovered the movement, and sent thousands upon thousands of troops after General McClellan's retreating army. All the secrecy and strategy had gained but the time between midnight and morning, and when each Federal soldier was tired enough to lie down anywhere in search of his so-much-needed rest, Rebel cavalry and artillery came rushing after him, and, with weary step, he had to wheel into line of battle. The most heroic bravery was the rule throughout the army, in fighting against the guerrillas who infested the rear. Hooker fought until his men dropped down from fatigue. Slocum relieved him. Sedgwick came to the rescue of Slocum, and the impetuous Kearney charged to the very centre of the enemy's lines. In every engagement the enemy were beaten, and the rear-guard, first one corps and then another, gathered laurel upon laurel in the hundred skirmishes of that retreat.

The march was fully protected. Excepting the cannon lost in battle, and one piece destroyed on the way, not a single valuable article fell into the enemy's hands. Thousands of dollars' worth of property was destroyed, because it could not be carried away; but the rear-guard kept behind the last wagon, not allowing a single team to be captured. Wood was burned, ammunition blown up, whiskey and molasses barrels broached, and wagons, whose horses died by the way from sheer fatigue, completely dismantled. Soldiers who threw away their knapsacks, but first spilled their contents or rent them to pieces. Muskets lying in ditches were bent and broken. But little left by that grand army in its wonderful retreat was of use to the enemy. Fire and water, the knife and the axe, did their work, and did it well.

The horrors of the march can never be forgotten.

Wounded and sick dragged themselves along, many a one lying down to sleep his last sleep under the grateful shade of the roadside woods. A confusion of wagons and soldiers and cannon, and the paraphernalia of war, blocked the passage; and, in addition to the Rebels thundering behind, and the long, weary, dusty way before, hunger and thirst began to stare them in the face. Thousands had thrown away their haversacks, containing all their food, and not a bite could they procure. Few streams or springs could be found to quench the thirst of the poor soldiers. They lay upon the ground, drinking from ditches filled with mud. Wells sometimes furnished a scant supply, but it was not one-tenth large enough for the army. Horses died from thirst, and were left lying where they fell. Everywhere could be heard the cry for water; but above it sounded loudly the voices of the officers who urged every one forward. Hunger and thirst came to the aid of Secession in the infliction of deep and painful wounds upon the Union army.

When the troops came in sight of the James River, away off in the distance, its muddy current swiftly coursing between its low banks, how many hailed with delight that glorious stream, which betokened the end of the weary, terrible journey! Malvern Hill was covered with gazers who feasted their eyes with the sight. The halt on the hill was short, and the river soon reached. Here was witnessed the most frantic glee on the part of the troops. Soldiers rushed down and plunged into the stream in a perfect frenzy of delight. Many, whose thirst had been most excruciating for hours before, standing neck-deep in the water, drank to their hearts' content. The horses, too, were relieved; their wants were cared for, and the hungry soldiers were the only ones left who were still in worse misery than the army generally.

Turkey Landing is a rude wharf, some four or five miles above City Point, on the Richmond bank of the river. A few hogsheads of tobacco sent away seemed to be the extent of the trade before the war,—although a rather large warehouse, somewhat tastefully decorated, showed the wealth and judgment of its owner. Otherwise it had neither beauty nor attraction. Low and flat, burned almost to a cinder by the heat of the sun, it seemed the most uninviting spot in all Virginia. To the tired troops, however, it was a paradise. They were allowed to encamp and find that rest of which they had been for days deprived. The sick and wounded lay down, and the surgeons attended to their wants. The stragglers were picked up by the provost-guard and sent to their regiments, and, quietly and speedily, order seemed to come out of the confusion.

On the evening of the 1st of July, General McClellan removed his encampment from Turkey Landing to Harrison's Point, and temporarily yielded the place to the enemy. This was the spot chosen for the encampment of the army and its restoration from the excessive fatigue it had undergone. The hundreds of vessels laden with supplies, which had left White House, were there, and every thing was in readiness to provide for the wants of the soldiers.

Wednesday morning, July 2, was ushered in by a severe and unrelenting northeast storm, which converted every thing into mud and mire. As the weary troops arrived, they were forced to pitch their little shelter-tents upon this disagreeable surface. Rain fell in torrents. The sick and wounded, granted a short rest at Turkey Landing, had again been inhospitably turned out, and were feebly and slowly tramping through the mud, to lie down in it, the rain beating upon them whilst they waited for the hospital-boats. There is always humanity in the army; and never were seen nobler instances of it than on the plain near Harrison's Wharf. Whilst the poor and helpless men were lying in the mire, or listlessly wandering about with despair in every feature, regiment after regiment of troops had their hearts touched, and generously gave up their tents for the wounded to creep under. Two hours raised quite a little town at the head of the wharf, and many a grateful look showed the gratitude of the poor fellows who had given health and strength to their country. The rain fell faster, and the mud grew deeper. One could scarcely walk; and Wednesday night lowered upon the army, perhaps the saddest and dreariest since it entered the field.

On that day and the next, all labored at shipping the wounded and landing commissary stores. Steamboat after steamboat passed down the James River, filled to overflowing with unfortunate victims of the week of battles. Craft of all kinds landed food, which was at once sent to the regiments and brigades, to feed the hungry. The enemy, too, on Thursday attacked the camp, but were worsted, numerous prisoners and a battery being captured. The rain did not stop until noon of that day, and the condition of the encampment was most sorrowful. Sunset, however, was clear, and better weather could be safely prophesied. The Fourth of July found the army fully protected by gunboats and earth-works, and prepared to hold its position against all odds.

The losses upon the great retreat were most fearful. General McClellan's official report sums them up thus :—

	Killed.	Wounded.	Missing.	Total.
Gen. Sumner's Second Corps,	176	1088	848	2086
" Heintzelman's Third Corps,	189	1051	883	2073
" Keyes's Fourth Corps,	69	507	201	777
" Porter's Fifth Corps,	873	3700	2779	7352
" Franklin's Sixth Corps,	245	1313	1179	2737
" Stoneman's Cavalry,	19	60	97	176
The Engineers,	.....	2	21	23
Total	1565	7711	5958	
Grand Total				15,224

The greatest loss in any single division was in that of General McCall. Nearly one-half of it was either killed, wounded, or captured. The numbers stand thus :—

Killed,	251
Wounded,	1223
Missing,	1607
Total,	3081

There has been no authentic statement of the enemy's casualties. A Richmond newspaper placed it at nearly eighteen thousand, but that, no doubt, is somewhat unreliable. Although they claim a series of victories, yet they acknowledge that General McClellan's army escaped from their hands by the superior ability of its commander.

Upon July 4, the Federal troops were quietly encamped upon the banks of James River, the men recovering from the fatigue of the terrible ordeal through which they had passed, and the officers preparing their reports and reorganizing their commands. It was a serene and peaceful day,—one worthy to be the anniversary of the natal day of the nation. During the afternoon, General McClellan reviewed the troops, and was received everywhere with the most enthusiastic demonstrations. Rounds upon rounds of applause from the regiments greeted his appearance. Whilst the review was progressing, the following order was read to the army. It is a fit close to the grand drama which ended the campaign upon the Peninsula:—

"HEAD-QUARTERS, ARMY OF THE POTOMAC, July 4, 1862.

"SOLDIERS OF THE ARMY OF THE POTOMAC:—

"Your achievements of the last ten days have illustrated the valor and endurance of the American soldier. Attacked by superior forces, and without hope of reinforcements, you have succeeded in changing your base of operations by a flank movement, always regarded as the most hazardous of military expedients. You have saved all your material, all your trains, and all your guns, except a few lost in battle, taking in return guns and colors from the enemy.

"Upon your march, you have been assailed day after day with desperate fury, by men of the same race and nation, skilfully massed and led.

"Under every disadvantage of numbers, and necessarily of position also, you have, in every conflict, beaten back your foes with enormous slaughter.

"Your conduct ranks you among the celebrated armies of history.

"No one will now question that each of you may always with pride say, 'I belong to the Army of the Potomac.'

"You have reached this new base, complete in organization and unimpaired in spirit.

"The enemy may at any time attack you. We are prepared to meet them. I have personally established your lines. Let them come, and we will convert their repulse into a final defeat.

"Your Government is strengthening you with the resources of a great people.

"On this our nation's birthday, we declare to our foes, who are rebels against the best interests of mankind, that this army shall enter the capital of the so-called Confederacy, that our national Constitution shall prevail, and that the Union, which can alone insure internal peace and external security to each State, must and shall be preserved, cost what it may in time, treasure, or blood.

"GEORGE B. McCLELLAN,
"*Major-General Commanding.*"

Upon the morning of July 5, the author left the camp at Harrison's Landing, to return to the North. The troops had almost recovered from the fatigues of the retreat, and were preparing, as they thought, for renewed efforts to capture Richmond. But it was ordained otherwise. They were destined to pass through a series of defeats under strange generals, but finally, when again directed by their old commander, to drive the enemy before them from Western Maryland, and add new laurels to his brow. May the endurance, patriotism, and courage of the army of the Potomac be ever found in the soldiers who fight for the Union!

CHAPTER XII.

THE CONCLUSION.

BEFORE closing this narrative, it is proper that the number of men contained in the Federal and Rebel armies, or an approximation to it, should be given. As the retreat was caused solely by a sudden increase of the force of the enemy, justice to every officer and soldier of the Union army demands that all information as to the number of men upon each side should be made public. The *exact* number of either army cannot be given, the documents necessary to great accuracy being very wisely kept secret whilst the war to which they refer is still being waged. Approximations to the true force, however, may be obtained sufficiently correct for the object in view, and in which if there are errors they equally affect both armies, and are thus, for all practical purposes, obviated.

General McClellan's advanced parties reached the Chickahominy River upon May 20, 1862, and on that day his entire army was marching upon Richmond. He had five *corps d'armée*, and one independent division. The average force of a division at that time was eight thousand men, which would make his entire strength as follows:—

General Sumner's 2d corps	16,000
" Heintzelman's 3d corps	24,000
" Keyes's 4th corps	16,000
" Porter's 5th corps	16,000
" Franklin's 6th corps	16,000
" Stoneman's division	8,000
Total	96,000

Each division contained from twelve to fifteen regiments, which made the entire number between one hundred and fifty and one hundred and sixty. The average number of troops in each was about six hundred and fifty. The Ninety-fifth and Ninety-sixth Pennsylvania, two of the strongest regiments in the service, scarcely ever reported more than eight hundred men each for effective duty. The Forty-ninth Pennsylvania had but five hundred and fifty. None of the five regiments composing the Excelsior Brigade mustered more than four hundred men. General Casey's entire division did not number five thousand. A year of constant service, sickness, wounds, and death had made sad inroads upon every regiment of the army of the Potomac. General McClellan, whilst he had more than one hundred and fifty regiments, mustered but ninety-six thousand troops.

The strength of the enemy must be calculated upon the same basis as that of the Federal force. When the battle of Fair Oaks was fought, they had eight grand divisions, besides cavalry, each one containing from twenty-four to thirty regiments, and each corresponding to a Federal *corps d'armée.* These eight divisions were defending Richmond upon May 20. Their force was as follows:—

General Huger's division	16,000
" D. B. Hill's division	16,000
" Longstreet's division	16,000
" G. W. Smith's division	16,000
" Magruder's division	16,000
" A. P. Hill's division	16,000
" Rains's division	16,000
" Ewell's division	16,000
" Stewart's cavalry force	10,000
Total	138,000

From the 20th of May to the 26th of June, or during the time the Federal army was before Richmond, it is estimated that the entire loss of Union troops, by wounds, death, prisoners, sickness, discharges, and resignations, was about twenty thousand. Almost one-half of these must have been lost in skirmishes and battles. Five thousand seven hundred and thirty-nine were killed, wounded, and captured at Fair Oaks, six hundred at Five Oaks, and three hundred and forty-nine at Hanover Court-House; and other contests were in proportion. The mortality from sickness was very great, and hundreds were discharged for disability. Calculating the enemy's upon the basis of the Federal loss, it amounts to twenty-nine thousand men, of whom five thousand two hundred and thirty-three were lost at Fair Oaks, and fifteen hundred at Hanover Court-House. This would therefore reduce the strength of both armies thus:—

	Federal.	Confederate.
Force upon May 20	96,000	138,000
Loss	20,000	29,000
Leaving	76,000	109,000

It only remains to add the number of reinforcements received by each, and an approximation will be had to the force of both when the retreat commenced upon June 26. To the Federal army, General McCall's division of thirteen regiments and eight thousand men was added upon June 18, being attached to General Fitz-John Porter's corps; and about the same date some two thousand troops arrived from Fortress Monroe. The Rebel army received upon June 5 a force supposed to be Jackson's, the strength of which has been variously estimated, but which could scarcely have been less than sixteen thousand; and upon the ten days previous to the retreat there were fifty thousand added to the enemy's number. Thus :—

	Federal.	Confederate.
Force	76,000	109,000
Reinforcements	10,000	66,000
Total	86,000	175,000

The Rebel army thus containing more than double the number of men that General McClellan could muster.

During the retreat, according to the official report, the Federal army lost fifteen thousand two hundred and twenty-four. No official statement of the enemy's casualties has been given. The army of the Potomac upon its arrival at Harrison's Landing was thus reduced to less than seventy-one thousand men. That the enemy had an enormous force during the retreat seems to be proven by the fact that at the end of August they were able to defeat the combined forces of Generals McClellan, Burnside, McDowell, Sigel,

Frémont, and Banks under the command of General Pope, and compel their retreat to the protecting trenches in front of Washington.

There have been few better armies than the one which besieged Richmond. Complete in organization, discipline, and that practice in combat which alone can make troops fully available, it was deficient alone in numbers. Mutual confidence existed between officers and men, and every exertion was made by all to further the plans of its commander. All arms of the service were well represented by sturdy, patriotic volunteers, whose soldierly conduct won the admiration of the country they were fighting for. Had force enough been given it, victory would have been inscribed upon its banners.

No braver men ever went to war than the soldiers of that army. Their feats of daring have already become history. Their confidence, coolness, patience, and courage will be the materials for many a tradition. Where are there more admirable evidences of that true bravery which alone deserves success than are found in the actions of the soldiers of the army of the Potomac?—in the bold adventure of the Fourth Michigan at New Bridge; in the gallant conduct of the Second Maine at Hanover Court-House; in the stubbornness of Casey's division at Fair Oaks; in the glorious charge of the Excelsior Brigade at that same bloody battle; in the contest of parts of the Forty-ninth Pennsylvania and Thirty-third New York with the enemy upon June 28; or in the resistance made by General Porter's corps on the previous day at Gaines's Mills? And where will be found more boldness than in the advance, amid the enemy's fire, of the single company to the Mechanicsville bridge, or in Colonel Cake's expedition to the swamps of the Chickahominy, or in Captain Keenan's reconnoissance to the James River? The men of the army were true soldiers: in battle, in advance, in retreat, they were alike courageous, confident, and merciful.

Their general officers were worthy of such an army, —the veteran Sumner, the cool but quick Heintzelman, the daring Fitz-John Porter, the fighting Hooker, the impetuous Kearney, the gallant McCall, and the numbers of others,—all of whom were true leaders, commanding every energy of their soldiers. Yet it is sad to know that two of them have fallen in battle,—two citizens of New Jersey, who had the most eminent military ability, and whose loss caused lamentation throughout the land. General Kearney was shot down whilst posting an out-picket near Centreville, and General Taylor died at Alexandria from a mortal wound received whilst defending the capital against those who would invade it.

But what shall be said of the commander of such generals and such men,—he who is received with such enthusiasm as he passes among his troops, who commands the admiration of thousands in the country, and whose military genius is acknowledged by all the soldiers of America,—the man whose modesty alone competes with his ability, and who, whilst he is famous for the campaigns he has fought, will be celebrated for the magnanimity of every action of his public life?

General McClellan is one of the very few American chieftains who is honored with the confidence of his soldiers. It is given him to the utmost extent. Nay, it rises higher. Not only have his followers faith in his ability; but they love him: all testify to it. His appearance is greeted with a shout. In camp his praises are sung; in battle every nerve is strung tighter and every energy taxed higher when he rides on the field. Nothing can deprive the soldier of his love for his general. When dying, he attests it; and the poor cripple who has left a limb upon the battle-field is never better pleased than when telling the virtues of his beloved commander.

There is no ordinary military ability found in General McClellan. From the beginning of the war his career has been a constant series of successes,—success in organizing an army of citizen-soldiers, success on a dozen fields in Western Virginia, success in driving the enemy from before Washington, in thrusting them from Yorktown, in thundering at the very gates of their capital, and, when a deaf ear was turned to all his appeals for aid, consummate success in extricating his army from the swamps of Virginia and the toils of the foe.

His character is equally brilliant. He joined the army as a soldier, and as such he still fights. No proclamation of his has given the Government uneasiness, or caused fierce faction among the people. He has not meddled with politics. Not a word from his lips nor a stroke from his pen has indicated a bias toward any party. A true Union man, he wishes to sink all differences among the people, in order to quell the rebellion. Toward those who have spent their time and their talents in misrepresentation and calumny he has been most noble. He has overlooked all. For the good of the country he has peacefully submitted to every indignity; and when his troops were taken from him, and he was left at his camp in Alexandria,—a general without an army,—he told the Administration he would tender his resignation if they wished it, but said, with a patriotism which could not be mistaken, "I have enlisted for the war, and shall serve to the end of it: if I retire from public life, it will only be to join a regiment as a private soldier, and still fight the enemy."

There are few men in America—there are certainly none now in public life—more capable of subduing the rebellion than Major-General GEORGE BRINTON McCLELLAN.

RESUME OF PLANS AND MOVEMENTS IN FRONT OF RICHMOND.

AS SEEN FROM THE CAMP AT HEAD-QUARTERS.

ANY truthful narration of events so momentous in their results, and at the same time so thrilling and absorbing in the steps of their progress, as those attending McClellan's flank movement in the Peninsula, must engage the attention of the loyal people of this nation, especially in the absence of the more studied and thorough representation which will come later, when, in the fulness of time, the historian and critic shall have weighed the bearing of movements on the grand result of the war, and analyzed the skill with which military dispositions were made for the successful accomplishment of deliberate designs. Again, the American people are entitled to the earliest information, imperfect though it be, of the conduct and leading of the army of the Potomac, so that, if merited, the ægis of popular opinion may be interposed between that gallant army and venal and designing politicians, who, finding no such element as patriotism in their own moral constitution, cannot conceive that citizens may face death from disease and the sword to achieve national regeneration, and who therefore use calumny and detraction as weapons against men who, unmoved by selfish considerations, and without any design of seeking political advancement, fondly hope for the time when the need of the country for their services shall cease, and they may return to private life in the consciousness of having sacrificed home and congenial pursuits in the discharge of a public duty.

Had General McClellan's orders been obeyed when he directed General McDowell to proceed to West Point while he attacked the enemy in the front at Yorktown, there would have been no siege of Richmond; for the enemy, with McClellan in his front and McDowell, forty thousand strong, in his rear, would have rendered Yorktown again famous by a second capitulation, rejoicing all loyal people and virtually ending a second war. But that McDowell was removed from McClellan's command after he had sailed and was committed to the completion of his plan in front of Yorktown is known to all. The reason and method of this interference must one day be explained at the demand of the country. After Yorktown was relinquished, an immediate pursuit was made, with an attempt to throw a force on the enemy's rear at West Point, where McDowell should have been: these efforts were attended with partial, though inferior, success, and General McClellan, having followed the retreat of the enemy with great activity, placed himself in front of Richmond, with a navigable river for his base, and a short line of railroad directly in his rear, which furnished all his supplies, and removed his sick and wounded, as fast as they accumulated, to hospital-boats.

Thus arranged, General McClellan found himself prepared to attack the enemy's works, that surrounded Richmond in a double line,—the first at a distance of about five miles,—and selected the early days of June for the assault. But the floods that swept out the canals and rivers of Pennsylvania came also in Virginia, and the Chickahominy, from a small stream, became an almost impassable river, overflowing the low country in its course. Preparatory to the assault upon Richmond, the left of the army had been thrown over the Chickahominy,—when the enemy, believing that river now impassable, fell upon this wing with his entire force, intending to crush it; but, being bravely resisted, and also assailed by divisions that crossed the Chickahominy with indomitable courage upon the remains of bridges afloat, and rocking with their burden, the water breaking over the guns, he was foiled in his purpose, and repulsed with great loss. This was the battle of Fair Oaks, on the 31st of May. General McClellan was only prevented from following the foiled and beaten enemy into Richmond at this time by the impossibility of passing the Chickahominy over the wreck of the two bridges that had already done such good service before floating off piecemeal.

The month of June was unprecedented in Virginia for cold and incessant rain, and the army suffered from camp-fever, a disease known to all armies, and a diarrhœa exceedingly general, but not of a dangerous character. During June, General McClellan contended with floods of rain, which obliged him to build numerous bridges, and lay corduroy roads over swamps and bottom-lands, often under the enemy's guns. These difficulties alone prevented him from attacking Richmond; for not only were the lowlands on the Chickahominy flooded, but nowhere in the alluvial soil around Richmond or on James River was it possible at that time to move wagons or artillery. During this delay, decreed by the elements, the enemy was engaged in assembling the entire South at Richmond, and, although the city was one vast hospital, this accumulation went on, and the conscripts of Virginia, North Carolina, and Georgia poured in by thousands. This General McClellan was fully aware of, and scarcely a day elapsed without bringing to his camp deserters and prisoners, some of whom had not been in Richmond over a week, and all of whom confirmed the above statement.

General McClellan now wrote repeatedly to his Government for reinforcements: he received in response one small division, the Pennsylvania Reserves, consisting of eight thousand men, commanded by General McCall. These raised General McClellan's command to nearly ninety thousand men. Five thousand more were tardily sent, and reached the White House too late to be of service. They were returned to Fortress Monroe, whence they joined the army of the Potomac the day after it reached James River.

General McClellan knew of the enemy's intention of attacking his right wing, and desired it, and when, on Thursday afternoon, June 26, the Rebel Hill attacked McCall at Mechanicsville, he was bravely met and repulsed with great loss. At dawn on Friday, the 27th, General McCall withdrew from his position, bringing his train, and joined General Fitz-John Porter in his rear, who also fell back with him, intending to cross the Chickahominy on a bridge to the rear of our front and centre, which lay facing Richmond from White Oak Swamp to the banks of the Chickahominy. The enemy followed with four entire divisions, commanded by Jackson, Hill, Longstreet, and A. P. Hill, and forced our right wing, consisting of two small divisions, to an engagement at a short distance from the bridge over which it was intended to cross. Up to this time every thing had proceeded entirely according to General McClellan's desire; he had toled four divisions of the enemy, some eighty thousand strong, out of Richmond, too far for them to return, and it now remained to be seen whether his brilliant design in so doing could be accomplished. Bridges had been built over the Chickahominy in sufficient numbers in case of mishap to retire upon the White House, a bridge had been thrown over White Oak Creek in case a flank movement toward James River should be necessary, and now General McClellan stood at the telegraph which communicated with all his commanders of the front and left wing, awaiting the auspicious moment when the enemy's front should have become so weakened by sending divisions to follow our right wing down the other side of the Chickahominy, that, by one brilliant dash, our left wing and centre could be swung over all obstacles into Richmond, crowning the enemy's double line of intrenchments and piercing his centre. But Fitz-John Porter had been forced to fight, and gallantly the regulars, Pennsylvania Reserve, and other troops of his division met the enemy, two to one. Here was the great battle of the Chickahominy, where, to save his right wing, General McClellan was obliged to reinforce from the left and centre with which he designed to charge into Richmond. At this hour, the want of reinforcements from the North saved the Rebel capital. The brigades of Newton, Taylor, and Bartlett crossed to the assistance of the right wing, and, when further aid was required, the Irish Brigade, under Meagher, crossed with a quick step and martial bearing at a critical moment that no one on that field will ever forget. At night this command was leisurely withdrawn, and although the enemy had poured eighty thousand men upon our right, and sent them too far to recall, still his front was strong, and he moved large masses toward our left, while using his artillery upon our centre with unusual vigor. Under these circumstances, having sent every man that could be spared from the centre to save the right wing, an assault upon Richmond was not the part of a general, and McClellan calmly turned to his other resources. To fall back upon the White House was to cease to threaten Richmond and let loose a Rebel army to invade the North; to make a flank movement to James River was to incur the greatest hazard to which an army could be exposed, while to make it successfully would be the most brilliant military movement on record, and still to threaten Richmond and hold the Rebel army in check. With a calm and brave confidence on the part of the entire army, first in its commander, secondly in its officers, and lastly in its matchless self, without haste, without bluster, but quietly, soberly, and sedately, the movement was made. The enemy was repulsed on Saturday, on Sunday, on Monday morning, in a general engagement on Monday afternoon, and in full force beaten and overthrown on Tuesday, when an obedient, brave, and confident army occupied its chosen position on James River, having gallantly fought and patiently suffered while obediently following the only man who could have so won their confidence as to successfully make a flank movement in the face of an enemy double his numbers, at home, too, upon the field of operations.

THE END.

www.ingramcontent.com/pod-product-compliance
Lightning Source LLC
LaVergne TN
LVHW010151110826
845151LV00002B/489